W9-COX-410

LadyMagic

The Autobiography of Nancy Lieberman-Cline

Nancy Lieberman-Cline with Debby Jennings

Foreword by Martina Navratilova

SAGAMORE PUBLISHING INC.
Champaign, Illinois 61824-0673

© 1992 Nancy Lieberman-Cline

Sagamore Publishing
P.O. Box 673
Champaign, IL 61824-0673

Production supervision
    and interior design: Brian J. Moore, Susan M. Williams
Cover and photo insert design: Michelle R. Dressen
Front cover photo: Bob Mader
Back cover and spine photos: Bike Athletic Wear Co.
Developmental editor: Dan Heaton
Copyeditor: Joyce D. Meyer
Proofreader: Phyllis L. Bannon

Printed in the United States of America.

10   9   8   7   6   5   4   3   2

ISBN: 0-915611-43-0
Library of Congress Catalog Card No.:91-60003

To my mother, husband Tim, my family and dear friends for all their love and support. And most of all, the Lord, who has given me more opportunities and blessings than one could ever ask. To all, I am truly grateful.

Contents

Acknowledgments vii
Foreword ix
Preface xi

1   The Fundamentals 1

2   What Will the Neighbors Think? 13

3   Keeping the Court 25

4   Take the "A" Train 31

5   A Far Cry from Far Rock 37

6   Recruiting Wars—for a Girl 49

7   Playing for Old Glory 57

8   Finding Father Figures 65

9   Fresh Outlook 75

10   Crowns for the Lady Monarchs 83

11   Adieu, Amateur Standing 97

12   Shining as a Diamond 107

13   Meeting Martina 115

14   With a Little Work 127

15   **Team Navratilova** 139

16   **The Team Disbands** 155

17   **Looking for Nancy** 171

18   **No Business Like Show Business** 181

19   **Making History** 187

20   **Wedding Bells** 199

21   **Comeback Kid** 215

Epilogue 231
Awards 237
Career Statistics 238
Foot Locker Scholarship Application 239

Acknowledgments

When writing an autobiography, so many friends, family, and others come to mind. It is not easy to go back in time without remembering the people who have had a major influence on your life. I am extremely thankful for their support and encouragement.

These people are: my mother, Renee, and my father, Jerry; my brother, Cliff, and his wife, Carol; my husband, Tim; my friend and business partner, Tom Thompson; my dear friends, Robin Roberts, and Wes Lockard (Burnie, the Miami Heat Mascot); my camp director, Teri Morrison; my former secretary, Vicki Arnold; my Pastor, Lance Bingley in Omaha; my attorneys, Robert Rose, Jeff Klein, and Bob Rossilli; Dr. Michael Iott; my husband's parents, Bob and Marian Cline; Pat and Dean Thompson; my trainers, Griz Zimmerman and Maureen Curren-Maksuti; the late Jack Wilkins; Carl and Connie Salland; Rosita Lee; Barbara Wood; Mark and Ellen Muchnick; Eric Muchnick; Rhonda Rompola; Jim and Ellen Howard, Sam and Gay Lattimer; and John Fitzgerald (J.P.); Mark Block; Adam McKenzie; Rita Haywood; Aunt Ruthie and Uncle Bob; Bob Zuckerman; LaVoiser Lamar; Jane Nisenholc; Sonja Hogg; and Dawn Marsh.

I must also thank Dan Heaton for his help on this book, but most of all, thanks to Debby Jennings for the hours of research, and for the friendship during the trying times of getting this book completed. (Thank you also to the University of Tennessee Women's Athletic Department for sharing Debby with me).

I would be remiss if I did not mention the sponsors who have supported me and my basketball camps: BSN Sports, Foot Locker, Park Place Motorcars of Dallas, Tony Roma's, Bike Athletic, and Converse.

Lastly, thank you to the folks at Sagamore Publishing for finally getting me through this book: Joe Bannon, Peter Bannon, Brian Moore, Susan Williams, Michelle Dressen, and a special thanks to Joe Bannon, Jr. Thanks also goes to Bob Mader for a great cover shot.

—N.L.

Acknowledgments

A number of people deserve a big thanks for their kind support, suggestions, and encouragement during the writing of this book.

I would like to extend my first big thanks to the Jennings clan—my parents, Mae and Jack Jennings and my numerous sisters and brothers, who failed to continually ask "Is it done yet?" Special appreciation goes to my 99-year-old nana, Josie Mae MacLean, who fostered my early love of words by playing endless games of SCRABBLE with me.

Secondly, a note of thanks to my boss Joan Cronan, secretary Gayle Irwin, and assistants "The Boyz"—Eric, Phil, and Bob at the University of Tennessee Women's Athletics Department for their encouragement.

Most importantly, I couldn't have successfully completed the manuscript without my circle of Knoxville friends. For all of her constant support, critiques, and painful honesty, I extend a warm and special thanks to a particularly good friend, Patsy Bales. To all the others and many, many more—ya'll helped to make this possible.

Finally, thanks to Sagamore Publishing for taking a chance on a rookie author. And to my dear pal, Nancy Lieberman-Cline—Lady, you are Magic.

—D.J.

Foreword

Overachiever. Motivator. Competitor. Great athlete. Dealmaker. Any one of these words would be appropriate to describe Nancy Lieberman. Nancy Lieberman is a person you would want on your team. She always gives her best and makes her teammates better.

When I first met Nancy in 1981 I was just going through the motions with my tennis career. The first time I saw her, I was in the middle of a match on Amelia Island, FLorida. I recognized her by her flaming reddish-orange hair, which stood out in the crowd. In those days I was not always concentrating on my matches the way I should have. I'd be playing somebody and I'd be thinking about dinner or an interesting conversation I'd had three days earlier.

I was in the middle of a match with Kathy Rinaldi when I spotted Nancy sitting in the players' box. I had never seen her play basketball, but I knew she was an All-American from Old Dominion who by 1981 was playing for the Dallas Diamonds in the Women's Professional Basketball League.

We began talking after my match and hit it off right away talking about sports, of course. It was the first time I had met a woman who knew as much about the subject as I did. She read the box scores and the standings; she knew about sports that women never play, like football and baseball.

I told her I had always thought Carol Blazejowski was the best basketball player in the country (even though I had never seen her play), and Nancy told me she'd always rooted for Chris Evert (and she probably had, up to that point). I enjoyed the jockeying and agitation the first time we met. Male athletes are comfortable teasing and testing each other, but women tend to be a little bit inhibited on that score. Coming onto the tennis tour, I wanted to belong and be liked. I could tell right away that Nancy Lieberman felt none of that inhibition.

It didn't take Nancy long to change my perception of things. By the time the summer rolled around, I was running sprints, lifting weights, doing things a world-class athlete should have been doing all along.

"Get up, dammit, get up," she screamed at me.

"I can't. I can't get up."

Nancy towered over me, hands on her hips. She was furious. I was crying. That was our first workout session together and both of us were making important discoveries. I was discovering true pain in my body for the first time in my life; Nancy was discovering that I did not like it.

Thus began an association that would last three years and help me reach the top in tennis. It was an association built on our dreams of being the best in our respective sports, helped along by our general interest in athletics.

Nancy made me realize that my career was not going to last forever and I'd better reach my potential in the time I had. Here was the best basketball player ever to play the game, with nowhere to show her stuff, ready to work her behind off, and there I was throwing it all away and not even caring. There is no telling where my career would have ended up without Nancy's help, but I know for certain it would not have been as successful as it turned out to be.

Nancy never thought she had more gifts than other people. She saw herself as an underdog. She always strived to be better and to work harder.

You could call Nancy the Billie Jean King of women's basketball. She is a pioneer of her sport, years ahead of her time. It was this kind of vision and dogged determination that drove Nancy early on in her childhood to succeed despite all the obstacles that lay in her path. She went over them, around them or through them — whatever it took, Nancy was willing to pay the price. And pay she did.

Whether you need motivation or not, I believe you will find Nancy's story inspiring. Perhaps it will move you, too, to bigger and better things.

MARTINA NAVRATILOVA

Preface

Sometimes, the commercial says, you've got to break the rules. OK, call me Nancy the rule-breaker.

The rules say little boys grow up playing basketball, football, baseball—competing. The rules say little girls grow up playing with dolls. Those little boys grow up knowing how to compete, and they carry that into the business world. Those little girls grow up knowing how to dress dolls, but a lot of them never have the chance to learn how to compete, and so a lot of opportunity is closed to them. If you don't know how to compete, your only option is to comply. There are those rules again. I've never believed in just going along with what everybody says is the way it should be.

When I was a girl, I used to scour the library shelves for books about female sports stars. I couldn't find any, and so all my role models were men. I want young girls now to be able to read about someone who broke the "rules" that say women can't compete in a "man's world."

I've always had the feeling that when one door closed another door opened. Things have always kind of fallen into place for me. My brother Cliff got the lion's share of attention when we were young, and that pushed me toward sports. My professional basketball league folded, and then I met Martina Navratilova, who desperately needed a training partner. I took a chance playing in the men's United States Basketball League and with the Generals on the Harlem Globetrotters tour, and that led to meeting my husband, Tim. I often wonder why I was given the ability and the opportunity to be a pioneer in my sport. It seems like God has a plan for me, and I just have to keep going through one door after another.

As far back as I can remember, the thing that kept me going was my competitiveness. When I was young, all of my confidence and success were tied to my athletic achievement. Without that experience, that success, I might not have developed the confidence to go on in sports. There is nothing like getting a taste of winning. Success breeds confidence, and confidence can sometimes make you win just because you think you can.

Sometimes in my career, the opportunities have been limited, but there was always a door open somewhere. I could easily have stopped playing basketball in 1980 when the United States boycotted the Olympic Games in Moscow, or when the women's professional league folded in 1981. Something told me to stay with the sport and to be active just in case the league rose from the ashes. Doors close, other doors open.

Besides, giving up has never been a part of what makes me tick. Everything I have accomplished has been triggered by adversity in one way or another. I had a tough childhood, but I really don't regret it because the adversity I faced growing up helped make me who I am. I hated the idea of failure, and a lot of my life is tied into trying to achieve and gain the self-esteem that is so important for anyone.

I think always being on the edge as a kid helped me take it to the edge as an adult and have the ability to make a quick decision. It might not always have been the right decision, but at least I learned to take a chance and make some decision. Some people never learn that.

Probably three of my best attributes are staying focused, not taking things personally, and taking nothing for granted. If a hundred people tell me I'm not able to accomplish something and I truly believe I can, I take it as a personal challenge, something to prove. I've never settled for second best, and I still have dreams of achieving so many things.

Looking back, it's kind of amazing, but I didn't realize what a big deal it was to be the youngest basketball player selected to the USA Olympic team or to have over one hundred scholarship offers in the early years of Title IX. I just looked at those honors as an affirmation that somebody cared about me—that I was special, talented, had something to offer. That gave me a very special confidence that I have always carried with me.

But whether it was riding the subway to Harlem to play basketball or stepping up to the foul line to hit a pressure shot, I always had an inner confidence. Growing up, I wouldn't show fear, cry, or act afraid of anything. I would use humor as my defense and deflect the pain with wit and laughter. Instead of crying, I would just make a joke. My childhood fears and insecurities were channeled into being the best—not by a little, by a lot. I felt like I wasn't noticed at home, and so it became very important for me to be noticed, period.

I've always set my goals in the stratosphere. I think that is why Muhammad Ali was my hero early on. The thing I admired about him was that he always backed up what he said he was going to do. "I am gonna win the title. . . I am gonna knock him out," Ali would say. Yeah, it was showmanship. But I thought it was great to show that kind of confidence and bravado.

We rarely see that kind of athlete in women's sports. Many female athletes are very private, quiet people who make the news only during a tournament or a controversy. The Martina Navratilovas, the Chris Everts, and the Monica Seleses may grab the headlines, but rarely will you read about an athlete from a team sport.

I know that there are other Nancy Liebermans out there who need an opportunity and a role model. They need to read about some of the pitfalls I went through trying to be taken seriously as an athlete. Fifteen years ago, I didn't have some of the opportunities that are available today. I made it and was successful because I believed in myself, worked hard every day, and had God in my corner. Some athletes out there today have everything in the whole world but will never achieve what they can because they are lazy or spoiled or complacent with their degree of success.

I rarely read my press clippings. If you start believing everything people are writing about you, you'll lose your focus, the sense that there is always someone chasing you. Even when I was at the top of my sport, I was still running. That never changed because I knew that right behind me someone was ready to take my spot. A lot of people get to the top and are exhausted from the climb. They want to rest and reflect on what they accomplished getting to the top.

I have never wanted to rest.

Chapter 1

The Fundamentals

 The early years in my neighborhood may have been the toughest of my life. I was angry. I wanted my father to be around. I wanted my brother to play with me and not be treated like an invalid. I wanted my mother to accept me as a tomboy and to accept the friends I brought home from school and the park, regardless of race or religion.

I was lean and mean, my body and my mind developing into a hardhead with an ego. When you depend on yourself for so long, you don't need to depend on anyone else, or at least you don't think so. Maybe that attitude hasn't always been the best thing for me, but that's just how it happened. To this day, I find myself being hardheaded sometimes, and saying things I later regret, and I chalk it up to the first instincts I picked up in Far Rockaway, New York.

My mom never really disciplined Cliff and me. She tried as much as she could to give us direction, but I think she was easy on us because Dad wasn't around and she didn't want to make things tougher on us. If anything, she was too easy on us. When there isn't a strong father figure at home, kids tend to get away with too much. My mother did all she could, but there came a certain point where I knew how hard I could push her. I believe that if you see stability, respect, responsibility and love, you will be able to build good habits and a solid foundation for good choices at an early age. Maybe if things had been different growing up, I would have thought things through a little more, not made so many emotional decisions. I might have saved myself some scars. But when you're young and trying to figure it all out, I guess making some bad choices is just a part of life.

We were Jewish, but we never had a solid religious base at home, and my roots never got very deep. I wish someone would have taken me aside at an early age and explained the respect, fear, love and understanding that goes along with praying to God.

I never developed a strong relationship with my mother as a child, either. I always walked around with a chip on my shoulder, and she never understood my passion for success. There were so many things I missed growing up that I look at it now and wonder how I managed to turn out OK. My whole value system came from playing team sports.

I learned responsibility because I had to be at a certain practice at a certain time. I always worked hard in practice because I wanted to earn the respect of my teammates. I learned how to respect and treat people the way they should be treated because I wanted the same in return.

Don't get me wrong—I had very good times; I mean I was not an unhappy kid. I had a happy childhood, but my happiness came from my friends and sports far more than from my home and family.

Sports, any sport—that's where I found inspiration. I could watch any athletic event on television and be happy. I'd watch the New York Knicks or the New York Rangers and just want to be doing what they were doing.

In April and May, I would go crazy watching baseball, basketball, hockey, and any other sport the networks would put on television. Watching sports was my escape. I didn't have to think about anything when I was fantasizing about sinking the winning free throws, stealing home, completing a hat trick. Sometimes I would chime in with John Condon, public address announcer for the Knicks, or Marv Albert, who did the play-by-play for the Knicks and Rangers.

I have always needed a challenge, and I guess growing up was my first challenge. I was born Nancy Ilizabeth Lieberman on

July 1, 1958, in Brooklyn, to my mother Renee and my father Jerry. I was the first girl, the second child. My brother Cliff was two years older, the apple of my family's eye.

As my mother tells it, I was about two weeks premature. Everyone was convinced that she was going to have another boy. When she went into the delivery room, the doctor asked her if she had a child at home. My mother told him she had a son.

As the doctor was delivering me, he said, "Mrs. Lieberman, you have another boy." The nurse corrected him. My mother was puzzled, confused, then happy—there was a little Lieberman girl.

She finally got to see me, a big baby, 9 pounds, 11 ounces and 22 inches long, with flaming red hair. I was a chubby baby with a round face, little rolls of fat all over my thighs and belly, and three chins. My mother called me gorgeous, as only a mother could.

I'm told I was an active baby who stayed awake all night and slept all day. A playpen was like a prison to me. I wanted to climb out, over, under everything. While Cliff was quiet, the perfectly content child, I was a hellion and wanted to be doing something all the time.

We moved to Far Rockaway when I was almost two years old. I guess it was about this time that my parents were having a lot of friction in their marriage. I don't remember seeing my father much. He would come in and see me at 5 a.m. before going to work. Sometimes he wouldn't return home until after midnight. He was a building contractor and built our house and some of the houses around the corner.

My parents were separated for years, then finally divorced when I was twelve years old. My dad was hardly ever around when I was growing up, and most of my recollections are negative ones. I remember playing outside one day when they were fighting, and a milk bottle came crashing through a window into the yard. I remember looking at the bottle and the glass and thinking that my father must be home.

After they would yell and scream and have terrible fights my mother would insulate Cliff and me from anything that happened. She never gave us any of the details, and we were left to figure things out on our own. I think that is why I became rebellious and started questioning so many things at an early age. I had to know why, and I wanted answers to everything.

Most of my memories of early childhood came from stories my mother has told me over the years. The one recollection I have of my parents being together is when I was three or four years old. One night I snuck into their bed and slept with them; that is the only time I remember them being together.

When my dad finally moved out of the house there was even more tension. We were all on edge, and there was a lot of arguing between my parents and both sets of grandparents. My father's parents had a yard that connected with ours, and it gave us a playing area large enough for football or baseball when the two yards were combined—"Miniature Yankee Stadium," we called it. Sometimes I would go over there and play.

The worst times were waiting for visits from my father. Sometimes I would sit around all day just waiting for him. He lived around the corner, just four houses away. When he wouldn't show up, I would call his mother, "Bubby" (Yiddish for grand-mother), and ask if he was there.

She'd always say something like, "What do you think? I got him in my pocket?" Eventually I'd start crying.

"He promised me. He promised me." I would sit and cry my eyes out until there was nothing left, and then I'd go shoot some hoops or wander around the house wondering how some-one could hurt me so bad. To this day, I can't find the words for the disappointment I felt. He was my dad, and —the way I saw it then— he didn't want to have anything to do with me.

I remember there were times when my mom had no money, but my dad wouldn't support us. Sometimes the lights and the heat were turned off because my mother couldn't pay all of the bills without the child-support money. Cliff and I would round up all of my mom's purses and dump them out looking for change so we could put gas in the car to drive down to one of the hotels my dad owned. We'd ask him why he didn't take care of us and send my mom the money she needed. Those were the worst times.

Cliff was always a good little boy, and I was always worse than ten boys. My grandparents would make little threats, saying that they were going to send me away if I didn't start behaving. They couldn't understand how I could be so bad when Cliff was so good. I heard that harangue so often that I began to resent my brother. He was studious and would stay in his room for hours, reading and being a good boy. I was the total opposite.

Then, too, Cliff had asthma, and the family just sheltered him so much it must have been suffocating. They treated him like he was frail, but Cliff wasn't frail—Cliff had asthma. He'd go through stages sometimes when he was young when his asthma was bad, but everybody around him—my grandparents, my mom—they were all such hypochondriacs, they just made it worse. They sheltered him, they didn't let him experience life, and they didn't let him fall down. Sometimes you have to fall down and scrape your knee to learn: "Oops, that's not the right way."

It made me so mad when my Bubby treated Cliff like he was gold. I'd ask for some little thing, and Bubby would say no; then Cliff would ask for a TV and get a color set. I asked for furniture for years, and Cliff got furniture. I asked for a car, Cliff got a Pinto. When you're young, and you see yourself wanting certain things and someone else receiving everything, you wonder why the treatment is different.

Sometimes I just wanted to have it out with my mom. "Mom," I wanted to say, "I'm not mugging people, I'm not stealing, I'm not drinking—why do you make me out to be such a bad kid because I choose to be out in the street playing ball, which is very healthy, but you think Cliff is the better kid because Cliff is in the house, in his room, studying, like all good boys should do? 'But my Nancy, I don't know where she is, she's in a schoolyard somewhere, running around with ten black kids. She's embarrassing us, she's a tomboy.'" You just get so tired of hearing it.

Looking back on it, it's easy to see that the treatment I got, the comparisons I always heard, none of that was Cliff's fault. But when I was a kid, I had mixed feelings toward my brother because it seemed like his being so good is what made me look bad.

Really, though, Cliff was a great kid and a good brother. Cliff didn't have my athletic ability, but I didn't have his cerebral ability either. I respected him for his smarts and his good grades in school. He's still probably the smartest guy I know, a brilliant doctor, brilliant in computers. But because he was sheltered and I wasn't, I was the street-smart kid while he was the book-smart kid who doesn't have street smarts, and I think today he gets taken advantage of sometimes because he never got the chance to develop that survival mentality.

When we were growing up he'd set aside a little of his allowance every month and pay me for some chores I did for him. We'd celebrate something called "Nancy Day" once a month: He'd take me to Morton's Army-Navy store and buy me something. Usually it was sports-related, like tube socks or sweat bands. Cliff just wanted to do something for me, and it meant a lot to me. When he was older, he worked at Playland Amusement Park. I'd come by to see him with my friends, and we would go on the rides.

Cliff and I were best friends then. I'd tag around him because he was two years older and he had to kind of watch me. I remember starting kindergarten and being very active. I loved the arts and crafts classes and making Wrigley's foil wrappers into chains. I guess I was always looking for attention because I remember getting into trouble for picking on the kids in my class. The teachers would constantly tell my mother I was yapping in the back of the room.

Sometimes I would sneak out of my classroom and look for Cliff. I always wanted to know where he was and so I would walk around the halls and look into classrooms trying to find him. When I would, I'd whisper through the crack of the door, "Cliff." He would look at me with a look that said, "Get out of here!" I'd giggle and go back to my room. I guess I just wanted my big brother to notice me.

Of course, we had the usual brother-sister fights, too. I think the times Cliff and I didn't get along came from my missing the discipline and companionship of my father. I always wanted Cliff to do things with me, to play the same sports I played, and to like the things I liked.

We were almost a total reversal. I was like the little boy playing sports and getting into mischief. Cliff was like the typical little girl, quiet and reserved and not sports-oriented. I was a smart-ass, using my cynical wit as a defense mechanism. Cliff was always polite and courteous to everyone.

My anger was rooted in the lack of love from my father. I grew up not wanting to appear weak in front of my family. I never cried. I rarely told my family I loved them. I was hard on the outside and a little hurt girl on the inside. The closer Cliff got to my mother and grandparents, the further I pushed them away, hiding behind my sports and games.

My father might not have gotten along with my mother, but he could at least have supported us. We had a nice house, but we didn't have any money. My dad was comfortable, and he was always working hard for a deal. He was a hustler. I don't use that word in a negative light. I think it's positive because he was always able to make money and be creative with it. I think he missed the boat with his children, though, because he neglected us when we were kids while he was pursuing more money for a better life. What I don't think he ever understood was that loving Cliff and me wouldn't have cost him a penny. All we wanted was a show of affection and a few minutes of his time.

I did let the resentment toward my father show sometimes. I remember filling out forms for school once, and for mother I wrote "Renee," and for father I wrote "deceased."

There was love in my home, understand, but my father's absence got in the way sometimes. My mother naturally was bitter toward my father, and she was always very emotional about it. At the same time, she thought I should handle my feelings about him better.

I know it hurt my mother because she was there all the time taking care of us, but I'd always be excited about seeing my father. He didn't really do anything for us, and I think she resented that we still cared. Sometimes she would pit me and my brother against my father. I'd be crying and she would say, "I love you, honey, and I'm always here for you, even though your father doesn't care." That would just make me resent my mother. She was right, of course, but the dig still hurt me. I didn't want to hear the negative because no matter what, he was still my father.

It would tear my heart out to think that my dad didn't love me. As I grew up, I had a hard time trusting anyone's care or love. I always wondered if they wanted something from me. My father would say, "I love you, Nancy," but he'd never do anything to prove it. I wanted my father to really be in my life, not just some voice over the phone. So I grew up not understanding what it meant to love somebody. They were just a bunch of words: "I love you." I wanted someone in my life who would back those words up and live them every day with me. Instead, I grew up with the notion that you shouldn't love unconditionally. Never, ever put your heart and soul on the line because someone might not love you back.

If it hadn't been for my grandparents on my mother's side supporting us, we probably would have been on welfare. My mother never worked until my grandfather died in 1976, and then she went to work for an eye doctor.

The area I grew up in was predominantly Jewish. We had ethnic Jews living next to us, and we grew up ethnically Jewish. My mother sent Cliff and me to Hebrew Sunday School classes. I wasn't ready for Hebrew School because I had no sense of religion in my upbringing. I hated it. I rebelled. I disrupted the class and the teacher by jumping out of windows, talking back, whatever it took. They would call my mother: "Mrs. Lieberman, you need to come and pick up your daughter because the other children in the class cannot learn."

Part of me didn't want to learn, and part of me couldn't understand why I had to be one kind of religion. I wanted someone to tell me why I had to be Jewish, to give me some background and explain why I had to go to school to learn about it. We celebrated both Hanukkah and Christmas because my mother's parents were Irish Catholics. We had a lot of mixed marriages in our family. But formal teaching was not my idea of a good time, and I grew up with very little understanding of what Judaism —or Christianity, for that matter— was all about.

I felt like I had a void in my life because I didn't have an understanding of religion, God, or Jesus Christ. I knew He was there, but I never understood His significance—who or what He really was in my life. I didn't have that inner peace or comfort knowing that someone else had control of my life. My peace and comfort came from scoring points and winning trophies. Even as a youngster, I knew that there had to be more to our existence than what I could see.

But at the time I was more concerned with figuring out why girls were treated differently from boys. It never made sense to me that my girlfriends growing up played with dolls. BOR-ing! My idea of a good time was racing around the school yard at Public School 104 with the boys. Cliff and I walked the one block to the school, but I couldn't wait to get there and run and play with all the guys.

I never had a long attention span in the classroom. The teachers all had the same gripe. Nancy's not paying attention in class. I couldn't sit still; all I wanted to do was go outside and play. Just sitting there all the time drove me crazy; I, in turn, drove my teachers crazy. I loved gym class but hated the recesses when I stood on the sidelines. The boys played football and basketball, while the girls played kickball and punchball. I knew there were no professional kickball leagues.

After school, I would go to the park with Cliff and our mother's helper, Irene, a neighbor who kept an eye on us for a few dollars my mother would get from her parents. I loved being outside, playing on the swings or the jungle gym or joining a group of kids for games. My favorite game was called knock hockey. When I got older, Cliff and I would go to the park and play whatever game was going on.

Sometimes Cliff's asthma would act up, and he couldn't go out and play with me. He was constantly being tested for one allergy or another and taking shots, and his physical activity was limited. I couldn't really understand why or how he was sick. He didn't look sick to me. Sometimes he could play and other times he couldn't. At times like this, Cliff was just another male figure who was letting me down, for no reason I could figure out.

One day when I was in the third grade I watched some older boys playing basketball in the gym. I liked the game, and I was intrigued with all the different moves and shots. Not long after that, I saw an NBA game on television for the first time. I couldn't believe the action and non-stop motion of the game. I was mesmerized. I really didn't understand the rules, but I knew I liked the constant movement.

The next day, while delivering papers on my route, I looked at the pictures of the game on the sports page and read in the headlines that the Knicks had beaten the Bucks. I was hooked. I was used to a 5-4 baseball score or a 24-17 football score, and I couldn't believe how many points were scored in a basketball game. The Knicks and the Bucks had scored over 100 points each!

I started going into the old gym in front of the school to shoot baskets before school and at recess. At first, some of the kids were amused at how I'd just throw the ball at the basket, not really shooting it. As I watched the guys in the schoolyard and the Knicks on television, I picked up the right technique to shooting a basketball. It would be years before I'd get any actual instruction.

Little by little, the guys started letting me play, and by the time I was in the fourth grade I was pretty good. We played indoors a lot and when it got nice I'd tag along to the park with them. I learned quickly that you have to be competitive to stay on a court at the playgrounds, where the winner plays the next challenger and the loser goes back to the end of the line to wait for another game.

I had always played a lot of baseball and football in my backyard. We had the biggest yard in the neighborhood, connected with my Bubby and Zadie's (grandparents') yard. There was a barn at the very back of the yard and it was a home run if you hit the barn.

If you hit the window, my Bubby would come out and start yelling at everybody. She'd tell us to get out of her yard, but I'd remind her that Cliff and I were her grandchildren no matter what my father did. She would get a nasty kind of mad, and we loved to egg her on. I think we eventually busted out every window in that old barn.

Other times, we would have non-stop games of tackle football, complete with pads and helmets. I think playing like that when I was so young helped me get the respect of the guys. Then, too, it was my backyard, and I got to call the shots. Well, except when we broke one of Bubby's windows.

At the formative ages, I think that boys and girls are pretty much at the same skill level at any sport if they start out together and get the same training. The boys weren't that much stronger or quicker than me, and I was able to keep up with them. They were better in some skills, and I was better at others.

I remember my disappointment when I was told I had to stop playing in the Police Athletic League when I was nine years old. After playing ball in the neighborhood leagues, you could move up to PAL baseball. I had made my PAL team as the starting left fielder and backup shortstop, beating out guys I had grown up and played ball with for several years. I had a good arm, and I delighted in blowing people away with a pinpoint throw from the outfield or taking away a hit deep in the hole and throwing the runner out by a stride.

The day before our first game, the coach, a guy named Smitty, came up to me and said I wasn't going to be allowed to play. He told me that it had to do with insurance. "Nancy, they won't insure you because you are a girl."

In those days, I didn't know what the word discrimination meant. All I knew was that I was crushed that I couldn't play ball with my friends. They would finish playing a game in the PAL, and then I would join them to play in the neighborhood games. It just didn't make sense to me: I could play with them at school and in neighborhood games, but not in a league, where statistics counted. That was probably the reason I wanted to play PAL ball anyway. Statistics are a measure of success, and I wanted to know how I stacked up.

Fortunately, there were fewer barriers in basketball. Shortly after being barred from the PAL, I signed up to play on a boys' age-group team (10-13 years old) at the Hartman YMCA. I was the tallest player on the team, and I played center. We had games every Sunday, and I loved the competition. Most of the guys were the same ones I played against in the neighborhood, but it was fun to have coaches and start learning the game.

Up to then, I had learned the game of basketball the same way the guys did—by playing half-court, one-on-one, which means you are the guard, forward, and center all wrapped up into one. I'd also get to play against both girls and guys in gym class at Junior High School 180 in Rockaway Beach, though there was no girls' team to play on. That was the first time I ever played with a net.

Every game that I could get into at the gym or park helped me hone my individual skills at a very early age. When I had the opportunity to play an organized game in the "Y" league, I was able to apply the skills I had learned on the playground to a full-court setting and a team game.

The toughest part was just making the transition to the full court, but looking back, I had the best of both worlds, excelling at both one-on-one and the full-court game. Not many players are fortunate enough to cut their teeth both ways so they have that versatility.

Those years also taught me one of the most important lessons of my life: If you proved to the guys that you belonged in their domain of a basketball court, football field, or baseball diamond, you could become a participant instead of just a cheerleader.

Chapter 2

What Will the Neighbors Think?

In the late 1960s you couldn't be a "female athlete"; you were still a "tomboy." That was a stage little girls went through on their way to becoming sweet young women. You'd grow out of it, and if you didn't there was something wrong with you. It was so frustrating being an athletically gifted girl and hearing that over and over again. Couldn't they understand? I simply loved sports.

One of the first times I remember being called a "tomboy" was on account of my shoes. I had always worn a pair of boat shoes called "skips," but all the boys in the neighborhood had white canvas Chuck Taylor Converse basketball shoes. Of course, I got it in my head that you weren't a very good athlete unless you had a pair of Cons. Sometimes I'd judge how good a player someone was by his shoes before he even stepped on the court.

I had saved and saved the money from my paper route to buy a pair of white low-cut Converse Chuck Taylor basketball shoes. I worked up the nerve and took my ten dollars to Morton's Army-Navy Store.

The salesman looked at me kind of funny when I told him what I wanted. "It's not a shoe for girls," he told me. I told him that's what I wanted and I'd wear them home, please.

I couldn't wait to show my mom and Cliff my Cons, but all they did was rag me: "Nancy's a tomboy. Nancy's a tomboy." At first I was mad, insulted and hurt that they would say that about me because of my shoes.

But then I turned the insult around. By calling me a "tomboy," they were saying I was like a boy. I took that to mean wearing the right equipment and all—my Chuck Taylor Cons. Yeah, that's OK. So tell me I'm like a boy; I'll take that as a compliment.

I was so proud of my Cons; they were limousines for my feet. Talk about protective! I was infuriated if I got grass stains on my Cons. I wanted them to always look fresh and white and just like new. I didn't care who saw me wear my "boys' shoes"; keep off of my Cons.

It took a while for my mother to get used to the sports I was playing. Every day, I would come home from the playground and my mother would ask me, "How many home runs did you hit today?" No, Ma, I play basketball. The next day she would ask, "How many touchdowns this afternoon?" No, Mother. I shoot baskets. Somehow, she had a hard time getting the sport right.

My mom was still waiting for me to grow out of this stage. In the meantime, she would look out the kitchen window to the back yard and see me and all the boys playing football.

At the time I didn't realize it, but I had a crush on the best boy athlete in our class, Steve Cohen. Steve and I always played football, basketball, and baseball together. One day, I was sitting across from Steve in school, and it suddenly dawned on me that he was a cute guy. I had never thought of guys that way before; they were just people to fill up a roster. I wondered if he looked at me as a girl instead of a tomboy. Did those cute guys think I was cute? Or did they consider me a girl who could help them win basketball games but not a girl they would like to take out? It was too much to worry about when I was in the sixth grade, so I never brought it up. We just kept playing sports together.

I guess my mother had taken notice that her tomboy was growing up. One day she stood grimacing in front of the kitchen window, watching us play football in the back yard. As she watched, she heard a loud "POP!" Out shot red hair from under a helmet.

"That's enough playing for you, young lady," my mother called out.

I remember coming into the kitchen and seeing that my mother had this disgusted look on her face. I could sense a serious mother-daughter chat coming on.

"Nancy, sit down for a minute," she began. "Look at you, dirty from head to toe. Nancy, you're a girl, and girls aren't supposed to roughhouse. I don't want you playing football with all of those boys. They're all jumping on top of you, and you'll get hurt."

"I won't get hurt," I shot back. "It's the boys you should worry about. I love my sports. Why can't I play?"

"Honey, it's not ladylike to play sports," she explained.

"But Mom!" I whined.

"Nancy, you are never going to be an athlete because it is for boys, not for girls."

I leaned up against the refrigerator, put my hands on my hips and grinned a defiant grin, I was a cocky ten-year-old.

"Yeah? I'll show you. I'll make history," I proclaimed, and walked out the door.

My role models and idols in sports were very important to me growing up, and it didn't matter that they were all males. Muhammad Ali was the greatest athlete overall in my eyes, and Willis Reed and Walt Frazier of the Knicks were my basketball idols.

Ali represented everything I wanted to be in sports. He was bold, brash, confident, and cocky, but he backed up everything that he said he was going to do. I always admired that because I came across a lot of athletes who would brag and then not back up their mouth with their game. I wanted to be such a good player that I could be just like Ali—brash and bold but able to back it up. I also learned from Ali that his attitude gave him an enormous psychological edge over his opponents. It's a real psych job when your opponent hears you say that you expect to beat him. I vowed to myself that I would never talk trash unless I was able to back it up.

I learned a lot from watching Willis Reed play the game. He had great leadership qualities and a lot of determination. He was the team captain and the glue that held the Knicks together. He always got the job done whether he was healthy or playing hurt. He left his blood and guts on the court.

Walt Frazier was cool, calm, and determined. As the Knicks' point guard, he had such style; he dictated and controlled the tempo of the entire game. I learned how to find the open man on the floor by watching "Clyde" play. He was always patient, and it paid off when he would come up with a timely steal and basket. The Knicks had the city wrapped around their little fingers, and I hoped someday I would be the toast of a town, too.

I remember the nights I listened to the Knicks games on the radio or caught an occasional game on television. I would get so caught up in the games, imagining myself playing like Frazier or Reed. If they happened to lose, I was convinced that I had done something to jinx the team.

My mom couldn't pull me away from a Knicks, Nets, Rangers, Yankees or Mets game on the television. I twisted that dial for years, season after season. I usually could be found out in the schoolyard after a game, practicing a move I'd seen Reed or Frazier make on television. I never lost when I played my playground fantasy games. Because of Frazier, I wore jersey No. 10 through high school, the Olympics, college and the pros.

In 1986, I finally had a chance to meet the man who wore No. 10 for the Knicks. I was doing a charity fundraiser at a sports bar in New York, the "Sporting Club," with a number of celebrities and athletes in attendance. As I was working my way across the room, I spotted Walt Frazier, and my eyes got as big as saucers. I stumbled through my hello, nervously told him about picking his number to wear over a dozen years earlier, then weakly walked away feeling stupid. Several years later, I had the opportunity to talk to him again and even promoted his N.Y. Knicks Fantasy Camp in Atlantic City. This time I was able to talk with him, and I found out that he had seen me play, that we both had homes in St. Croix and were both very involved in charity work. I told him that I talked about him so much growing up that my mother thought for years that he was a playground buddy of mine. In a way, he really was.

I guess you could say my imagination was my first basketball coach. I would go out and shoot early in the morning, go to school, and then play basketball again until after dark. A lot of times I would shoot around by myself and imagine that I was making a move against Frazier. Then I'd pretend I played for the Knicks and I was making my move against Dr. J., Julius Erving.

I would create shots and dream that I was beating all these NBA stars. I can remember so many times when I tried to hit a winning shot at the buzzer in my make-believe games. I tried them all: the half-court "Hail Mary" shot, the length-of-the-floor shot, the drive to the hoop past five defenders, free throws with no time left on the clock. It was a big deal when I hit half-court shots at the buzzer three games in a row at Old Dominion. What the spectators didn't realize was that I'd been practicing those shots all of my life on the playgrounds.

By that time you could see I was going to be a good athlete. I had been successful playing Pee Wee football, softball, baseball, and basketball. I was well-coordinated and was accepted by my male counterparts as a winner. I loved the competition and the winning. I just didn't know how to get that through to my mother.

And she didn't know what to say to me. I was trying to build my self-esteem. My brother was smart. I didn't have good grades in school because I had a short attention span, and I was distracted by what was going on at home. Sports were something I could do to feel good about myself. I just wanted to stay out of the house and play every sport I could to block out my other failures. When I had to be in the classroom, I was a real troublemaker.

"Mrs. Lieberman, your Nancy, she disrupts the class. The other day the class was so quiet, taking a test, and all of a sudden Nancy starts quacking like a duck and disrupts the whole class." Another way to get attention, make myself the focus.

When people would talk about what a good athlete I was or the big basket I had hit, I wanted my family to hear it. But it really didn't matter—no one in my family was a sports fan, and they wouldn't have understood anyway. Grades—that's what my family understood: Nancy got C's and D's, Cliff got A's and B's. It didn't matter to them that I was a good athlete. I thought of myself as dumb because of my grades, but I caught on quickly that I could use my basketball to give me the self-esteem I couldn't get in the classroom.

Growing up, I guess I drove my mother nuts. All she ever wanted was a frilly little girl, but here I'd come in from the park and start banging a ball in the house. My mother grew up with Bell Silverman, who became opera star Beverly Sills, and I think she expected to put me in dresses and make me into an opera star, too. My grandmother was always buying pretty little dresses for me to wear, too. She wanted to dress me up like a doll—I was having none of it.

It was shattering for them to realize that all Nancy wanted to do was race around in sneakers, tube socks, cutoffs, and t-shirts. I wanted to play ball. I *had* to play ball. Instead of sitting in my room and crying about my family, I would wrap myself in my sports.

Most summers for about five or six years, my mother would pack me up and send me off to camp for a few weeks. I felt like they sent me to camp just to get me out of their hair for eight weeks of peace and quiet. I hated being away from my friends and the playgrounds for so long, but I did my best to make camp an interesting experience.

I attended a wonderful place called Camp Surprise Lake. I was as disruptive at camp as I was in school, getting into fights and mouthing off to other kids. I couldn't hide behind my basketball here. It was arts and crafts, canoeing, hiking, horse-back riding. Nowhere for me to shine and win acceptance from the other campers. One time I remember throwing a bunk bed out the door because another girl camper made a remark that I didn't like. I was terrible, and there were few days when the camp director wasn't calling my mother about me.

The more I didn't want to be at camp the more she insisted they keep me there. I'll admit now that going to camp really wasn't all that bad. Some years Cliff wouldn't go because he was so choked up with his allergies and had to be on oxygen and shots, but one of my best summers at camp was one year they let him go, too. Cliff was on the teen side of the camp, and I was on the younger side. Even if we didn't always get along, it was nice to have my big brother nearby.

Sometimes in the middle of the night we would signal each other with flashlights across the lake. Then we'd each get in rowboats and row out and meet each other in the middle. It wasn't a huge lake, but it was fun to be daring and have the adventure. We'd meet and talk for awhile, then row back and sneak in before the counselors found us missing from our bunks.

Still, I never liked the idea of being shipped off to camp without my mother even asking what I'd like to do with my summer. I did make some good friends at Camp Surprise Lake, but I'm sure there's more than one counselor who recalls the times I nearly tore my mother's dress off fighting to keep from being loaded onto the bus for camp.

Sometimes my mom's parents would take Cliff, my mother, and me to Florida to vacation at the Surfcomber Beach Hotel in Miami Beach. When we'd go to Florida, I had the beach and pinball machines as my escape instead of the blacktop and asphalt of the basketball court. I always had fun on those trips, but it was never too soon to get back to the neighborhood.

On those trips, Cliff and I usually got along well because we had to be each other's best friend. Cliff's secret mischievous streak would come out, and those are the only times I remember both of us getting into trouble equally. One time we went to a gag shop and bought a laughing box, and we had it along one night when my grandmother took us to a Las Vegas-style nightclub show at the hotel. We were bored, and in the middle of the act we pulled out the laughing box. The box started going "ha, ha, ha, ha, ha" while the performer was in the middle of a song. As everyone turned around to see where the noise was coming from, my grandmother grabbed Cliff and me by the ears and pulled us out of the show. She yelled at us all the way up the aisle and to our hotel room. It hadn't dawned on us that we shouldn't have pulled the stunt.

My most memorable trip to Florida was the summer before I entered the sixth grade. I had saved my money on the trip and ordered a pet alligator for $9.99 before I went back to New York. About eight weeks later the alligator came in the mail. My mother couldn't imagine what I could have ordered. I remember running through the kitchen screaming that my alligator had arrived, but my mother was apparently under the impression that it was a stuffed animal. When I tore into the box punched with holes and stuffed with shredded paper, she should have had a clue.

The alligator was six inches long and very much alive. My mother still thought it was stuffed until she touched it and it moved. She went nuts.

"Nancy, you can't have an alligator in New York. You are getting rid of it right now. Cliff is probably allergic to it," my mother screamed at me. Now I knew that Cliff was allergic to just about everything in the world, but I wasn't buying that alligators were included.

My grandmother tried a different tack—bribery. "Nancy, I'll give you $25 for the alligator," she said. I shook my head. "$30?" I still said no. There was no way I was going to get rid of "Al" the alligator.

When I went to camp, I gave Al to a friend for safekeeping, and my family thought they were finally rid of him. No such luck, they found out when I returned. Al stayed in the picture a few more months, and my family finally gave up complaining about him until the day I lost him in the house.

I had taken Al out of his tank and let him run around inside the house after school one day. I lost sight of him and couldn't figure out where he had gone. All I knew was that I couldn't have him loose in the house or I was going to be in trouble.

I saw him scoot under the refrigerator so I rolled the big white box away from the wall. All I could see was dust—no Al. I figured he must have crawled into the motor, so I found a screwdriver and took the back panel off the refrigerator just as Cliff walked into the house from school. As soon as he saw the mess he knew he was going to be in trouble if he helped me. About the only way Cliff ever got into trouble was trying to bail me out.

Neither of us could see Al, so we started taking the refrigerator apart. After a while we still couldn't get to him and figured that we were going to have to turn the big machine on its side. We felt pretty stupid as everything started falling out of it, but we found Al stuck behind the motor and got him out. Then we worked like crazy cleaning up the mess so no one would be the wiser about our afternoon adventure.

The next time my grandmother bribed me to take Al away, I surprised her by giving in. My grandparents took Al and put him into Sheepshead Bay. I guess the deal I cut with my grandmother over Al was the beginning of my business career.

My grandparents, Lou and Eva Saks, helped fill the family void. Whether it was good advice, a scolding, a hug, or a palm full of change, they were always there for Cliff and me. My grandfather made his living as a pianist. He loved jazz, and people would come from all over to hear him play.

Both of my grandparents had performed in vaudeville. Grandpa Lou even performed for silent pictures. He was a real master at the piano, and he could lay a towel over the keys and never miss a note. I could never figure out how he could do that. I guess that's what I remember best about him.

Grandpa Lou was so quiet that sometimes it was like you never knew he existed. My grandmother was just the opposite, a "Type A" personality who always ran the show. Sometimes my grandmother and I would be arguing, and Grandpa would just walk over to the piano and start playing the Cavalry song or the William Tell Overture like it was the silent movie soundtrack for this big fight scene. He wouldn't say anything, he'd just keep playing, and then gradually you'd start to realize what he was doing and—"Hey, cut that out—he's making fun of me"—and I'd forget I was arguing with my grandmother.

Grandma Eva was the type of person who always seemed to do things right. I remember her always being in a dress with lovely jewelry. She was an elegant lady who would never think of going out without a matching dress, shoes, and handbag.

She would often take Cliff and me to Brooklyn to walk in the parks, shop, or play bingo. She always tried to dress me up like a little doll, but I told her I wanted to dress like the boys. She was always a little disappointed that her granddaughter was a tomboy.

Cliff and I were also close to my Uncle Al and Aunt Bea, my mother's sister. I spent a lot of time hanging out at their house. It was a great place full of things that were really neat to a kid. Uncle Al and Aunt Bea collected everything from African wood carvings to slot machines. I think I clung to my Uncle Al since my dad wasn't around. He and my grandfather Lou were the dominant male figures in my life.

My aunt and uncle owned a store called Tile City. I would go over there every day and talk to Uncle Al and watch all the carpet and linoleum go in and out of the store. My uncle always told me funny stories and jokes and laughed a lot. He gave me the attention I was missing growing up. Maybe he sensed that I missed my dad. Anyway, I was always his little girl.

Their condo was across the street from Beach 17th Street, the place in that neighborhood to play basketball, right on the water. All the college stars would play ball there, and if you could get into a game on Beach 17th Street, you were really something. I would watch the guys at Beach 17th and dream about playing the same way. I tried to copy their moves and add them to my repertoire.

By the time I was a sophomore in high school I was going to Beach 17th to watch the big dogs play, in hopes that I might get into a game. One day, Brian Winters, who later played with the Milwaukee Bucks, and Levern Tart, who played for the New York Nets in the ABA, said, "Come on—let's let the girl play."

Once they saw I could play, I never had any trouble getting into a game. In fact, Levern took me under his wing and brought me with him to a couple of parks to play ball. One time we went to play in Harlem, and I was the only white player out of several hundred there. I was really scared, but Levern told me to just go out and play and relax. Later, we played in a tournament there at St. John's Park and I came away with the MVP trophy. I never dreamed when I started going to my aunt and uncle's house across from the Beach 17th playground that one day I'd get to play in that world.

I think the black guys on the playground accepted me at an early age because I was trying to make the same moves they were. I never saw color growing up, and it didn't matter to me who I played with just as long as they wanted to win and keep the court. These guys were just teammates and friends. I couldn't understand other people's prejudices. Maybe it was because I was a red-headed, white, Jewish tomboy. How could you expect me to understand prejudice?

I think I was always looked at as a ballplayer first and a girl second. I was just one of the "guys," and most of us grew up and learned the game together. Our favorite times at P.S. 104 were at recess, when we played on a rim that was only 8 1/2 feet high. I can still remember my first slam-dunk on that rim. Sometimes I'd take all my buddies, black and white, to my house for lunch at recess.

My neighbors didn't know what to think when they saw me walking down the street with eight or nine guys, most of them black. We'd come in the house and I'd buzz my mother on the intercom and say that I had brought some friends home for lunch.

"That's nice, dear. I'll be right out," my mother would say.

She would take one look at the assortment of guys I brought home and call me into her bedroom. "What are the neighbors going to think, you bringing home all of these boys?" she'd ask me. I told her time and time again I didn't care what they thought.

These were my buddies. Growing up I think the words most repeated out of my mother's mouth were, "What will so and so think?"

Chapter 3

Keeping the Court

The schoolyard shaped the basketball player I became. It taught me how to compete, survive, rely on myself and others, and win. The skills I showed later in the Olympic Games or at Old Dominion were skills I had honed on the schoolyard and by playing streetball. They were moves I made thousands of times and visualized thousands more.

I was doing cybernetics before it became popular. I'd come off the court at night and go to bed thinking about a move I saw that day. I would do the move 100 times to perfection in my mind's eye. Sometimes I would watch myself dribble in the mirror to check my form. So much of the game became muscle memory for me because I repeated the moves so often. I loved my sport, and I lived it.

My early basketball experiences were exercises in survival. Today, so much is set up and orchestrated for kids. In the summers they attend elite camps, team camps, and AAUs and rarely step onto a hot blacktop court for a pickup game. At camps, you learn to play, but in the pickup games, you learn to survive. You have to win to keep your court, and if you lose, it might take a whole day just to get your court back.

Keeping the court—I thrived on that kind of competitive situation. I played a lot of one-on-one because survival means depending on yourself to win. Playing the game taught me a lot about responsibility. I look back at some of the lessons the playground taught me 20 years ago, and they still apply to my life.

Something as simple as lining up in front of all the kids on the court to take your turn trying to touch the rim or the backboard was a really big deal. There was peer pressure, the potential of failure, and the realization everyone would see the result. Since I was the only female out there, I felt like if I failed, their perception would be that *all* girls had failed.

The competition was always there. It was like, "C'mon, can you touch the backboard?" We'd have contests to see whether we could touch the backboard, and then it wasn't the backboard, it was the rim. I remember the first time I dunked on that 8-foot-6 rim. I mean it was a major, major event in the neighborhood. Here I was a girl, 5-foot-8, dunking with those boys, and it earned me enormous respect.

We'd play one-on-one or two-on-two for the right to use the court. It was pretty cut and dried. Either you win or you step aside. I knew that first impressions were everything, so I'd walk out on the court like a jock. I concentrated on technique and form when I was warming up because I knew a lot of people would be watching the girl if they'd never seen me play. If they saw me shoot like a guy, then I had instant acceptance. Once I got on the court, I'd play hard to hold it all day. When some kids would head home for dinner, I'd just be catching my second wind. I can remember my mother and my grandmother standing on the corner yelling down the street to me.

"Nancy, let's go. It's time for dinner and it's getting dark," they'd call. "In a minute," I'd answer, but that minute usually meant two or three hours. There were very few indoor courts, so we stayed outside as long as weather permitted. It didn't matter if it was dark because there was usually one good street light around and that was all we needed.

At night, we would play a game called "radar ball." It would be pitch black out and we would shoot hoops by whatever street light happened to be closest. We had a good idea where the basket should be on the court, and the metal rim would make a pinging sound when someone scored. If you couldn't see the ball, you just followed the sound of the bouncing ball. Sometimes we'd lose track of the sound, and the ball would be lost until the next morning. On some nights, that was the only thing that could end the game.

One of the guys in the neighborhood finally had a light put up on his basketball court. Mark Muchnick lived around the corner, next door to my Lieberman grandparents, and his court became the place to play in the neighborhood at night. The only drawback was the constant complaining from my grandparents. They would scream out the window to tone it down, turn off the light, and quit bouncing the ball.

My mother disapproved of my being out at night playing basketball, of course. I would get the same lecture every time I came back into the house: "Nancy, why can't you be like other girls? Why do you have to stay out half the night playing basketball? This can't be normal."

She didn't approve of us playing in the snow, either. We would get out there and shovel the snow off the court and play with gloves, jeans, and a couple of sweat shirts. If the weather got really bad, I'd invite all the guys over to my house to play. We improvised by taking bumper stickers and wrapping them around a coat hanger for a rim and using a piece of cardboard for the backboard. I tacked this apparatus up on my bedroom wall, and we'd play two-on-two with a Nerf ball, the rules otherwise basically the same as those for outdoors.

As busy as I was, playing every game I could find, I still wanted a job. My mother said, "No, Nancy, you don't need to work. You're only a kid."

But she didn't understand my motivation. I knew we didn't have much money, and I wanted to earn some dollars to buy the sports equipment that I wanted. I wanted to buy shoes, footballs, basketballs, baseballs, a glove, and a bat. All I wanted were the necessities of my sports.

I told her I wanted to deliver newspapers.

"Nancy, this is for boys. Delivering papers is a job that girls just don't do," she explained. Naturally, before long I was delivering the *Long Island Press*.

I have to admit I don't know how my mother put up with me and all of my sports. I would jump in the house at night to try to improve my vertical leap. I'd stand next to a wall and jump up and slap it with my hand. Sometimes I would run out of my room and jump up and slap the doorway. I wanted to be able to jump just like Julius Erving, Doctor J., whom I watched every time he was on television. I wanted to master some of the incredible moves he made, and it made sense to me to work on my jumping, too.

As I got older and bigger, my jumping improved. Gradually, I worked my way up the wall and the doorway, and sooner or later I was able to touch the ceiling. Of course, I'd usually try these stunts when my hands were filthy from playing in the streets or dribbling a ball. Little by little, the fingerprints worked their way up the wall until they turned into hand prints on the ceiling.

My mother finally had enough. "Who put all of these fingerprints on the wall and the ceiling?" my mother would ask.

"I don't know. I guess it was, uh, Cliff?"

Cliff would look at me like I was crazy. I knew it was time to get out of the house for a while. When I came back, my mother was cleaning the walls and ceiling.

I had another habit that drove my mother nuts. I always wanted to work on my ball handling, especially when the weather was bad in the winter, so I would dribble for hours around the house. One day my mom was in the back of the house with a headache, and she'd had enough of my dribbling.

"Nancy, stop that right now. It's making me crazy—all that bounce, bounce, bounce."

"No, mom, I can't stop," I yelled. "It's too cold outside and I need to work on this crossover dribble."

She came charging out of the room with a screwdriver in her hand and punched a hole in my basketball; then she went back into her room thinking that she had won the battle.

But my paper route, plus money from Grandpa and Grandma Saks, kept me well supplied with basketballs. I got another one. Bounce, bounce, bounce went the hollow sound of the rubber basketball on the linoleum floor.

"Nancy, where did you get that basketball?" Mom bellowed.

She punched another one with her screwdriver, and another, and another until she had deflated five of my balls.

I had more.

It got to the point where it was comical. I was laughing, and she was puncturing the balls, one after another. As my supply got low, I suddenly stopped laughing and realized the joke was on me. She told me to get out of the house and dribble outside before she punched holes in all of them.

"Mom, how could you do that?" I finally said. "I can't believe you would do such a thing. How will I ever get better at my sport if I have no cooperation or support from my family?"

There was a stage in my life around my early teens when I became very aggressive. If my mother punctured my basketballs, then I had to find a way to get back at her. I felt like she and Cliff constantly ganged up on me and I had to fend for myself. I had a choice at that point: leave the house and escape by playing ball or stand toe-to-toe and fight with them.

One time Cliff was picking on me, and pretty soon it turned into a fight. In my mind, I was just defending myself against my older brother. But I was pretty good with my hands and he'd been sheltered, so invariably Cliff would get the bad end of the deal. Except when I got busted as the nogoodnick by my mother.

"Ma, Ma. Cliff was beating me up," I would cry. But she would just have caught the tail end of the fight: me getting a good lick in on Cliff, I became the bad guy.

"What are you doing to your brother?" my mother screamed one time, picking up a chair and cracking it over my head. I couldn't believe it. It was just like a scene out of a Western barroom brawl.

The next time we came to blows, I decided there was no way Cliff would get the better of me. The minute he raised his hand, I just clocked him and knocked him down. I grabbed my coat and left the house, heading for the basketball court. Sometimes in the winter I would keep my coat on the railing just in case I had to grab it and leave quickly. Many nights I left the house and hid out in the yard, standing next to the fireplace. When the coast was clear I would sneak back into the house in the middle of the night.

In those days, I never had a best friend whose house I could have gone to when all hell broke loose at home. I think most of the girls in my class were scared of me because I hung around with all the guys, both black and white. I was friendly with the girl next door, Wendy Miller, because her brother Steve would let me play ball. The other girls in my class would invite their friends over to lunch at recess while I was playing ball or having all the guys over for lunch.

I never went to parties or dances because I spent all my time playing sports. I couldn't tell you what song was on the radio, or what the big fashion was, and I wasn't into the typical adolescent female concerns. I was busy breaking the rules or, rather, playing by my own rules, playing ball.

Chapter 4

Take the "A" Train

I'll be the first to admit I was a handful growing up. If I was rebellious as a youngster, it was nothing compared with my teenage years. I was full of anger, full of sarcasm.

My mom took Cliff and me to a psychologist for kids when I was 14 years old because I had really started to pick on Cliff and her. I felt like Cliff would always take up for her when she and I got into a fight. After a while, Cliff was like my mother's defender, reprimanding me for fighting with her.

"Nancy, don't yell at Mother, and don't pick on her," Cliff would say. I would say something like, "What? Are you two married or something?" This is when a father might have stepped in and showed me a little discipline for making such a stupid comment.

I told my mother that she and Cliff were the ones who needed the psychologist, not me. I'd head out the door and call over my shoulder, "If the doctor needs to talk to me about your evaluations, he can reach me at home."

I dealt in pure sarcasm, something more powerful than a lethal drug. Eventually, I did go to see the psychologist, just to embarrass my mother. I played around while taking all of the tests; putting square pegs in round holes was one of my favorites. I also purposely described wild things out of inkblots and if they asked me to describe certain colors, I would make up colors to confuse them. My mother would overreact and that just made matters worse.

I was very comfortable, in comparison with my home life, playing on the schoolyards at P.S. 104. But my real challenges began when I took the "A" train out of Far Rockaway.

In my first year at Far Rockaway High School, a guy from the boys' basketball team came over to the girls' gym to deliver a message to me. He told me that a guy named LaVosier Lamar from Harlem had seen me at some tryout camps and wanted me to come into the city to play ball with his team. He said they practiced every night after school and played in AAU competitions. I couldn't believe it. I was 13 years old, and I was being recruited to play for one of the best AAU teams in the city, the New York Chuckles.

I was so excited when Coach Lamar asked me to play. He told me he'd meet me at the subway station and take me to the gym. I was going to play in Harlem.

There I was, 14 years old, the only white girl riding the train to go shoot hoops. I was so scared going down there that I would put on a couple of sweaters under my coat just to look bigger. Then I'd get on the train, have this real mean "don't mess with me" look on my face and look people in the eye so they wouldn't know I was scared.

My mother would beg me not to go.

"Nancy, this is driving me crazy," she said. "You know you'll be killed if you ride that train to play ball. I'm afraid someone is going to get hurt."

"Mom, don't worry. I promise I won't hurt anybody," I'd tell her.

She just stared at me, a look on her face like, "What are you talking about?"

I'd ride the train and get off at my stop, either East New York in Brooklyn or Harlem, then walk as quickly as I could to the schoolyard. Many times Lamar, a rotund black man with a heart of gold, would meet me at the train. Other times I would have to walk to the gym. Then sometimes I'd go straight to the parks, walk up to the guys waiting to play, and say, "All right, who is next?" There'd be guys with names like the Terminator, and I'd say, "I wanna see the Terminator," and this big guy with a deep voice would say, "I'm the Terminator." I'd be throwing an attitude and the guys would just be looking at me. If they didn't say anything, I'd usually announce that I was next, and if they wanted to play they needed to see me. And they'd look at me like, "I can't believe she's talking to me." It's no wonder they eventually nicknamed me "Fire."

I 'd walk across the park and sit down to wait for the next game. The guys didn't know how to take me at first. Here was a 14-year-old red-headed Jewish girl taking over their game. But once I got the court, it didn't take long to gain their respect. We all realized we were out there for the same thing, to play ball.

I won my share of trophies while playing with the Chuckles and the Harlem Hellraisers in the AAU and summer leagues. Most of the trophies I won came from all-star games and tournaments in Harlem, 4-foot monsters engraved "Most Valuable Player." I loved winning trophies because it was another incentive to play hard. One time, I was playing in a tournament at City College and I was the only white player on the floor. At the end of the tournament color didn't matter. Outstanding play is what got you a trophy.

Lamar was my first mentor, always teaching, pushing, asking as much of me as I was capable of giving. He taught me that there was no color and to accept others no matter who they were or where they came from in life. In that world, *I* was the minority, and they accepted me because I was a ball player... just like them.

One Saturday my mom was getting calls from people on my route who hadn't gotten their papers. Then she got a call from me.

"Ma, I'll be home soon and I've got to talk to you and Grandma."

"Nancy, where are you? I've had people calling me and complaining all afternoon looking for their paper."

"You don't understand. I've got something to tell you when I see you." When I got home, my mother drove me on my route. In between tossing papers and driving house to house through the neighborhood, I told her I had gone to a USA basketball tryout at Queens College. She had a blank look on her face, so I tried to explain.

A few mornings earlier, one of my friends from school had called and told me about an article in the paper. There was going to be an open tryout at Queens College for the USA women's basketball team. So we said, "Let's go play ball."

We went down to Queens and found ourselves with about 150 other players in a line to pay the $5 registration fee. It was the first time I'd ever seen so many female basketball players, the first time I realized there were a lot of girls like me who could play the game well. I wasn't so strange after all. Other girls had grown up loving sports too. I was tired of people telling me I would outgrow sports and being a tomboy. For the first time, I started to think of myself not as a tomboy, but as an athlete. The word "athlete" had a lot more dignity, commanded a lot more respect.

We were split into teams and each given a number. We played from 10 o'clock in the morning until 5 o'clock at night. We'd scrimmage and do drills for an hour or so and then the coaches would make cuts and post a list of survivors. Every time I checked the list my number would still be there. I was just a 15-year-old playing ball and having fun.

I was in the last group scrimmaging when they made the final cut. They started announcing the list: Michelle McKenzie, Carol Blazejowski, Nancy Lieberman . . . .

"Nancy Lieberman!" I couldn't believe it.

I had made a team. A USA training team. They had picked just ten players out of the 150 to go to Albuquerque for a three-day pre-camp tryout, and I was one of the ten.

The players at Queens would join players from three other regional camps, forty players in all. The plan was to select ten players at the end of the pre-camp to go to an actual training camp with players like Carolyn Bush, Lusia Harris, Ann Meyers, Pat Head, and Julienne Simpson—who were the super-duper stars of college. I was so excited to tell my mom.

"Mom, I made the team. I'm only a kid!" I said. I told her I was going to Albuquerque.

"Like hell you are," she said. "Where do you expect us to get that kind of money to buy you a plane ticket?"

I think my mother and grandmother really wanted to send me, but we just didn't have the money. But three people who were very instrumental in my development as an athlete spearheaded a drive to raise money for my trip. My basketball coach

Larry Morse, my softball coach, Barbara Sakrowitz, and her husband, Brian, made my trip possible, along with the whole Far Rockaway community. They rallied around me and raised the money for plane tickets for both Coach Morse and me.

The coaches of the team were Alberta Cox and Carolyn Moffitt. I really didn't know who the big name players were at that point. All I knew was that I was one of ten players selected for the pre-camp, and the rest of the girls trying out were collegiate All-Americans. I constantly walked around asking people about the different players, but I was young and having fun. I didn't know what intimidation was at that point.

Coach Cox ran the tryouts like Marine boot camp. Her theme was that the ball was an extension of your hand. You had to carry the basketball with you at all times, even when you were sleeping or eating. After some drills one day, I ran to the water fountain for a quick drink. "Lieberman. Where is your basketball?" she bellowed across the gym. I was embarrassed enough not to forget my basketball again.

I barely had my sweat pants off in practice one day when I collided during a rebounding drill with Joan Bonvicini of Southern Connecticut State College. Joan was trying to keep me off the boards when I caught an elbow to the ribs. After only two days of drills, I knew the pain in my left side was more than just a muscle pull.

I kept playing until I started having difficulty breathing. I remember sitting in my hotel room, lying on the bed—with my basketball, because I didn't want somebody to squeal on me to Coach or for her to walk in and catch me without it—and I was just gasping for breath. I was sitting there trying to talk myself out of thinking it was anything serious. "I've never played at high altitudes before," I thought. "I'm tired because I'm not used to doing all this running and full-court drilling." I had my pride; I didn't want to come back to Far Rockaway and have people think I was a loser.

But it was so sore—it had to be for me to finally go to the coach. I was 15 years old, real skinny, 5-8 and 118 or 120 pounds. And in this little girl's voice, I said, "I think I got hit, and it hurts. . . . I'm having a little problem breathing." Like that was an afterthought, "Oh, by the way. . . . "

So they took me for an X-ray, and they found I had some

fractured ribs and an enlarged spleen. The doctor said, "I suggest you go home and give it a rest. I would let you play, but the injury is right where your spleen is, and I'm afraid if you take another blow, you'll be hurt, seriously hurt." My tryout had lasted only three days before I was sent home.

As I was being driven to the airport by Coach Cox, she wished me luck and told me to get ready for the 1980 Olympic Team. I told her I was thinking more about making the 1976 team. She just smiled at me and gave me a look that said, "not a chance." I asked her what she thought I needed to work on and she said the fundamentals of the game. As I returned home, I felt a sense of mission to make the 1976 Olympic Team.

Chapter 5

A Far Cry From
Far Rock

 When the USA national team came to the Felt Forum in New York later that year, I went to see them play the Soviets. I wanted to be out there playing with them, but my time hadn't come yet. I kept the souvenir program pinned to the wall in my bedroom for years dreaming that one day my name would be there: "USA uniform No. 10, Nancy Lieberman."

When it finally sank in what I had done at the ripe old age of 15, the media began calling and setting up interviews and sending photographers. Even Cliff got into the act. "Nancy, do you realize that you are one of the 40 best players in the United States?" my brother asked me as he looked at the list of the players who attended the tryout.

I had never thought about that. I think, maybe, for the first time he shared my excitement. Suddenly my mother began to take an interest in what I was doing, too.

Once the invitation to the USA camp sank in, my mother realized this was no longer playtime in the school yards. She realized it was a very keen competition, something she could finally take seriously.

So many reporters came around, from *News Day*, the *Long Island Press*, and ABC Sports, and I think at first my mother was overwhelmed by it as much as I was. Soon they began to pepper her with questions about my basketball upbringing.

"Mrs. Lieberman, what do you think about this? What do you think about that? Did you really puncture Nancy's basketballs with a screwdriver? Is it true that she rode the trains to play ball?"

As my mother took a more active interest in my basketball career, I think she sensed that she was losing a daughter and gaining a sports celebrity. Yes, I was still her daughter, but I was also fast becoming a public figure, too. She knew she had to become more knowledgeable about all of the basketball questions she was getting. Now when I devoured the sports page in the morning she would ask me questions about what I was reading. She would quiz me when I cut out the baseball standings. Little by little, she began to understand how important sports were in my life. And little by little she became a sports fan herself.

All of a sudden she had a handle on my basketball career. The woman who used to yell at me for watching sports on television all of the time began to join me in front of the set. At first, it was obvious that she didn't want to look bad to all these reporters, but as she followed the sports pages, she gradually became a genuine fan.

If mom was cramming for a final exam in a crash course, she passed it with flying colors. It wasn't long before she was fielding questions from reporters with ease. She knew about every phase of my game. Before long, she began to sound like Dick Vitale.

"My daughter Nancy, the basketball player, you know, she has such a great jump shot. Youngest player to make the U.S. team, you know?" my mom would say.

After a while, she started accumulating newspaper articles and would carry my scrapbook around in her giant purse. Sometimes she would pull it out and show it to total strangers. I often wondered if she thought she would get seated in a restaurant faster or get a better parking space because she was my mother.

My mother's increased interest parallels the public's greater awareness of women's sports. My mother had never been interested in seeing me play basketball while I was growing up. In her defense, I don't think she saw it as a big deal because she never grew up with sports. She couldn't relate to my love of sports. As a matter of fact, my only recollection of her coming to see me play was one time in my senior year of high school. She never had to car pool me to practice or really get involved in it. She never took my love of sports seriously. Today, I'm excited when I see so many parents getting involved in their daughters' athletic careers.

I think my mother was naive about what athletics could mean to your life. I guess it just shows you the sign of the times. These days, women's basketball is commanding regular season coverage on CBS, taking a share of the news hole in *USA Today*, and for better or worse, drawing the occasional investigation by the National Collegiate Athletic Association for recruiting violations. Female athletes today also have the benefit of the Women's Sports Foundation, which has been the leader of grassroots programs for women through studies, awareness and lobbying for equality.

The WSF and the Bike Athletic Wear company have teamed up to promote awareness of women's athletics. Bike is going to be a 1992 camp sponsor for me and is featuring me in an advertising campaign. They did a poster of me shooting and a young girl staring up at me with an expression of, "Wow, maybe that could be me one day." Off in the background, I'm standing on the Olympic platform with my medal, the American flag behind me. Bike and the WSF are trying to instill in young girl athletes something that's always been a motto of mine: "Never stop working, wanting, or dreaming."

My mother understands the importance of sports now, but back in my high school days, Cliff was my biggest fan in the family. He watched me on the school yards, and he came to most of my high school games. We never won any titles in high school, but our Far Rockaway team was very competitive. In my junior year, we were only going to play 15 games for the season and I knew that we needed to play more. A lot of my friends had played for more than one team at a time in those days because the rule against it was unenforced by the Public School Athletic League.

One of my Far Rockaway teammates, Mary Ann Aida, and I starting playing for St. Francis de Sales on the weekends, but then the PSAL decided to crack down, and we were suspended for the rest of the season from our high school team. At the time, Far Rockaway and St. Francis were both undefeated. In my senior year, Far Rock advanced to the semifinals, where we lost a one-point game to Fort Hamilton.

When I came back from my first experiences on the USA team, it was apparent that all the great competition had helped me to elevate my game. But I was hungry to learn more, and I asked Lucille Kyvallos, the head coach at Queens College, "Coach, what can I get better at?" She handed me five brochures and said, "Go to a basketball camp," and I just picked the top one: Howie Landa's All-Pro Camp. Maybe it was "All-Pro" that caught my eye because I thought I wanted to be "All-Pro," but anyway I went to his camp, and that was the first time, at 15 years old, I got any extended, structured instruction.

I dribbled with my head down for the longest time, and I shot the ball with two hands for the longest time. It wasn't until I went to camp that Howie Landa showed me how to hold a basketball. I had a side rotation on my shot because I would spin it, using my left hand too much. It wasn't until I went to basketball camp that they were able to break me of that habit. We'd do drills where I'd have to keep one hand behind my back, and they had these little blinders where you'd dribble and you couldn't see the ball. I learned a lot there.

I learned how to box out there, too, there and at the Albuquerque tryout, and how to pin my player in the post. I was so aggressive I would always box out. That got me some more attention in the pickup games, too, where everybody just ran and shot, and nobody paid much attention to the fundamentals.

People would be running full speed to the basket, and I'd see the ball, plant, pivot, turn, and —boom— my butt below the guy's belt. "Unnnnh!" I became known for putting my butt in the guys' cups—but of course nobody on the playground wore a cup, just like nobody on the playground boxed out. That earned me a lot of respect—or at least fear.

During the summer between my junior and senior years I was determined to make the Pan-American Games team after having to go home early from New Mexico the summer before. I had used that experience to improve on my weaknesses. Back in those days, I didn't do any sprint work on the track, weight training, or long distance running for endurance. All of my workouts were in the gym, where I just played and worked on my shot.

I spent hours in the gym that summer with Brian Sakrowitz, dribbling in and out of stationary cones, dribbling and shooting with both hands, and improving the other fundamentals of the game. The summer before when I went to New Mexico, I thought I was a really good player. A year later, I knew I had a lot sounder foundation.

Barbara and Brian Sakrowitz drove me to the regional trials at Ursinus College in Pennsylvania. I was nervous, but well prepared and glad to be there. After I advanced through the regionals, the next hurdle to make was the actual Pan-American Team, in Warrensburg, MO. I felt like I had accomplished something no one expected the year before, getting as far as I had in the trials. Everything I did the last time around was "Gosh, unbelievable, how did she do that?" And so now I was going to be playing against people like Joan Bonvicini, Dottie McCrea, Marianne O'Connor—some really great players—and I'm going up against them, but now it's a year later and I'm supposed to be good. Now I have something to lose.

At the same time, I didn't feel the intimidation I had felt as the new kid. I had heard a lot about a hot-shot player named Anne Meyers and I really wanted to meet her. One day before the tryouts started, I was walking down the hall in the dorm and someone shouted for Annie. I started to approach her when another girl walked up. I asked her for her autograph. Anne turned on her heels and told me she couldn't be bothered, or something to that effect. I couldn't believe it. How could someone be so cocky as to turn down an autograph? At that point, I decided that Anne Meyers was going to be my personal mission at tryouts.

I planned to dog her from one end of the court to another. What did I know? I knew most of the players didn't want to guard her because she was so good that they were afraid of looking bad. Every time we drilled or had a scrimmage I always made sure that I got Annie because I wanted to see if I could stop her. If I did, I figured the selection committee would want to know who that gutsy 16-year-old was who stopped Anne Meyers.

My game was physical and I played more on talent than on brains. I did all the flashy things—blocked shots, behind the back passes, steals that turned into easy baskets for my team. I knew

I had Anne's attention when I caught a sharp elbow to my chest and she was whistled for a foul. As I was trying to catch my breath, I stole a glance at the committee and saw a few smiles. They had noticed Nancy Lieberman.

Another time in a drill, a teammate put up a shot, and I was on the weak side. Dottie McCrea was on the other team, about 6-1, but wide, thick, a strong girl and a very experienced player. The ball hit the opposite side of the rim, I came in from the weak side, and I jumped over her—boom!—got the rebound and kicked it back out. We moved the ball around the offense, and I got it on the wing. I drove the baseline and went up for the shot, and McCrea went up with both hands to block it. I changed hands with the ball while in the air and went right past her and made the shot.

Sometimes you'll make a move and think, "How'd I do that?" How I got around her and made the shot was unbelievable to me, to the coaches, and to the other players. When you're competing for spots in a tryout and other players rave about a move, you know you've done something. The committee was just open-mouthed. It really impressed them because everybody there could shoot and everybody could dribble, but not everybody could physically do stuff like that.

Waiting for a cut list is sheer torture. I remember peeking my head out of my dorm room in Warrensburg, waiting for the list to be posted, hoping my name would be on it. When the list finally appeared there was a rush to check it. When I saw my name I got a huge lump in my throat. I'd really made it!

There was a lot of tension between athletes during the Trials and after the names were posted. It wasn't like, "I hate you," but players like Carol Blazejowski and Marianne Crawford wanted to be on that team, and they were really upset when they were cut. There was a lot of talk like, "She doesn't belong on that team," and a lot of that was directed at the little 16-year-old from Far Rockaway.

Well, I might not have belonged on that USA team, but years later Billie Moore, who was one of our coaches, told me they picked one player for the future. Their rationale was, "We're going to have an Olympic team, a Pan-American team—the 12th player's not going to play much anyway. Let's pick that spot for the future of USA women's basketball." We didn't have a developmental program, we didn't have an Olympic Festival, we didn't have three U.S. teams going out during the summer like we do now. Now we have the World University Games, and then there are two or three teams every summer that go out, so instead of just 12 girls, maybe 36 are getting experience. So they picked that spot for the future, and it paid off for them.

The team, under coach Cathy Rush, was going to play in South America in the World Championships before going on to Mexico City for the Pan-American Games. When we arrived in Bucaramanga, Colombia, a bunch of tall women, many of us black, we were objects of curiosity to the natives. Both they and we got some cross-cultural education. It seemed like every time we'd walk the streets around our hotel, we'd be met with stares, and even in the hotel we'd see people looking in through the windows at us like, "So that's what Americans look like."

I couldn't believe the awful conditions. Their five-star hotels were like typical motels in the States. I didn't recognize some of the food, and being a finicky eater, I didn't eat much besides some candy we brought from home. Having police escorts and armed guards became a way of life for the team, and we were instructed to go out in groups, never alone. We weren't well-liked, and being young, I didn't understand why. Politics went over my head then, and I didn't realize how much people from a poor and struggling country could resent our country's wealth and power.

Still, USA garb was a hot commodity among the tournament teams. You could trade your USA t-shirt, pins, or just about anything with red, white, and blue on it for blankets, jewelry, or clothes. It was an education in the barter system and in negotiation.

From Bucaramanga we advanced to a regional site in Colombia, a much bigger and more progressive city, but still a long way from my experiences as a New Yorker. Cars crowded the streets here, but there were also donkeys pulling carts for transportation.

In Colombia, we shopped, traded, and learned a little about a different sort of culture. Communication is so important on this kind of trip. Even the simplest things were a major effort, like asking, "More bottled water, please, no ice." That was the saying on the trip, of course: "Don't drink the water," because everyone had told us it would make us sick. Talk about taking things for granted! We found out that Americans are pretty pampered. But to tell you the truth, I couldn't wait to play and get back home.

We didn't play very well in Colombia, winning the consolation bracket. I'd never seen so many talented women players from all over the world before.

By the time we got to Mexico City for the Pan-Am Games, the team had really come together and we were playing with confidence. It was fun staying in the Athletes' Village, meeting competitors from all over North and South America. But the best thing was the special camaraderie among all the U.S. athletes in the different sports. I met some of the players on the men's team and spent a lot of time talking to Ernie Grunfeld. Ernie is now the Director of Player Personnel for the Knicks, and we still see each other from time to time at celebrity and charity functions in New York.

I only played three, four, five minutes per game when the competition started, so I knew it was important for me to have good practices to help my teammates get ready. But it was hard for me to be sitting on the pine since I was so used to running the show in my own backyard. Once I was sitting next to Pat Head with two minutes left in the game when the coaches looked my way. I turned to Pat and told her that there was no way I was going to be embarrassed going in with only two minutes left. I picked the wrong person to complain to.

"Nancy, you'd better learn to take what you can get and make the most of it when you have the opportunity," Pat said. "If you get in, take advantage of whatever time you have by being alert, intense, and ready." Pat's probably the most intense player I've ever stepped on the court with. She probably doesn't realize what an influence she has been to me as an athlete and a person. I never saw anyone work harder to come back from an injury than Pat did when she hurt her knee in 1975. Her effort was just amazing. When you're 16 and see something like that, it stays with you a long time.

Pat's lecture made me work harder in practice, but sometimes I played too rough. I was always picking my teammates up off the floor. Julienne Simpson, our team captain, told me I wouldn't see my 17th birthday at the rate I was going. To this day, I still appreciate the kindness and patience my teammates showed me when I was the youngster on the squad.

Our coaches, Cathy Rush and Billie Moore, gave us a great game plan to execute game-in and game-out, a gold-medal game plan. No matter how many times you see a medal being placed around the neck of a champion, their flag going up, the national anthem of their country playing—that's a moving ceremony that never gets old. Imagine the feelings when the medal's around *your* neck, *your* flag is being raised, *your* anthem is being played!

I felt so many overwhelming emotions when we won the gold medal and went through the ceremony. We headed back into the locker room and everyone was jumping around, hugging and kissing each other, just like you see on TV. It's such a different feeling because you tried out for yourself, but you're winning for the USA. Everyone back home is a teammate, and you pull energy from that feeling. I was young, emotional, and so proud to be a part of that moment.

We got back to the village and I could hardly eat at our victory celebration at some restaurant—who noticed the name? I talked well into the night with my roommate, Charlotte Lewis, who was heading back to Illinois State in Normal. She was 6-3 and could dunk—I'd never seen that before. She took good care of me on the trip, talking, listening, and just being a great friend. Then suddenly it was over and I was on my way home to start my senior year of high school after a storybook summer.

I came home to a hero's welcome in Far Rockaway. A lot of people met me at the airport with signs and banners. For weeks I walked around with my gold medal hanging from my neck. Everything was so hectic with reporters and interviews and with college coaches recruiting me. It seemed that my simple way of life was changed forever after that summer.

More people knew me, and now everyone was proud to be part of my success. Just like people say, I found friends and relatives I never knew before. I felt so much pressure and responsibility to live up to what a gold medalist should be. Act differently, talk differently, improve as an athlete— those became my rules to live by. Can't rest, have to work to be better.

I wondered how my high school teammates and classmates would treat me, whether they'd be happy for me or jealous. I didn't want my friends to think all this had gone to my head. I wanted to share my medal, uniforms, and loads of "freebies" the team received with all my friends. My mom couldn't understand how I could do that. "Nancy," she said, "you can't give the whole world everything." I thought I could.

But I knew things could never be the same again, either. I didn't have the free time I used to have. Still, I stayed close to my best friends, Barbara Wood, Debbie Kurkomelis, and Rosita Riggs. We spent a lot of days talking about our future.

I even had fun pulling pranks on the media. Our local paper, the Far Rockaway *Wave*, sent a writer named Kim Butler to do a story on me at my home, and I had my friend Rosita meet her at the door.

"Nancy?"

"Yes."

"How are you? Congratulations!" Kim was expecting this athletic-looking kid, and here's this skinny 5-6 girl with long brown hair and a bit of a stutter. Kim sits on the dining room couch and starts her interview, asking questions and taking notes, and meanwhile I'm hiding in the other room. Finally Rosita and I burst out laughing. Kim and I became good friends over the years despite the trick, and Rosita went to Old Dominion and became one of the managers of our team, one of those indispensable, underappreciated supporters you never hear about.

To get away from all the commotion, I went up to Julius Erving's Basketball Camp. Mark and Eric Muchnick took me to Dr. J.'s camp and told Julius that I was a sure bet as an Olympian and that I had just won a gold medal. He was so nice to me and took a genuine interest in my achievements as a basketball player. This was the first time I met Julius and it marked the beginning of a long friendship.

Dr. J. was so kind to me. He didn't take what the guys had said as boasting. He took me for real and he was kind and compassionate to me. He had a great impact on my life at that point and continued to be a role model for me for many years. We see each other periodically at charity functions and I've stayed at his home a few times. Late in the day he and his wife, Turquoise, and I would sit around the kitchen table and talk for hours about athletics, his career and mine, family responsibilities, and my relationships with my mom and Martina. We also talked about his Christianity. I had so many questions for him. It was amazing how together he was—stable, hard-working, a family man, a Christian, and a role model loved by millions—and he put on a move or two on the court in his day, too. I cherish the times I've had with Julius and Turk. For the last ten years, the first Christmas card my mother has received has been from Julius and his family.

After Julius' camp, my whirlwind summer was coming to an end, and my senior year at Far Rockaway H.S. was beginning. I set a goal of leading my team to a championship. I also started thinking seriously about college. We didn't have enough money to send me to school, so I knew that I would be looking for an athletic scholarship to pay my way. And I knew I wanted to take my game to the next level.

Chapter 6

Recruiting Wars—for a Girl

 Going into my senior year at Far Rockaway, it was awfully hard to concentrate on school and graduating. All I wanted to do was play basketball in the gym during P.E., at lunch, at practice, after school, in Harlem, and at any other conceivable time or place. My focus was on the upcoming 1976 Olympic Games team trials, and I wanted to make sure I improved on every one of my weaknesses.

I wanted to show the committee that I wasn't too young or inexperienced to make the team. I wanted to be in better shape than anyone out there and I planned to use my senior year to experiment with other positions. Since I had grown to 5-foot-10, I played center in high school, but I knew from hundreds of letters I was receiving from college recruiters that my future was as a big guard or a power forward. To be more marketable, I wanted to handle the ball more and shoot from the outside. That would give me a better all-around game.

I was also well aware that I had to have a great senior year to chase away any doubts that I had belonged on the Pan-Am team. I felt pressure to win and to show dramatic improvement in my own game, but at the same time I didn't want to feel like I was overshadowing my teammates. Sometimes it's tough to reconcile team goals and personal goals.

The most important goal, of course, is winning, and team chemistry is vital if you're going to do that. My senior year we had great players—Rita Haywood, who now coaches at St. John's; a good point guard in Debbie Kurkomelis, who knew how to get the ball to the right players at the right time; and good role players like Annie Nisenholc, a longtime friend of mine. We played hard and to win, and we also played to bigger crowds than ever. It's amazing how much harder we played with the gym full.

I had so much fun with those girls. Between basketball season and softball season, my athletic career couldn't have been more fulfilling. As a matter of fact, I thought softball was my best sport until college, though to tell you the truth, Barbara, our first baseman, saved me more errors than I can count. I was the shortstop, with lots of range, a great arm, and the mistaken notion that I could throw batters out from short left, center or the parking lot. I suspect some of the long heaves I made back then are responsible for the elbow problem I'm living with now.

After a great season, our basketball team lost to Fort Hamilton High in the semifinals of the Public School Athletic League championships. I'll tell you, in those days, winning the PSAL championship would have been like Olympic gold to me.

My exposure to the international game in 1975 had caught the eye of college recruiters. I never knew I had so many friends, supporters, and confidants. I was amazed by the attention. I had over one hundred scholarship offers. When you are 15, 16, 17 years old, if you're good in your sport you know it. But nothing can prepare you for the pressures that go along with being good, especially the recruiting process.

All of my self-confidence came from basketball and softball. Suddenly I was hearing all these recruiters tell me how great I was and that's hard for a kid to handle. It builds up your ego. And of course, everybody trying to recruit you shows you their best side. When you are young, it's hard to know who's for real, and who's a phony.

Throughout the whole process, I never met a coach who didn't have the best school in the country. Everyone had the best school, the best academics, the biggest and the newest facilities.

Back then it was a real selling job because women's programs didn't have the benefit of television exposure. Sometimes I would get a letter from a recruiter and I would have no idea where the school was located so I'd pull out a map of the United States. When Old Dominion started recruiting me my mother started looking at the map, too. I think she was wondering how far her Nancy would travel from home. With cable and newspaper exposure these days, there are fewer "unknowns." Back then, it was a selling job all the way.

I knew there were certain things I wanted to accomplish when I went to college. More than anything, I wanted to play in Madison Square Garden. It was a personal goal of mine all the years I was growing up. All my idols had played there and someday I wanted to score a basket on their goal and sit in the same seats on the bench they sat in. In my mind, I could hear John Condon say, "Welcome to the magic world of Madison Square Garden. Starting in the backcourt tonight, No. 10, Nancy Lieberman."

I also wanted to play for the national championship on network television. Back then, the only way you got to play on television was in the title game.

It's funny what coaches and recruiters are willing to do and how they compromise their values when they find out what a blue-chip athlete has for goals. Suddenly, lots of coaches were telling me of their plans to schedule a game in the Garden. Others gave me a timetable for making it to the championships, always pointing out that I was the player they needed to get them to the top.

Everyone had their subtle ways of recruiting, and sometimes the rules would get bent. Women's sports were governed by the Association for Intercollegiate Athletics for Women until the NCAA took over in 1981. Under AIAW rules there were no paid recruiting visits but it was surprising the number of paid visits that were offered. Some programs offered money for signing scholarship papers, others offered money for points and rebounds, and several schools promised bonuses for advancing to the regionals and nationals. This was pretty heady stuff for a 17-year old girl to handle.

Out of over one hundred schools that recruited me, probably five or six made illegal offers. Only one or two were really blatant about it, but others would say, "You won't have to worry about stuff; we'll take care of you; we'll fly you home." I had heard about illegal recruiting of guys. It made me feel kind of special that I was receiving the same treatment for my basketball talents.

It's hard to turn away from the money and the inducements when you haven't had a lot your whole life. But all I knew was that I wanted to play basketball in college. If I took the illegal offers, my school could be put on probation, and that would cut me off from the goals I hoped to achieve. Basketball was my identity.

The hardest part of being recruited is that in the end you have to pick one school and tell all the other ones "no." So many of the schools interested me, and I was confused for so long. Some kids rely on Mom and Dad to make the decision, but I decided I wanted that task. But all the questions—Where do I go? What will I major in? Can I handle the work? Wow, is that place really that big?—just made it more confusing. I like this coach, I like those players—it's really tough. Then, after you've decided, the dreaded calls back to coaches: "Well, I think maybe, well, I've decided, I've narrowed it down. . . . It's not that I didn't like your school."

It's not easy, believe me, to tell a coach who's been recruiting you for two or three years that you're going somewhere else. It was especially tough saying "no" to the coaches and players at Queens College and St. John's University. I had grown up playing at those schools and knew the people.

Vicki Kress was the coach at St. John's, and I remember playing a pickup game there against her team. Somebody shot the ball, and I went up and got the rebound in the air. Before I came down, I hit the outlet pass; then when I came down, somebody tripped me, and I fell. I got up, ran the floor, was the first one down, and made the layup. Vicki called time out and started screaming at the team: "The girl got the rebound, threw the outlet, tripped, fell down, beat the defense and everybody on the offense down the floor." She was really letting her team have it, but at the same time she was making me feel pretty good about myself.

It would have been nice playing at home in New York, but I knew that I wanted to get away from the city and try someplace new. I needed to grow and escape, even if it was just for four years. I wanted to see how other people lived. I wanted to get away from the city's asphalt and enjoy green lawns and fresh air.

I wanted to go to a school where basketball was the No. 1 sport on campus and would get a lot of attention. I really didn't know yet how far away from home I wanted to go. At one point I wanted to play for legendary coach Billie Moore, but I would have had to go to Cal State-Fullerton. Billie had been one of my Pan-Am coaches and would be my Olympic coach in 1976. I had learned so much from her that I knew she could help my game, but I wasn't convinced that I wanted to go all the way across the country. Besides, by this time my mom was becoming a fan, and I knew that she would want to see me play once in a while.

At the time, I heard rumors that Billie might be going to Arizona. It scared me because the only reason I'd go to Fullerton would be to be coached by Billie. If she left, I'd have to transfer someplace else and pay my way for the first year under the old AIAW rules. My family's financial situation meant I couldn't afford to change my mind.

Since there was no way of knowing what Billie might do—she later accepted the head coaching position at UCLA—I took a look at Old Dominion. The coach at the time, Pam Parsons, spent a lot of time calling, writing, and just paying attention to me. In those days women's recruiting rules were a little bizarre. Coach Parsons and her assistant coach Cindy Russo really did a great job.

Coach Parsons went to Jack Wilkins, owner of Wilkins Chevrolet and a big ODU booster, for $500.00 to fund plane tickets to come and talk to me. Mr. Wilkins told me the story years later.

"Coach Parsons would call and pester me to give her the money to go to New York," he said. "She swore that there was a red-headed Jewish girl named Lieberman who would change the course of women's basketball. I thought, 'what the hell, they might have something.'"

One time Pam called at 10 p.m. and said she'd be right over. We had roomfuls of people camped out all over, and Pam spent half the night talking to my mother and me. She was always around, making the extra effort to persuade me. That was impressive to a 17-year-old kid.

ODU didn't promise me anything illegal, just a good atmosphere for playing basketball and pursuing my degree—just what I was looking for in a school. Cindy Russo had a really low-key approach to recruiting and I got along great with her during the whole process. I liked her as a person and respected her as a coach.

I felt like ODU was just far enough away to get out of New York, but close enough so I could always get back to my environment. It gave me a chance to see another part of the country. Norfolk, Virginia, is in the middle of a beautiful area with friendly people and a lot to do. I fell in love with the city of Norfolk and the school, and I really liked my teammates.

It didn't matter that nobody had heard of Old Dominion. I wanted to be a part of building something great so that years later people would remember ODU and Nancy Lieberman, her teammates and their awards and accomplishments. The bottom line was that I wanted to play and to win and I had made a decision it would be Old Dominion.

My mother was a little disappointed when I finally decided on a school. As much as she complained about all of the phone calls and mail, I think she really loved the attention. If I was out playing ball or didn't want to talk to the recruiters, she'd be on the phone with them for hours. In one breath I'd hear her say, "I can't stand that phone ringing for hours and hours." The next thing I knew she was talking to coaches for hours and hours.

One time she talked to some coaches from the University of Nevada at Las Vegas. They told my mother they would roll out the red carpet and put my name in lights all over Vegas if she let me go to school out there. I think she envisioned something like "Introducing Nancy Lieberman and Mother" at Caesars Palace.

The people from Old Dominion made my mother feel good about the opportunities I would have there. The mayor even called her up and told her how exciting it would be for the city of Norfolk to have a great women's basketball team at ODU. She knew what my dreams were, and when I made the decision she supported it.

However, a lot of coaches said to me, "If you go to Old Dominion, nobody will ever hear of you again. You will never be an All-American. You will never make the top USA teams. You probably won't improve, and don't expect to win a national championship." They kept telling me to go to a school where I could contend for the title—theirs, in other words.

All of their talk triggered something inside of me. I decided to go to Old Dominion and prove to all of them—and myself—

that I could succeed. It was like my childhood all over again. I had a challenge. People were discouraging me, but I knew I could do it. There are few things I enjoy more than a good challenge. After my four years, there would be no one who could say, "I told you so." Instead, we told everybody in the nation that the best place to be in women's college basketball was at Old Dominion.

The day I left for school I had a shiny white and burgundy Pontiac Firebird. You could hardly even tell it was a hand-me-down. My dad had promised he'd buy me a car before I went to college. My Aunt Ruthie, who lived in Great Neck, had bought the Firebird new for my cousin Ilene. When it had 5,000 miles on it, Ilene was ready for a new car, so Aunt Ruthie sold the Firebird to my dad, who gave it to me. Maybe it sounds ungrateful, but that hurt a little bit.

Uncle Bob and Aunt Ruthie had money and always looked great, and their kids, Ilene, Drew, and Todd, always had everything. I was always getting their hand-me-downs. It was always, "Oh, Ilene wore this shirt for three years, and now she's giving it to you." It wasn't Ilene's fault, but after a while I started resenting her because she was pretty and I was a tomboy, and "Ilene's got boyfriends, and you've got a basketball and black friends." So little things like that made me resentful. Ilene gets a new Firebird, and I'm getting her old one. I was really grateful for the car, but I was also hurt. If Dad had just said in the first place, "Nancy, I'll get you a used car," then maybe it would have been OK.

Coach Parsons sent her brother to New York to ride down to school with me. He arrived a few days early and just hung around with us. I guess Pam had sent him to make sure I'd show up at ODU.

While I was getting ready to leave for school, my best friend Barbara Wood came by and asked if I wanted to do something with her and her boyfriend, Raymond. I was busy getting ready to go, but she said, "He wants us to come down to Shea Stadium to help him shag balls for a couple of injured Yankee players, Elliott Maddox and Ron Blomberg."

Her boyfriend was a Yankees batboy, and the Yankees were playing at Shea Stadium while Yankee Stadium was being renovated. I didn't care if I was leaving for the moon that day, there was no way I'd miss an opportunity to shag balls for a couple of Yankees. I got to see the clubhouse and the behind-the-scenes areas I had always wondered about as a kid.

But now I was sort of grown up and it was time to actually leave home for the first time. The thing that sticks in my mind is looking at my Grandpa Lou as we were leaving. Both he and my grandmother had helped me financially to get ready for college, and he was as much a father figure to me as anyone.

I had never shown much emotion but as I got ready to leave, I realized I was crying. I was scared as I looked at my family. I had always been rough and brazen and boastful—I could take care of myself, thank you. But now I wasn't so sure as I looked at the people who meant security to me. It was a strange feeling not knowing what was ahead of me, new people to meet and places to go and challenges to conquer. I painted a picture of my family in my mind and I thought a lot about my grandparents in the coming months.

My grandfather looked really sad. I didn't know it then, but he would be dead six months later. We just locked eyes for a minute, and I remember I had the strangest, saddest feeling.

When I left that day, I knew I was gone for good. Basketball was a way out for me. My scholarship represented independence, and I was really on my own. I would have some financial aid, a little money from my family, and my scholarship.

In Norfolk, Coach Parsons had arranged for a furnished apartment off-campus and had me all set up when I arrived. I walked into a lovely place about three miles from campus complete with a great roommate, Ruthann Burgun. Ruthann was from a small town in Pennsylvania and I was the big city girl from New York. We got along great, the start of a great friendship.

I couldn't wait to meet my teammates.

Chapter 7

Playing for Old Glory

 My senior year in high school had been hectic and the recruiting battles both tiresome and exciting. No matter what happened during 1976, I was focused on the tryouts for the 1976 USA Women's Olympic basketball team.

Once again the Trials were held in Warrensburg, Missouri, and I felt more comfortable as I walked into the familiar surroundings of the gym. I was no longer an unknown player. This time around, the selection committee would be looking to see whether I had improved my level of play from the previous year. Over the next several days they were going to be looking for fundamentally sound team players, loaded with talent and able to play at a controlled tempo. We heard the words "team chemistry" a lot during the Trials.

As the Trials progressed, it seemed I was drawing three-time Immaculata College All-American Marianne Crawford in most of the drills. She had been the point guard on a team that ruled women's college hoops in the early 1970s. She was only 5-foot-6 but had a great vision of the floor, shot well, was sound on defense, and was a great passer. I knew that the committee was paying special attention to our match-up.

My game was different from Marianne's. At 5-10 I was more physical, and I ran and jumped like a guy. The style of play in the international game gives a bigger and more physical player an edge.

The Trials were no-nonsense. It would be the first time in Olympic history women's basketball would be a medal sport. We were concerned about more than just winning: we needed to made a good showing to boost the awareness and progress of the game.

The drills were tough and competitive. You always had to be alert and hustling to prove your mettle against other talented women. Shooting drills, defense, on the ball, off the ball, coaches yelling and pushing you to your limit.

In between sessions, as names were constantly being sliced from the list of candidates, we ate and rested. Here's Nancy, 17 years old, ice packs on each knee and shin, taking advantage of a break to write in her journal, trying to capture the feelings of the day. Entry: "We went 2 hours this morning—I believe they're crazy—yes, the coaches—we ran 3-man weave, 5-man weave, 3 on 2, 2 on 1, 11-man drill, shooting, man defense, zone defense— deny, head on ball, full-court 1 on 1, then, 'Ladies, let's scrim- mage.' Scrimmage—I can't breathe or walk. Need some sleep. Next practice session at 2:00."

We endured the same type of session two or three times a day. It really taught me that your body won't quit if your mind is strong. I guess mine was young, dumb, and strong; I was just happy to be there.

The tension in the dorm was unbearable as we waited for "the list" to be posted. I can never recall being as fidgety or nervous in my entire life. Finally, a shout went out: One of the managers had posted the list in the hall. There was screaming and crying all at once as players registered their emotions after looking at the list. I slowly walked down the hall ready to take my turn, praying that my name would be there. Somebody must have been listening to my prayers: "Lieberman, Nancy." I couldn't decide whether to scream or cry. A phone. I had to find a phone to call home and tell my family the news. I talked to everyone: Mom, Cliff, my grandparents, and Barbara Wood. Everyone was so excited for me. Me, too, but now the work begins.

There were many familiar faces from the previous summer on the team. Billie Moore was the head coach, and Sue Gunter, now of Louisiana State University, was her assistant. These coaching maniacs sent us through one drill after another. Their favorite thing to make us do was run, run, run, run, and run some more. We were counting down the days to when the training camp would be over and we would go to Hamilton, Ontario, for the pre-Olympic Qualifying Tournament. Our rigorous program would begin to seem worthwhile then—at least we hoped it would.

Although the drills and practices were new and tough for me, I felt my body getting stronger and saw my skills improving. I stopped complaining on a regular basis and saved it for special occasions. One day in practice I was playing the back of a 1-3-1 zone and was so tired I was slow getting out to cover the player with the ball. Billie stops practice and says, "Nancy, my grandmother could have gotten there quicker!"

Now I'm both tired and embarrassed, but I think to myself, "Billie's grandmother doesn't know how to play the back of a 1-3-1." I must have been getting a little smarter, too; I didn't share my observation with the coach. We came through boot camp in great shape mentally and physically. A high school kid just doesn't get the opportunity to learn what I did then.

Teams must qualify to go to the Olympic Games in basketball. The only teams automatically invited are the previous Olympic gold medalist and host countries. The competition in Hamilton was the first step and the only step to the 1976 Games. Two teams would qualify to go to Montreal.

I played some in the first three games, but I didn't get in at all when a plane full of people from Old Dominion flew up to see me in our fourth game with France. A few weeks earlier, I had signed with Old Dominion assistant coach Cindy Russo at the Olympic Trials. I was going to be a Lady Monarch. I was so disappointed and embarrassed that so many people from my new university had come so far to see me ride the bench. After the game, all I wanted to do was hide in the locker room.

I realized that I was being selfish; I knew that the good of the team should come first. I just wanted to contribute and not let anybody down. I was about to get my chance.

In the next game we drew a tough team from Bulgaria. Billie had us in a 1-3-1 zone, and our guards were getting smoked by a sharpshooting Bulgarian who was knocking it in all night from the baseline. Anne Meyers and Sue Rojcewicz were chasing back and forth in the back of the zone, and we had a hand in the shooter's face as she released the ball, but nothing was working. Bulgaria and the USA were two of the teams to beat in the tournament, so this was a big game.

I was sitting at the end of the bench, still a little pouty from not getting in against France. I was looking around the gym and watching the game, but I lacked the intensity I should have had on the bench. About that time a teammate taps me on the shoulder and I hear Billie yelling for me.

She tells me to check in for Annie Meyers and gives me instructions to stop the Bulgarian.

"Nancy, be aggressive in the back of the 1-3-1 zone," she said. "Run at the shooter as hard as you can, but when she gets ready to release the ball, step to the side." I was so excited to be checking into the game. "OK coach, I've got it," I told her. I take the floor looking like a woman on a mission. I follow the ball to the corner and run at the player as hard as I can as she is leaving her feet to shoot the ball. As she went up on her jump shot, I left my feet as I was running toward her and my knees hit her square in the chest and sent her sprawling into the bleachers. As I stepped over her I saw Billie motioning to me, "To the side of her. To the side of her!—I told you to get out of the way!"

I was a little sheepish about decking the Bulgarian player because she never returned to the game. We went on to win the gold medal to earn our spot in the Olympics, and the Bulgarians took the silver. I celebrated my 18th birthday in Hamilton with a party thrown by my teammates. Life couldn't have been better. Well, except for the braids my teammates put in my hair. Boy, did I look stupid.

When we arrived in Montreal, I couldn't believe the security measures for the Games. The International Olympic Committee was still reeling from the senseless murders four years earlier of eleven Israeli athletes in Munich, and no precaution was spared this time. There were metal detectors and security officers with machine guns. Of course, as a New Yorker, I took this in stride, but some of my teammates were quite spooked.

I loved being in the Olympic Village around all the various athletes. Our USA contingent was huge, and it was fun meeting so many different people. It wasn't until after some of the athletes' magnificent accomplishments that I realized   I had spoken to them in the Village or shared an elevator ride. Early on I bumped into   Bruce Jenner and Nadia Comaneci but I didn't realize who they were until after their gold-medal and record-setting performances.

I had fun trading pins, clothes, and hats and trying to communicate with athletes from all nations. Anything with USA on it went for premium prices and was always good in a multi-item swap. The Soviets wanted blue jeans or U.S. currency and would trade almost anything to get it. Most of the high end, sophisticated trading took place in the evening after dinner, down in the courtyard.

However, as luck would have it, ours was the opening game in the women's competition—the first Olympic women's basketball game ever— and we had a pretty strict curfew. The game against Japan tipped off at 9 o'clock in the morning, about five days after we arrived. The coaches made us go to bed at 7 p.m. and wake up at 5 a.m. to eat breakfast so we would get used to being up and moving around. They hoped that would make us more alert at game time. I couldn't believe I was at the Olympic Games in bed while everything was happening at night.

The coaches' plan was good but we ended up losing to Japan in the opening game nonetheless. Lusia Harris of Delta State University scored the first two points ever in women's Olympic basketball competition. As the games went on, we played Bulgaria, Canada, the Soviet Union and Czechoslovakia.

Billie made sure I got into the opening minutes of the game with Bulgaria to remind their hot shooter that I was still around. She remembered me from Hamilton: Every time I would look her way, she would get rid of the ball in a hurry. We beat Bulgaria, and then Canada, and our next test was against the Soviets.

They were the most dominant team in the world at the time, led by 7-foot-2, 260-pound Iuliana Semenova. The game started out like the Green Bay Packers against the Chicago Bears, more physical play than I've ever seen in my life. The Soviets took a 17-4 lead and were killing us in the 1-3-1 zone when Billie put me in to mix things up a little.

I was a little shaky on offense because the Soviet players were so physically imposing. I threw an errant pass that ended up in the hands of a Soviet guard who took off with Semenova down the floor. Trying to atone for my mistake, I hustled back on defense, but they had the numbers on me with a two-on-one break. I faked at the ball and the guard passed to Semenova, and I was struck by a terrible realization: I was directly in the path of this charging 260-pound juggernaut. All I had time to do was close my eyes and say a little prayer.

I was seeing stars—the kind you see painted on a Russian tank. I was plastered to the floor, and I remember people running out to me and telling me not to move. Billie, the trainer, and my teammates—it sounded like a chant: "Don't move. Don't move. Don't move." My mother was in the stands crying and my childhood friends Mark and Eric Muchnick just stood transfixed as I was helped off the court. I was OK, though. I was young and resilient—and foolish for taking a charge from Semenova.

After our loss to the Soviets, we had to beat the Czechs for the silver. It seemed from the minute we left the Olympic Village that there was a special feeling among the players, a quiet assurance. Loud music was playing, people were singing and talking—we were a close team, and the locker room before the game was confident. Our leaders—Lusia Harris, Pat Head, Julienne Simpson—had a look in their eyes that said they wouldn't be denied. That's where preparation and experience pay off. We knew the Czech team was bigger and strong, but we were big and quick and had great athletes.

With 17,000-plus spectators in the Montreal Forum, we played our best game of the Olympics, holding the lead from the start. The Czechs made a run at us, but in the second half, we opened it up again. I even got into the game, so you know the coaches weren't worried about the outcome.

The clock winds down, and we're all smiles—not cockiness, pure happiness, proud to be Olympians, proud to be Americans. As the buzzer goes off, the crowd goes wild. Chants of "USA! USA!" and red, white, and blue waving everywhere. I look for my mom, for Mark, Eric, and for my high school teammate Annie Nisenholc. Strangers are hugging me. It's like a dream. And then the thrill of standing on the podium and having a medal placed on my neck.

When we got back to the Athletes' Village, we were congratulated by members of our delegation. A medal for basketball is a medal for the USA and everyone was thrilled with our accomplishment. I drew extra special duty after the medals ceremony when I was randomly selected for drug testing. Hours—and several gallons of water—later, I was able to produce a sample in front of my courier. Yet another Olympic experience.

I had such an incredible time on my first USA teams. I was 16, 17, 18 years old, traveling around the world and seeing different cultures. Missing out on my high school graduation was disappointing, but what better reason to miss it than the Olympics? Anyway, I was getting an education here like I'd never had at school. I had never been a good student in the classroom, but I was making up for that through my experiences. I got to go to places like South America and Mexico. And as a team, we had learned how to trust and rely on each other. To someone who grew up in the New York environment, that was a new and important lesson.

Later, as a member of other USA national teams, I would travel to Europe, the Eastern Bloc countries, and the Far East. I began to appreciate the world around me and the cultures of other people. You learn how to deal in another language and currency. You also learn responsibility, like knowing where your passport is at all times. You learn about patriotism, and you find out just how much your country and flag mean to you. You find out quickly about the bond keeping your delegation together.

When there are just 20 of you in the traveling party and the American flag goes up and they play the "Star-Spangled Banner," you can just feel the cold chills and hear everyone's heart pound. There is so much caring and trust that goes into traveling internationally with the USA team. These players are like your family and they usually become friends for life.

Chapter 8

Finding Father Figures

 From the moment I stepped on the Old Dominion campus, I could see women's basketball was a star attraction there. I was part of a "dream class" of seven freshmen, and the Lady Monarchs were the talk of Norfolk. I couldn't wait to practice, to have media day, to play in my first collegiate game.

Coach Pam Parsons had assembled quite a collection of talent. Her "dream class" included Inge Nissen, Angela Cotman, Sue Richardson, Sandy Burke, Heidi Doherty, Linda Jerome, and me. We had power, finesse, strength, height, basketball smarts, and lofty goals. All we were lacking was a coach who shared our goals.

The Pam Parsons who recruited us and persuaded us to sign with ODU was not the same woman in the gym with us day-in and day-out my freshman year. Coach Parsons was a manipulator, with an aggressive and domineering personality. Most of us had never seen that in a female coach before, and we really didn't quite know how to take her. She knew that she had a young and impressionable team, and she took advantage of us.

If she had wanted us all to get along and bond, as a team needs to do to be really successful, she could have accomplished it with ease. Instead, she wanted to create mistrust and distance between us. She liked to keep everyone guessing, and she convinced many of the players that she was the only person on the team to be trusted.

Coach Parsons constantly sent mixed messages and never allowed us to develop rapport with our teammates. One day in practice she'd be telling the team that our 6-foot-5 center, Inge Nissen, and I were the All-Americans, the ones who would lead ODU to a national championship even though we were just freshmen. We were the heart and soul of the team. The next day, if we happened to disagree with her or do something that she didn't like, suddenly we were idiots, scum of the earth, plain old pieces of crap. Our teammates had to wonder what the heck was going on.

Matters weren't helped any when *Sport* magazine sent a writer to Norfolk to do a feature article on me. Robin Finn from *Sport* came to the Old Dominion campus in September 1976 and followed me around for a couple of days. She wanted background on me as a person and a player, and she wanted to see my interaction with my teammates, coaches, and fans.

I was excited about a major magazine doing a lengthy article on me, and after a weekend of interviews, I felt like Robin had some really good information for her story. In the weeks that followed, there was a lot of anticipation about the story.

While I was sitting in the bleachers before the start of practice one day about a month later, Coach Parsons came up to me and slammed down a copy of *Sport*. At first I thought she was just kidding around, as usual, but it quickly became apparent that her anger was genuine. I couldn't understand why until I read the article.

Robin Finn had totally distorted the picture she had seen that weekend, and the article did not represent ODU or me in a favorable light. She painted the ODU players as arrogant and hateful people. I was depicted as a slick, brash New Yorker who came to the sleepy, country hick-town of Norfolk, Virginia.

My teammates were great people and wonderful basketball players, and they didn't deserve their negative portrayal. Neither did Norfolk, which is far from "sleepy" or "country," and whose people are generally kind, cultured and well-educated.

There was quite an uproar at practice that day as more and more people read the article. The Old Dominion administration immediately contacted the university lawyer to review the article for possible damages. After Mr. Wilkins read the story, he told me I needed to contact a lawyer, too, to protect my own interests. He set up a meeting with his attorney, Jim Howard. It didn't take Mr. Howard long to let me know I had cause for damages.

For several weeks thereafter, there were back-and-forth meetings and phone calls with *Sport*.   Finally Mr. Howard decided that our last resort was to file a lawsuit. More months passed, with an army of the magazine's lawyers taking depositions in hopes of being able to discredit me.

Eventually, *Sport* agreed to settle out of court for $5,000. Mr. Howard advised me to take the money. It was exciting to have that kind of money, and I used it toward my expenses at Old Dominion.

I never dreamed that I'd be swept up in such a crazy event to start my college career. All I wanted to do was play basketball, go to school, and get to know the people around me. Unfortunately, at the beginning of my playing days at ODU, even that was too much to ask.

I had a hard time handling all the mind games Coach Parsons was playing with us. I just wanted to prove myself on the court and not have my Olympic press clippings thrown up in my face. I came to school with so much hype and pressure because I was the youngest player on the Olympic team. Sure, I had played on the Olympic team, but I was far from a star; I was a role-player. But without having scored a collegiate point yet, I was expected to be a Superwoman at Old Dominion.

Coach Parsons would pit me against my teammates when all I wanted to do was blend in. I was 18 years old, just trying to get along; she made it very tough on a freshman. There were times when I just wanted to say "to hell with it" and quit the team. I couldn't stand the ridicule. Sometimes Parsons would sit on top of the bleachers with a bullhorn yelling, "pass and cut, pass and cut." She was like a Hitler barking out orders to us. The team would joke about her behind her back. It was hard to respect someone who strutted around like a peacock with her feathers out.

After a while we learned to tune out Parsons' four-letter words and verbal bashing. Fortunately, I had some teammates who were there for the same reasons I was—hoops and books. One of my biggest allies was Inge Nissen. I had helped to convince Inge to go to school in the United States when I visited some French club teams before the 1976 Olympic Trials.

During my senior year in high school, one of my friends from the New York Chuckles, Lynn Robbins, talked me into visiting the Claremont University Club in France. If I decided not to go to college in the States, I could play in Europe and make a lot of money while maintaining my amateur status. While visiting the CUC, I met Inge, who was interested in going to school in the United States.

As I was trying to decide about the contract the French team had offered me, Inge came by my hotel to talk. She was from Denmark and very elegant and sophisticated. "Nancy, let me fill you in about the situation here," she said. She was smoking Marlboros and drinking a glass of wine as she told me about the life of a club player.

The more she talked, the more I realized I really didn't want to be that far away from home, especially with my grandfather sick. I was too young to head out on my own in such a big way. Before I left France, I told Inge that I was thinking about going to school at Cal State-Fullerton or Old Dominion. I also told her I would put her in touch with Coach Parsons. I had a feeling that we'd make a good team.

Coach Parsons knew she had one of the best inside-outside combinations in the country with Inge and me, but she constantly berated us. Inge had one advantage over me: She had heard this kind of verbal abuse while playing on the French club team, and she knew how to tune it out. One Saturday morning, a few weeks into practice, Parsons let Inge have it.

"Inge, get the hell out of my practice," said Parsons.

Inge appeared unfazed as she collected her things. She began walking out of the gym, then turned around. Parsons had been letting Inge use her car to get to and from campus, and Inge reminded her, "I need the keys to the car."

"Here are the keys," Parsons yelled. "Now will you get the hell out of my practice?" We all tried not to laugh, but it was so ridiculous. Our team was out of control.

Inge had a style of her own. One day we were scrimmaging against men, and Parsons told us to turn over our pinnies—practice jerseys with a different color on each side. We'd been working out for some time, and Inge's t-shirt underneath was soaked. She asked Parsons if she could change it, and when the coach said yes, Inge just peeled off the shirt and was standing there in a sheer bra. Jaws dropped, especially the guys'. I guess that's no big deal in Denmark or France, but in Norfolk, Virginia, people were a lot more at ease when Inge finally put on a new shirt.

At first I was shy and quiet. That may seem hard to believe, but I was looking for a comfort level. I was different from my teammates because of the experiences I had already accumulated at such an early age. I think a lot of people took that as being stuck-up and having an attitude, but that really wasn't the case. Growing up in New York, people just mind their own business. You walk with your head down, and you don't look people in the eye.

When I first got on campus, that was the way I walked to class, head down, full steam ahead, rarely speaking to anybody. However, I quickly learned something about people in the South. They'll speak to you walking down the street whether you are looking or not. "Hey, how y'all doing?"

I'd look up and wonder if they were talking to me. I couldn't figure it out. I didn't know them and they were speaking to me. I kept on walking without acknowledging the greeting. It wasn't that I was a stick-in-the-mud, but I was very introverted . . . until I met Wes.

One day after school started I was walking through the Student Center with a couple of players from the men's basketball team when I saw this guy walking through the mall area outside. All of a sudden, he starts falling up the stairs with a open umbrella that just has the spokes in it. No covering or cloth, just spokes.

He's getting soaked because there is nothing keeping the rain off of him. As I watched, I couldn't help but think of Chevy Chase as Wes Lockard went through his antics. He finally opened the door and walked in after falling down a few more times.

Wes spotted me and came over to meet me. I knew nothing

about him, but somehow I sensed I was about to be embarrassed by him. He put his arms around me and rolled me down to the floor while singing, "I Want to Kiss You All Over." I couldn't believe he was doing this to me. And I wouldn't have believed it if you'd told me Wes Lockard would become one of the dearest friends in my life. We have experienced so many great times together, and our years at Old Dominion were a laugh a minute with him around.

Wes started out as the mascot for WTAR radio in Norfolk, parading around in a 7-foot-tall seagull costume. From the seagull, he graduated to Duncan, mascot of the New Jersey Nets, and now he is Burnie, mascot of the Miami Heat.

Stories of Wes and me have become legends at ODU, and the legends didn't end with our graduation. Nancy and Wes drive backward into Jack-in-the-Box at 3 a.m. Wes puts Harry and Pam Lozon's telephone into the freezer and doesn't bother letting them know where it went. Wes on the make at the SuperStars competition.

I guess that one requires some explanation. He had come down to the SuperStars with me and Martina, and we were having dinner with 1988 Olympic gold medalist Louise Ritter, among others. We kept trying to slip his room key to a young lady who was very shy and didn't know what to make of him. Join the club.

I try to give people advance warning before introducing them to Wes. Background is vital here! When he met Martina for the first time in 1981, he climbed up the back of her BMW, jumped head-first through the sun roof and started kissing her. Uh, Martina, this is Wes. I had tried to warn her beforehand, but sometimes with Wes, a warning isn't enough.

And if you think he's crazy in normal clothes, catch his act in costume. He has cracked up fans and athletes alike since college. Ask any NBA player, and he will tell you Wes is creative, funny, and spontaneous on court and a great guy off of it. He's also my secret liaison to the players: "Hey, Wes, when Michael Jordan gets to town, tell him to stop changing his phone number and give me a call. I need to ask him about camp." Wes relays my message, and it keeps my phone bills down.

Besides his friendship, the most valuable thing Wes has given me is the ability to laugh at myself. He's taught me not to take things so seriously and to look for humor in stressful situations. He's a loyal and caring individual who has added so much to my life. He's also a great listener, no matter what the situation, and, his apparent insanity to the contrary, he gives sound and sincere advice. He has been there for me in tough times with Martina and my family and when I had knee surgery. And in happier times, he was the witness for my marriage to Tim. Anything that means anything, he's been there. He's married now to a great gal named Wendy, and together they're keeping Miami in stitches.

Wes isn't the only person from my days at Old Dominion who has turned out to be a life-long friend. Another person who literally changed my life and had a profound effect on how I verbalized my emotions was the late Jack Wilkins.

I always had a hard time saying "I love you" to anyone until I met Mr. Wilkins. It was hard for me to tell my mother or father that I loved them; I just couldn't get it out. And here I found myself telling this older gentleman, a big booster of ODU, that I loved him.

I met Mr. Wilkins when I was being recruited by ODU. I instantly looked at him as a father figure. He was sarcastic on the outside and pure gold on the inside, kind of like I'd hope to have people think of me, I guess. Mr. Wilkins taught me about family values and how important a family, be it good or bad, was in life. He encouraged me to ease up on my mother and to treat her with more respect. He also introduced me to Harry and Pam Lozon, who would become like family to me.

The Lozons and Mr. Wilkins provided me with the family atmosphere I never had growing up. The Lozons had two young boys, Jason and Chad. I was like a granddaughter to Mr. Wilkins and a daughter to Harry and Pam. I couldn't have asked for better people to love and care for me. Harry was the dad I never had growing up, and I was his jock daughter. Harry had been a standout player at ODU, one of the school's all-time leading scorers. Mr. Wilkins had helped recruit him way back when. In my first year at ODU, Harry volunteered to help Coach Parsons with the team. The Lozons were always around when I needed advice or a friend to talk to.

Their house became home base for me and my friends. We would watch movies or cook out; it was always a family setting at the Lozons'. I can't remember Pam and Harry ever missing a home game. They even went to many of the away games and to both of our AIAW National Championships. Many of my most-prized trophies had a place on their mantel.

It was Mr. Wilkins who had hired the private plane for the ODU outing to see me sit on the bench in Hamilton in 1976. I got a phone call from Pam Parsons. "Nancy, this is Pam. Mr. Wilkins and a few others from Norfolk are flying up to see you play in the tournament in Hamilton."

"Wow!" I thought, "these people don't know me and they are flying up to see me play!" I was so excited I could barely warm up. There was Mr. Wilkins and his group, and I couldn't wait to show off. The game started and ended, and I hadn't seen a second of court time. I was so embarrassed I wouldn't come out of the locker room after the game. Mr. Wilkins waited and waited and waited, but I wouldn't come out. He finally left and called me the next day.

"Lieberman, we hire a private jet and fly all the way to see you play," he said. "Heck, even the ball girl got into the game, and the water girl had her warm-ups off and was ready to go." Then he dropped the sarcastic facade. "Don't worry about it," he told me.

It drove me nuts not to have been able to play, and it embarrassed me that someone would come to see me play and I wouldn't get into the game. I was surprised when Mr. Wilkins started joking around with me about it. I wasn't used to being on the receiving end of sarcasm.

That was the icebreaker of our relationship. He turned out to be one of the most positive people in my life. He genuinely liked me as a person. It wasn't just for four years while I was a player. If I had missed out on a father when I was growing up, now I had two father figures—Harry Lozon and Mr. Wilkins.

Mr. Wilkins would do anything for me, but he never just gave me what I wanted, I had to work for it. "Super Jew," he would say, "come on over to the house. I need some work done." I would go to the house after practice or on weekends and clean the house, shine the brass door knobs, run errands. In the four years I was at Old Dominion he never once called me Nancy; it was always Lieberman, or Super Jew.

"If you're going to represent yourself, your game, and your

university," he would tell me, "you are going to need to look and feel good about yourself." So he would pay me for doing the odd jobs around the house and tell me to go buy a dress and some nice shoes to wear to a banquet or a speaking engagement. He knew I didn't have any money for those things, and he wanted to help me.

There was not a day that went by that Mr. Wilkins didn't say, "Lieberman, I love you." He wanted me to feel good about myself beyond being a basketball player. He was just incredible. There was never a time that we would get off the phone without him saying, "Lieberman, I love you and I care about you." If I didn't respond, he would just sit and wait and say something like, "I don't hear you." It was just so hard for me to express my love for anyone else. He made it OK for me to say "I love you."

I finally felt the love that I wished my father had shown to me when I was growing up. Many days I would stop by Wilkins Chevrolet just to sit and talk. Some days we would talk about school, or classes, or cars, or boys. Sometimes we would just sit there and not really talk about anything at all. I always felt a closeness to him and will for the rest of my life. When Mr. Wilkins died in December 1990, it was a big hurt for me. I had kept in touch with him weekly and had come to Virginia Beach to stay with him several times before he passed away. I was so glad to have him meet my husband, Tim.

I know I can't replace the love and the kindness he gave me, but there will always be a special place in my heart for him. A few weeks before he died I called and we were having one of our usual talks, but it was more emotional than usual. Before he hung up, he said, "Hey Nancy, I love you." He had never called me Nancy before. "Mr. Wilkins," I said, "I love you too." I was all choked up and crying, he was all choked up—I couldn't help it. I knew I was losing time with him, and I wanted to be sure he couldn't doubt my love. My mom called the next day and said he had called and told her about our conversation. He said after he'd talked to me, he had cried like a baby, the first time he'd cried in years.

There are so many other very special people I met while at ODU that to try to mention all of them would certainly leave a few people out. Another family, that of Carl and Connie Salland, became close friends. Carl had grown up in Far Rockaway and had gone to my high school. As soon as he heard that I had signed with ODU, he called the basketball office and left his number for me to call him.

Connie and Carl were wonderful to me all through college. They came to all my home games and to the nationals, giving me support and encouragement. Along with the Lozons, they were like a second family to me. It was so nice to get away from school and watch television, go to church, or eat a home-cooked meal with them. When I moved back to Virginia in 1983, we lived about 10 minutes apart and our friendship has strengthened through the years. I always love to stop by Carl's store, Digital Sound, and rummage around in the boxes looking for good deals.

I had so many wonderful people around me when I arrived at Old Dominion, and it helped my transition to college life. The ODU fans deserve special mention, too. They treated me like family. There was always a special bond between our fans and players. We went to their homes, knew their names, ate dinner with their kids; they came to our games in heat, snow, and rain. We were their pride and joy, and they inspired us to play our best. The mutual feeling was warm and genuine. Nobody wanted anything from the other but love and friendship. Maybe the word "fans" isn't good enough to describe our friends who watched us play. Our championships weren't just ours, but theirs as well. If it hadn't been for the support I received my freshman year, I don't know how I could have made it through the basketball season.

Chapter 9

Fresh Outlook

 Coach Parsons was difficult to understand; it was hard to know what direction she was coming from. All I wanted to do was win basketball games, but it seemed that she was more concerned with winning mind games with us.

My hectic summer and freshman schedule provided me with a case of mononucleosis prior to the start of my first season, and I missed the first five games. Coach Parsons gave me a hard time about being such a big-deal Olympian and then not being able to play. She called me at midnight after our opening game at North Carolina State and cussed me out because we had lost. She was even madder after the team lost to Longwood College. She berated me over the phone because the team had turned the ball over too many times.

I was in bed with mono, truly sick, and I had to listen to her cussing me out over games I hadn't even played in. Night after night, game after game, it was the same screaming woman calling me and telling me I was good for nothing, pressuring me to get back on the court. I couldn't stand the verbal punishment, so I decided to find a doctor who would let me play to get Parsons off my back. It really angered me that she was treating me this way. Better than anyone at Old Dominion, she should have known I'd do anything to play the game.

Our trainer, Marty Bradley, and the doctor weren't keen about my playing. Somehow I managed to talk them into it when I was able not to wince when they poked and prodded me. They both warned me to take it easy, but I was so excited at the thought of getting into my first game that "taking it easy" would be hard.

We were playing James Madison at home, and my first time down the court, I dove into the stands trying to save a pass. I looked over at the bench with an expression of, "No problem." A couple of plays later I took a charge. You can't take a player who only knows how to play the game one way—all out—and tell her to take it easy. Instincts take over, and you just play the game.

The 1976-77 season was our first year of Division I play. We went 23-9 and won the Virginia state title, 81-54 over James Madison. We were one step away from the AIAW Sweet 16 when we lost to Tennessee, 61-60, in the regional finals in Memphis. Playing against my Olympic teammates, Pat Head and Trish Roberts, gave me more incentive than usual to play well. Unfortunately, I missed a shot from the left side with six seconds to go. I thought I was fouled, but no call for the rookie. That game was one of many meetings with Tennessee in my career. We were still invited to the National Women's Invitation Tournament (NWIT) in Amarillo, Texas, where we lost to Mississippi College and UCLA. I was named to my first All-America team, the NWIT team.

As a rookie, I led the team with 20.9 points and 7.9 assists per game. I felt I had played pretty well despite the on-again, off-again dealings with Coach Parsons, but I couldn't stand her constant manipulation and jealousy. One time when we were playing Virginia Tech, a film crew was at the game to get some footage for a story ABC's Dick Schaap would be doing a few days later. About nine minutes into the game I had already scored a dozen or more points and was having a good game, but when I threw a bad pass, Parsons yanked me off the floor and started screaming at me. As I sat at the end of the bench, she came by and started yelling and cursing at me again. When I asked her what I'd done wrong, she just screamed, "Shut the f— up!" I decided that playing was no longer fun with her around. After the game, I cleaned out my locker and got into a shouting match with her at her office. Later, I went over to Harry Lozon's house to talk, and the next day I told our athletic director, Dr. Jim Jarrett, about Pam's tirades.

I told him I didn't think I'd be coming back to school for my sophomore year. I vowed that I wouldn't ride the roller coaster again. Coach Parsons' favorite saying was *"My* way or the highway." A lot of us hoped ODU would show *her* the highway, and we got our wish when the school hired Marianne Crawford Stanley. Coach Parsons ended up at South Carolina.

I still thought a lot about transferring to another school. I wanted to go to the University of Tennessee because two of my Olympic teammates had transferred there and loved playing for Pat Head, the co-captain of the Olympic team. Pat didn't want me to leave ODU for the wrong reasons and urged me to give Coach Stanley a chance.

After my freshman year, I was invited to play on the USA junior national team and had the opportunity to be coached by Pat, formerly my Pan-Am and Olympic teammate. The Amateur Basketball Association was starting a program to develop younger players with an eye toward the 1980 Olympic Games. It was going to be different playing with people my own age after having been the youngest player on the USA squad for the past two years. Now I would be the senior member of the team, with a Pan-Am gold and Olympic silver medal to my credit.

With such a young crop of players, no one expected much from us, except for Coach Head. She put us through the same intense conditioning the Olympians had endured the year before. I was in the best shape of my life and had never had more fun playing basketball.

Maybe it was just a pilot program, but we went 11-0 and won both of our tournaments, in Squaw Valley and Mexico City. Everyone on the team complemented the abilities of everyone else. We were young and didn't know better, so we weren't awed going into games where we were the clear underdog. This was Pat Head's first international coaching experience, too. She had retired from playing after the 1976 Olympics and had just finished her third year of coaching at Tennessee. The ABA was not only testing the waters with us, but they were also trying to develop a young coach for the future.

My teammates were players who just a few months earlier had been intense collegiate rivals. This team was the beginning of some of my long and enduring friendships with people like Denise Curry from UCLA, Holly Warlick from Tennessee, Gina Beasley of N.C. State, and Kris Kirchner of Maryland. We all became All-Americans during our collegiate careers and ruled the roost in USA women's basketball into 1980.

I had such a rewarding basketball experience that summer. I averaged over 30 points per game and I can't remember having so much fun. I remember one time Billie Moore was watching us play. Somebody shot the ball, I think it was Denise Curry, and the shot hit the right of the rim. I just happened to be running down the floor and it was right in front of me. The rebound went off the right of the rim, and I was falling out of bounds, but I caught the ball with my left hand and tipped it in. Billie just jumped out of her seat, looked at me, and said, "I have never seen anybody do that with her left hand." What a boost to my ego that was! How good to hear a coach say something like that after the season of abuse I'd taken from Coach Parsons. I hoped that the dark cloud of my freshman year had passed and that this was an indication of good things to come.

It was going to be different having a new coach to start my sophomore year, especially since Marianne Crawford Stanley and I had gone head-to-head for a spot on the Olympic team just a year earlier. I remembered her as a very knowledgeable player on the floor who directed her teammates on the court like a coach does from the bench.

I knew there would have to be some adjustments with a new coach. I had been accused of running Pam Parsons off, and I knew that would be an intimidating story for a new person in the position. Our coach-player relationship was shaky at first, but after we broke the ice, the lines of communication opened, and a lot of positive things started happening.

Marianne came to us from a Catholic college in Philadelphia, and I wondered how she'd adjust to some of my more brassy teammates. As it turned out, she didn't have a problem because our individuality was very important in her scheme of things. I remember the first time Inge lit up a cigarette and drank a cup of coffee in the locker room during Marianne's pre-game talk. After going through half of her spiel, she casually turned toward Inge and said, "Inge would you cut that out?" Marianne had handled it without making a big deal out of it.

One of the first things Marianne did was adjust the chemistry of the team. She called me in and told me she felt I could contribute more to the success of the team if I switched to point guard. I didn't know what to think. I had been a power forward or center all my life. My game was built on being aggressive, rebounding, blocking shots, and scoring a lot of points. I think my ego got in the way when she first proposed the move, but eventually she made me see the whole picture. She wanted the ball in my hands, and she wanted me to be her coach on the floor and direct the team. She had been an All-American in college, so I trusted that she could teach me the position.

The move turned out to be a blessing in disguise. By taking me away from the basket, it lessened the wear and tear on my body and added to the longevity of my career. I became a thinker and a creator as a point guard and developed a whole new sense of the court and the game. There were times during my sophomore year of 1977-78 that I wondered whether I was really suited to this position, but the proof came when I was named to the prestigious Kodak All-America team for the first time. The bigger dividends of the switch would be paid off in national championships for the next two years.

My switch to point guard helped me earn a nickname. My responsibility was to create opportunities with my passing, and my favorite was a no-look, behind-the-back blind pass. During my sophomore year, the Michigan State men's team came to Old Dominion for a tournament. The star of the MSU team at the time was Earvin "Magic" Johnson. In the Norfolk papers the day after MSU played, some writers commented that Magic passed the ball like Nancy Lieberman. After that, the nickname "Lady Magic" began finding its way into the headlines.

Marianne gave us the direction to have a successful season from her first year as head coach. We all had our share of differences, but Marianne respected our individuality, focusing her concern on our on-court performance. We won 12 games in a row at one point, and Inge and I were having a ball with our inside-outside scoring punch. I averaged a little over 20 points a game that year and she averaged around 19 as ODU went 30-4, its first 30-win season.

What a difference a year made. Once again we won the state title, but we still couldn't get over the regional hurdle, losing

59-57 to N.C. State. Inge fouled out, and I missed a shot at the buzzer that would have tied it. I kept thinking that sooner or later we were going to win a regional and get to the Final Four. Instead, we went back to Amarillo for the NWIT and won this time, defeating Texas in the title game, 70-60. Later that summer, I played for Texas head coach Jody Conradt as a member of the U.S. national team that traveled to Czechoslovakia and Bulgaria. Basketball was fun again, and I was having the time of my life playing.

However, sadness hit my family during my sophomore year. I was playing in an invitational tournament in Knoxville, Tennessee, and we had just won the title when my family called me home to be with my grandmother, who was dying in the hospital. It was hard for me to see my Grandma Eva on life support and so weak. "Ma, please let Grandma go. Let her be at peace," I told my mother.

Mr. Wilkins and Harry flew up from Norfolk for the funeral, and I flew back with them right afterward in Mr. Wilkins' private plane. We had a game that night and nobody expected me to play. I had other ideas. I didn't get to the gym until right before the end of the first half. I peeked into the gym, and as usual it was packed. I was still in a daze from the emotional events of the day when I went into the locker room and changed into my uniform.

When I went into the gym, the fans started clapping for me. I was focused in a really strange and peaceful way. It's a feeling I've only experienced one other time in my life, and that involved Grandpa Lou. He passed away my freshman year, and two seasons later ODU played in Madison Square Garden, a day before what would have been his birthday. He would have loved to have seen me play in the Garden that night.

Sometimes, the littlest things can inspire me. Before the game against Queens College, one of the Lady Knights players was quoted as saying I was the most overrated player she'd ever seen. I was shocked and hurt she would say something like that. New York is my hometown, I had almost gone to Queens, and here's this player ripping me. She obviously didn't know me or how I'd react.

Between the emotion of wanting to play well for my grandfather and wanting to prove my opponent wrong, it was a career night. I scored 33 points, was 14 for 16 from the floor and had double figures in rebounds and assists—a triple-double before anyone had heard of such a thing. The record for points scored at the Garden was 52 by Carol Blazejowski. I never went for individual records, but I wanted that one, and I was very disappointed that Marianne took me out midway through the second half. Marianne and Carol were good friends, and while I guess I'll never know for sure, it has always stuck in the back of my mind that Marianne may have been trying to protect Carol's record.

As I was sitting on the bench the last nine minutes of the game, I remember feeling like Grandpa Lou had been watching me play. Both then and after Grandma Eva died, I remember hearing and seeing everything so clearly on the court. But it was as if the "Mute" button was pushed in and I was just floating through all my experiences on the court. This time I had another great game and left the floor thinking that night that both of my grandparents were together again and watching over me.

Chapter 10

Crowns for the Lady Monarchs

When we had our annual media day to start the 1978-79 season, I was asked how I thought we were going to do. It was a standard question, asked every year. This time I wasn't going to give the standard answer.

"Well first of all, I don't ever want to wear goat horns again, and second, I don't see too many teams on our schedule who can beat us this season. Old Dominion is going to win the national championship," and with those comments I sat down.

No one could believe that I went out on a limb like that to start the year, but I really believed what I'd said. It was the old Muhammad Ali approach: Tell 'em you're the greatest, then back it up. ODU won 26 games in a row and was the hottest women's basketball team in the country before we lost our first game in late February. Inge was the team's leading scorer, averaging 22 points to my 18. We had great balance and seemed unstoppable until we traveled to South Carolina in February of 1979.

It was the first meeting between Old Dominion and South Carolina with Pam Parsons as the Lady Gamecocks' head coach. Inge stayed home with an ankle injury. The rest of us made our way to Columbia by bus through a snowstorm. Travel was so slow and the roads so bad that we had to change into our uniforms on the bus. We didn't reach the gym in time for our normal pre-game dressing and taping ritual.

We wanted to beat South Carolina in the worst way. Those of us who had played for Coach Parsons as freshmen had a score to settle. Wanting so badly to win, we played tight and terrible and left Columbia with a 73-49 loss. I had one of the worst nights of my career: six points on something like 3-for-21 shooting. To top it off, my roommate, Rhonda Rompola, got into a fight, and when I tried to stop it, I got bounced from the game. Oh well, I wasn't helping much anyway. As it turned out, that loss to South Carolina would be the only blemish on our record that season.

We knocked people off left and right heading toward our first Final Four appearance in Greensboro, North Carolina. We drew UCLA in the first game, and I can remember how tight and nervous everyone was before tip-off. I was sitting through Marianne's pre-game talk trying not to hyperventilate. I tried everything— standing, sitting, walking, yawning, even scratching my head— to distract myself from my rapid breathing, but I knew that when the ball went up I'd be OK.

It wasn't "just another game," but we had to treat it that way. Maybe the only player who really wasn't nervous was Rhonda, a freshman. Rhonda knew how important it was to me to get into the title game. She went out and scored 25 points, leading us to an 87-82 win over Billie Moore's UCLA Bruins.

Some people just help make you what you are, and Rhonda was a sparkplug for me in the two years we played together. Rhonda and I were such fierce competitors, that if you didn't know us and watched us practice, you'd have thought we were bitter enemies. We wanted to guard one another in every drill, and be first in sprints, defense, everything. Most people backed off from me; Rhonda attacked. We loved the competition; it made us both better.

On nights we couldn't sleep, we'd have campus security open the gym at ODU's field house at midnight or 1 in the morning so we could go in and play 21 or one-on-one full-court. She was a great shooter, pound for pound the best I've ever seen. If there had been a three-point line then, she would have owned it. Rhonda, still the competitor, is the head women's basketball coach at Southern Methodist University in Dallas now.

With Rhonda's help, we had made it to the championship game. This was it. A game dreamed up on the playground so many years ago. It would also mark the first time the championship game would be carried from start to finish on NBC-TV. Our opponent was Louisiana Tech, who shot 70 percent from the floor in defeating Tennessee to earn a spot in the title game.

We had a lot of nervous energy after our pre-game meal the morning of the championship. My roommate, Sue Davy, had a little too much nervous energy, it turned out. She was running from room to room going out on the balcony and yelling to other players. Sue was running out to hide on a teammate's balcony when she went flying through a closed balcony door. Glass flew everywhere as Sue crashed through the door. Fortunately, the railing stopped her from falling off. There was glass everywhere. The paramedics bandaged and stitched Sue up and she was OK, but it was going to be hard for us to keep our minds on the game.

This is it, all our dreams. Marianne gives the pre-game talk, we know each other inside and out. Our fans are packed in the Coliseum. Usually I'm very calm and confident. My teammates have always looked at that to gauge what type of game we're in. This night, I'm walking around the locker room, white as a ghost. My hands are sweaty, and my heart hurts it's pounding so hard. Even in pre-game warm-ups my body's tight, I'm not breathing right—basically I'm scared as heck!

We played tight, scared, through the first half. We were a transition team—rebound, run, create points from our defense, pressure others into mistakes— but this night we were slow, playing a half-court game, and not being patient at that. Fans usually loved to see us play because we were structured but creative. This time we were downright boring. We trailed by a dozen at intermission.

I was mad, embarrassed by our first-half performance, especially after so many busloads of fans had traveled to the game from Old Dominion, not to mention the national television audience. In the locker room at halftime, Marianne handled us with care, not allowing us to get down mentally. She pressed us to relax, have fun, and chip away at the lead slowly.

Tech's point guard, Mary Nell Kendrick, had a bad habit on her spin dribble—she'd leave the ball behind her. I told Rhonda, Angie Cotman, and my other teammates that I felt I could deflect the ball off her spin. Sure enough, I had three steals in the second half. Inge and forward Jan Trombly played tough inside, we found our running game, and my fast-break greyhounds, Rhonda and Angie, started to cut loose. We pulled together and gradually got back into the ball game. Inge scored 22 points and I added 20 as we finally prevailed over the Lady Techsters, 75-65.

Being the best is all you ever dream about when you compete at this level. Nobody ever remembers who came in second, and a championship had been my dream from the first day I signed with Old Dominion. I wanted to be the best player on the best team in the country. When it finally hits you that you've won, the feeling is overwhelming.

When the buzzer sounded, we all rushed to the center of the court. I couldn't believe we were the champions. As we headed to cut down the nets, fans, friends, and family were all over the court. I remember cutting the cord and putting the net over my head as my teammates hoisted me into the air, my finger up in the classic "We're No.1" gesture. It seemed like everything was in slow motion.

I saw my mom, and our eyes locked. I went to her, and NBC and the other media captured our moment together. We still have that picture—and that moment, frozen in time—at my mom's house.

The party started at the Coliseum, continued in the locker room, and wrapped up early the next morning at the hotel. We all were exhausted, but it was the happiest kind of tired. At the press conference afterward, I was asked to share my views on our season, our fans, women's basketball in general, and how it felt to finally be the champs.

Weeks later, I made the USA national team, and we toured Bulgaria and Czechoslovakia for some much-needed international experience. I didn't get much rest that summer, but when I returned to Norfolk in August, I was ready to help defend our title.

My senior year was going to be another learning experience. We were the defending AIAW national champions, and everybody would be gunning for us. The pressure would be on to match our 35-1 record of '78-79. We had almost everyone coming back, seven seniors and Rhonda, a seasoned sophomore; we had Chris Critelli, an Olympian from Canada; and 6-foot-8 high school All-American Anne Donovan would be joining us. We lost my Pan-Am teammate Jan Trombly to a knee operation, but still had plenty of firepower with our other starter, Angie Cotman. Individually, I knew that I would probably break the record as target of the most box-and-one defenses in a single season. It figured to be a challenging year.

About nine games into my final year, the USSR women's national team came to Norfolk to play Old Dominion during its U.S. tour. Little did I know it at the time, but this game would be the closest I got to the 1980 Moscow Olympic Games. The Soviets had not been beaten since the early 1960s. They were steamrolling their way across U.S. campuses, beating our best college teams by an average of 40 points.

When the Soviets arrived at the Norfolk Scope for the exhibition game, they were greeted by what was then the largest crowd ever to see a women's basketball game, 10,237 spectators. It was a very physical game, and at halftime there was just a two-point margin separating the teams. Many of the players from the 1976 Olympic team were on the Soviet squad including my old friend, Uliana Semenova. We hung tough, but the taller, more physical Soviet team beat us, 76-66.

A couple of games later, we lost to Louisiana Tech in Madison Square Garden by a bucket, 59-57, right before the Christmas holidays. That loss was a dose of reality for us. It told us that if we took things for granted, we weren't going to get that second championship that meant so much for us. It was our wake-up call. We wouldn't lose again that season, while rolling off 27 wins.

I was doing more interviews, columns, talk shows, photo layouts, and appearances than I ever dreamed possible. I found myself becoming the spokesperson for women's basketball. In November, I received an invitation to attend an Olympic fundraiser at the New York Stock Exchange Building. I had heard a rumor that Muhammad Ali might be there, but after walking around with my mother and my friend Barbara Wood for an hour, there was no sign of my idol.

All of a sudden, a slew of security appeared and out of the middle emerged Ali. I couldn't believe it. My idol was right there in the same room with me. He was heading toward some stairs and I knew if I was ever going to have a chance to meet him I had to catch him then. He passed right by us, but the security and his bodyguards kept us back.

As he passed by on his way to the elevator, he noticed my gorgeous friend Barbara and winked at her. That was all the opening we needed. I grabbed Barbara and my mother, and we took off after him. Again, security turned us away, despite my pleas, but my resourceful mother went up to another security guard and explained that she had left her coat upstairs on the second floor. She led us upstairs where we were met by another roadblock.

"We're here to see Muhammad Ali," we announced in chorus. "You and everyone else," the guard's look seemed to say. Suddenly, a door opened and there was the Champ! He stuck his head out and saw the three of us standing there. A few minutes later, a man came out and asked Barbara to come inside; Ali wanted to speak to her. I couldn't believe it when he returned and beckoned us inside too.

Once inside, I also recognized Howard Davis, a boxer on the 1976 U.S. Olympic team who had won a gold medal in Montreal. My mom made straight for Ali.

"You know, my daughter Nancy is the greatest," she told him. He tilted his head and gave her a quizzical look. "No, no, no! What I mean is she is the greatest basketball player in the world."

Ali saw me talking to Howard Davis and called over to us. "Howard, who is she?" he asked. "She's the greatest basketball player in the world," Howard replied. "Is that so?" my idol asked me. I stammered something unintelligible and the Champ started playing around, proclaiming that he was the greatest.

Later, he invited us over to his suite at the Plaza Hotel. I couldn't believe that I was actually meeting one of my all-time idols. We went up to his room and chatted. We discussed boxing, and then he recited some poetry and talked about the historical misunderstandings between blacks and whites.

As we got ready to leave, I told him no one back at Old Dominion would believe I met Muhammad Ali. I asked him to do me a favor and talk to Harry Lozon back in Norfolk. It was midnight when I called Harry and told him I had someone I wanted him to talk to. When I put Ali on the phone, Harry was at a loss for words.

I still felt like I was dreaming when I left the hotel. We exchanged addresses and phone numbers as he walked us out to our car.   He planted a goodnight kiss on each of us and we giggled like little school girls all the way home.

A month or so later he called me at my apartment in Norfolk. Wes answered the phone and told me The Champ was calling. Ali wanted to let me know he appreciated the card and photos my mother had sent to him. He also told me he had read the 11-page article Curry Kirkpatrick had written about me in *Sports Illustrated.* "He said you are the greatest, Nancy," Ali told me. "Just don't forget that *I* am The Greatest."

The team had been rolling along, winning and winning and winning. In addition to playing and going to school, I was on the road a lot receiving a number of awards like the Broderick Cup and the Wade Trophy. Just when I didn't think I could do anything else, the phone rang one day and it was Raymond, Barbara Wood's boyfriend, who worked for Reggie Jackson of the New York Yankees.

"Nancy, Matt Merola (Reggie's agent) got you a spot in the SuperStars competition. You will be competing in the Bahamas and they'll pay your way and the way for a guest."

I couldn't believe it. I had always watched the SuperStars on television and thought that I should be out there competing with them. In the back of my mind I knew I could win because I considered myself an all-around athlete. This was the invitation of a lifetime, but I had to wade through a lot of red tape to go.

The SuperStars competition is for professional athletes, so I had to get permission from the AIAW, the U.S. Olympic Committee, and the Amateur Basketball Association of the USA to be able to compete without losing my amateur status. I told them I wasn't after the prize money. I just wanted the opportunity to compete and to experience the "thrill of victory."

Paperwork in hand, I started training for the competition. I was in great physical shape because we were in the middle of the season, but I wanted to work out with a track coach to learn some of the basics of running a 400-meter race. In December of 1979, Barbara and I flew down for the competition. I had never been to the Bahamas before, and I couldn't believe how beautiful it was.

On the first day of competition you have to pick seven of the ten events to compete in, excluding your specialty sport. After

I picked my sports, I realized I had only two sports on the first day and five on the second day. I'm a good athlete, but even I knew that there was no way I could handle that agenda.

My first event, at 8 a.m., was swimming. You'd think it would be hot and sunny in the Bahamas. No way. On this morning it was 50 degrees and overcast. As the other competitors got on the blocks I was still standing there shivering in my sweats. I was finally ready and was looking around to see what the "mark" position was when the gun went off. I'm left standing on the blocks as the field takes off. I manage to belly-flop into the pool but I am so far behind the field that it's really not funny. Not to me, anyway.

I'm swimming like crazy, my head bobbing side to side, when I look up and see the field coming back toward me. When I finally make the turn and come off the wall, I notice Annie Meyers is already out of the pool doing an interview and volleyballer Linda Fernandez is toweling off. Heck, the underwater camerawoman beat me to the finish.

OK, *now* it was funny. I ended up drinking half the pool because I was laughing so hard. I finally finished the first and last race I would ever swim in the SuperStars competition. I think Joe Frazier and I share the SuperStars record for coming the closest to drowning.

I managed to get through my only other event of the day, bowling, without any mishaps.

The next day was torture. In the morning I had rowing and golf; in the afternoon there was the 60-yard dash, the quarter-mile run, and the obstacle course.

In the dash, I had to come out of starting blocks. I'd never come out of blocks before so I really didn't know what to do. I ended up pushing off Barbara's feet and fell into tennis star Betty Stove's lane, pushing her out of her lane and totally disrupting the race.

I figured I'd make it up in the quarter mile. I could sprint the whole thing, I reasoned, since it was just one lap. I took off flying and opened up a huge lead on the field. I think I came through my first 200 meters in 27 seconds and I had blown by everyone in the race. About 50 meters later, as I was thinking about the finish, I hit the wall. I couldn't get air in my lungs, and my legs felt like lead weights. I struggled to finish the race, literally walking across the finish line in 77 seconds.

When the final standings were posted for the 1980 SuperStars, Linda Fernandez was the champion and collected about $54,000. I somehow finished second, and won $27,500, which as an amateur I couldn't collect. As Barbara and I were flying back to Norfolk, I kept thinking that I could have won had I known anything about track and field.

My senior year continued to be a three-ring circus. We were playing one of the toughest schedules in the country under the pressure of trying to repeat as AIAW champs. By late February, I was exhausted by the go-go pace I had been on.

I had fallen into the "can't-say-no" syndrome. On top of my playing ball and going to school, hundreds of people were asking me for interviews, speeches, and appearances. In addition, I was personally answering every piece of the 2,000 to 3,000 letters I was receiving at school. It seemed like I didn't have any time for myself or my friends, and it was getting to me in a bad way.

Don't let me kid you, I loved the attention, every bit of it. The stories were positive, and we were the hottest team in women's basketball. Yeah, I felt good. But I was also going through the least private time of my life, sharing my every thought and my every day with the public and the media. Sometimes I just wanted to go away and hide. Coach Stanley gave us the weekend off before the state tournament in early March, the start of our post-season. I knew I had to get away from Norfolk for a few days. The road to the 1980 AIAW championship was going to be rough, and I wanted to be ready, well-rested, and relaxed.

One night, around this time, I was on the phone talking to Sonja Hogg, a good friend who also happened to be the head coach at Louisiana Tech. At the time, ODU and Tech were ranked as the top two women's basketball teams in the country by the Associated Press. I was telling her how tired I was of dealing with the media and all the pressure.

I had gotten to know Coach Hogg after I took care of her star player, 6-foot-5 center, Elinor "Sweet E" Griffin, one summer when she was stranded in New York after the U.S. national team returned from Bulgaria. Elinor was a real country girl, petrified at the prospect of having to stay in New York alone when her flight out was canceled. I took her home with me that night, then got her on a plane home the next day. A few weeks later I received a nice thank-you note from Sonja Hogg.

Later that year, I met Sonja at a media day and we just started talking. During my senior year, we stayed in touch, and she was a great sounding board for me. After we lost to Louisiana Tech by two points in Madison Square Garden my senior year, we sat up and talked all night. She was a great listener and always gave me sound advice. In fact, two agents from Detroit had come to watch me play in the Garden and wanted to sign me to a contract after I graduated. When my mother and I met them for dinner, I invited Sonja to come along and listen to their offer.

I viewed Sonja as more of a friend than I did Marianne Stanley. Despite our rivalry with Louisiana Tech, I always knew I could talk to Sonja and she would be honest with me.

"Sonja, I've just got to get away for a while," I told her. "I think I'm burning myself out and I still have four weeks left in the season and then the Olympic Trials."

She agreed wholeheartedly that I needed to take a break. Her solution? "Nancy, just hop on a plane and come on down to Ruston for the weekend and rest. You can come watch us play and just take it easy," she said.

I started laughing. How was it going to look to the press at Louisiana Tech if Nancy Lieberman of archrival Old Dominion just happened to show up in Ruston for the weekend?

"Besides," I told Sonja, "we'll probably be playing you guys again for the AIAW title in three weeks."

She convinced me that the only people who would know that I was in town were herself and her husband, Bert. I've always lived a little bit on the edge so I thought, what the heck, this would be incredible. If anyone had found out at the time, it would have been the biggest scandal in women's basketball.

I had a great three days of fun and relaxation with Sonja. Tech had a game that weekend so I just stayed at her house, made dinner, listened to the game on the radio, and watched television. Later, I went by her office in a disguise—hat and dark glasses—while she was working late making recruiting calls. I felt like a fugitive on the run. I was at the height of my visibility, hanging out in a town where they knew women's hoops and who Nancy Lieberman was. We had beaten the Lady Techsters for the AIAW title just the year before.

Basketball and rivalries didn't matter that weekend in Ruston. I just had fun and got the relaxation I so desperately needed. I relished the fact that for three or four days, nobody knew where I was and I could come and go on my own. When I got back to Old Dominion after that weekend, everybody asked me what I had done during the time off.

"Oh, nothing. I just rested," I told them.

Sure enough, ODU and Louisiana Tech met in the semifinals at the 1980 AIAW National Championships three weeks later in Mount Pleasant, Michigan. This time, it was almost too easy; we had about a 25-point lead with eight minutes to play. Everything was clicking: Inge was unstoppable inside; 6-8 Anne Donovan would swat away a shot and start the fast break; I was running the show, and my greyhounds, Rhonda, Angie, and Chris, were flying the wings—inside, outside, it was one of those nights. If Dick Vitale had been calling it, you'd have heard, "Tech needs a T-O baby!" but there was nothing they could do to stop us that night.

In fact, we almost got carried away. Marianne pulled the starters at the eight-minute mark, while Tech was still giving it all they had. Their starters brought them back, and with three minutes left, it was a 13-point game. Here come the starting troops back in, and we wrap up a 73-59 win. And now, our confidence soaring, we play Tennessee, which beat Pam Parsons' South Carolina team in the semis.

What a moment for women's basketball—national TV, two great coaches in Pat Head and Marianne Stanley, and player matchups made in heaven: All-American Jill Rankin vs. Inge and Anne Donovan; All-American guard Holly Warlick, one of my closest friends, vs. me. The game is for bragging rights for the summer, when a lot of us will be seeing each other on the USA teams.

The scouting reports? Tennessee is known for its suffocating defense, forcing a lot of turnovers; the Vols run a patient half-court offense. ODU is electrifying off the break, big, strong, rebounds well, and shows personality on the court.

We controlled the tempo from the start. Anne and Inge again shut down the paint. We took a halftime lead and never lost control of the game. With a few minutes to go, I fouled out for the first time in my career—not counting an exhibition against the Soviets—and one by one my teammates joined me on the bench, joy written on everyone's faces. This is it!—four years, where did it go? We are going out winners, baby! Now it's over, a 68-53 final, and the locker room is crazy. I pull off my jersey, forgetting that assistant coach Jerry Busone is coming in for a post-game prayer. Outside are our fans who have made the trip— Wes is there, and Mark Muchnick from Far Rockaway and his wife. It's the second championship, but the feeling is new, and wonderful.

Fouling out against Tennessee reminded me of the only time I ever had a technical foul called on me during my collegiate career, at the University of the District of Columbia during my sophomore year. We were killing them—we ended up winning 89-34—and the starters were out of the game laughing at the end of the bench. Marianne caught me cutting up and sent me back into the game with three minutes to play.

The minute I walked on the floor I heard the official blow her whistle. I couldn't believe it! I didn't even have to open my mouth to get a technical. I asked why and the official pointed to my jewelry. I always kept my PSAL medal I had won in high school taped to my leg and hidden by my sock when I played. It was my good luck charm. After the game, I would wear it around my neck. When Marianne put me back into the game I completely forgot I had put it on my neck, and I was whistled for the only technical of my career.

Now I had fouled out of my final collegiate game, almost as if I was being made to reflect on the past four years. My college career was over. We finished 37-1, and both Inge and I were named to the Kodak All-America team. Inge led the team in scoring again with 17.4 points per game to my 15.2, but we had so much balance it didn't matter who was the leading scorer. Six players would be graduating from the team in 1980. For four of us who had weathered the stormy beginning with Pam Parsons—Inge, myself, Angela Cotman, and Susan Richardson—winning the title was especially sweet.

As an athlete, winning a national championship is all you ever dream of and more. There is nothing in the world that can compare with being the best at your sport. A year after we finished playing for the Lady Monarchs, the University brought Inge and me back to campus to retire our uniforms. Before the Lady Monarchs tipped off, my Dallas Diamonds played an exhibition game against Inge's New Jersey Gems. It was a very moving ceremony and a great tribute to us, the first female athletes at ODU to have our uniforms retired. As we stood there again before our loyal fans and friends, with Dr. Jarrett, our athletic director and a major force behind ODU women's athletics, saying kind words about us, Inge and I looked at each other with tears in our eyes. We were individuals for four years, but we were really one. We needed, depended on, and supported each other, though we didn't really know each other well. We will always be bonded by those ties, those successes. And for my money, Inge Nissen is the greatest center ever to play the game.

Later, my uniform was also retired by the National Basketball Hall of Fame. It hangs proudly in Springfield, Massachusetts.

Chapter 11

Adieu, Amateur Standing

 My final year at Old Dominion was rewarding, but it was the most taxing time I've ever spent with the sport. Along with the winning and the notoriety came a lot of demands on my time. I barely had time to celebrate the championship with my teammates before flying to New York to receive my second Wade Trophy, awarded to the outstanding female basketball player of the year. To date, no other player has won the award twice.

The Wade was special to me because it was named after a legend in women's basketball, coach Margaret Wade of Delta State University. She did so much to help further the game, and the award bearing her name was the highest honor any female collegiate basketball player could receive.

When I went to the Wade Trophy press conference, I was besieged by the New York media. I was asked to rehash my career at Old Dominion and talk about the impact my teammates and I had on the game. It was as if I had been hit by a bolt of lightning: My collegiate career was really over. I sounded like a talking history book going over the things we had accomplished while I was at Old Dominion.

I was peppered with questions about the upcoming Olympic Trials and the fledgling women's pro basketball league. Did

I expect to be the impact player on the Olympic Team? Was I going to be the savior of the pro league?   I didn't have the answers.

After the dinner and ceremony, former Wade Trophy winner Carol Blazejowski of Montclair State and I took a private jet to the Olympic Trials in Colorado Springs. We were dead tired when we got to practice and had to drag ourselves down the floor.

I ended up playing well in the Trials, but I was exhausted even though I was in the best shape of my life.

Kansas All-American Lynette Woodard and I had some incredible practices going one-on-one, but something was missing. Maybe I was mentally and emotionally burned out on basketball. All I know is that I was having a hard time staying focused.

On top of everything else, President Jimmy Carter was talking about boycotting the Moscow Games to protest the Soviet invasion of Afghanistan. We had the best women's basketball team and the best individual players in the world that year ready to put it on the line for the USA. When Carter finally pulled the U.S. athletes out of the 1980 summer games, it was my biggest disappointment ever as an athlete.

In 1976, I was the baby on the Olympic team. I wasn't in the position to help lead the team because I was still learning the game. But four years later, I was ready to be the leader. I had had the best seat in the Montreal Forum in 1976. My lot this time would be on the court, not on the bench where I had a silver medal from 1976, and I was ready to add a gold when President Carter dashed our dreams with the boycott.

I know it was a tough decision for the President. I felt that we had to separate ourselves as athletes and Americans, but Carter was in a no-win situation.

For days I had been talking to Harry Lozon and Mr. Wilkins about the looming boycott. I was tired. I couldn't imagine continuing to practice and prepare for the pre-Olympic qualifying tournament when the President said we wouldn't be going to the Games. What would be the use?

Looking back, I think I made an emotional decision to leave the team in 1980. They had just selected the 12 best players to represent the USA in the   Olympic qualifying tournament in

Bulgaria. If this team qualified, it would be our Olympic team and would represent the United States if President Carter suddenly changed his mind about the boycott. I discussed my feelings, my indecision, with Harry and Mr. Wilkins. I knew they had my best interests at heart. They told me to do what I felt was best for me, and in support of the President's decision, I left the team, went home, and got ready for the pro draft.

I don't regret siding with the President, but I should have stuck it out with my teammates; they were the ones most hurt by the boycott. I already had an Olympic medal, and many of my teammates in 1980 never got another chance to play on an Olympic team. I wish now I had listened to the people who said, "Lieberman, stick it out and hang in there for another month. Do something for the good of the team."

Selfishly, I guess, I just wanted someone to tell me what I wanted to hear and Harry and Mr. Wilkins were able to do that.

It was Easter Sunday when I informed my Olympic coaches, Sue Gunter and Pat Summitt that I was leaving training camp. I could tell they were disappointed in my decision and in me. Most of my teammates felt like I was being selfish and deserting them. And the decision created a lot of hard feelings between me and Bill Wall, Amateur Basketball's executive director. He had been watching me grow up on the courts since I was 16, and he didn't want me to make a mistake. I don't think anyone understood all the emotions that led me to such an unpopular stance.

ABAUSA called a press conference for me to explain my reasons for leaving and my stance on the boycott. I faced a barrage of questions.

Why? Why? Why? Why? Every question began with a why? My answers were pretty pat. I told them that I thought it was a tough decision for the President to make but in light of the circumstances with Afghanistan he had no other choice. I told them I tried to separate being an athlete and a U.S. citizen and I decided to support the President.

It was becoming the roughest time of my life. I remember leaving Colorado Springs feeling so isolated and alone. As I was walking through the Denver airport, my eye caught a television in a bar. On the news was my press conference and the story about my leaving the team. I had created this big stir, and it was a very strange feeling. I had never felt more tired in my life.

When I got back to Norfolk it was more of the same. More reporters asking the same questions, "Why? Why? Why?" My lawyer, Jimmy Howard, and the Old Dominion sports information director had planned a press conference in Mr. Howard's office when I got back. It was packed, and I felt obliged to spend a lot of time with the media who had followed my career so closely. That day seemed to last forever.

I look back almost a dozen years later and I am still sorry about my decision from the bottom of my heart. I guess I really was being selfish, putting myself ahead of my teammates, because I was on the verge of exhaustion. Yes, I did support the President, but more to the point, I was supporting myself. When I think about the people who were my good friends and teammates all those years, I wish I hadn't let them down.

I went back to the Lozons' in Norfolk to regroup. I had lined up some camps and speaking engagements before I went to the Olympic Trials, and now I was trying to decide who else I could contact for a job. I was in a financial twilight zone waiting for the Women's Professional Basketball League to draft me. For now, camps and speeches would be my only sources of revenue. It doesn't sound like much now, but $50, $100, $200 to speak was a lot of money to me.

It would be the first summer that I wasn't traveling internationally with a USA team. It dawned on me that I was finally out on my own, fending for myself. No more pampering, no more financial aid, no more athletic scholarship. Rhonda Rompola and I booked as many functions as we could. That summer, we just jumped in the car and hit a ton of speaking engagements all over the country. I must have made about $7,000, and it came in handy when I moved to Dallas to play for the Diamonds.

One day Rhonda and I were sitting around the Lozons' house trying to figure out our summer schedule. I went out to get the mail and it was the usual ton of fan mail that follows a national championship. But among the hundred or so letters that day was a check: $27,500 from the SuperStars competition.

"Hey Rhonda," I said. "I'm rich!" I had initially rejected the check to remain an amateur, but now my collegiate eligibility was over and my Olympic dreams were dashed. Someone had taken notice of my decision to leave the Olympic team and mailed me the check. I took it to the bank and cashed it. I was a pro.

Shortly thereafter, I went out and bought two cars. The first one was for me, a brand new 1980 Datsun 280Z black and gold anniversary edition. Then I selected a green Cadillac sedan for my mom and had it sent up to New York with a bow on it.

Growing up I had always read stories about athletes who got their first big bonus or paycheck. It always seemed like they bought their mother a car or a house or something. In a way, I felt like it was my responsibility as a big-time athlete to buy a big car for my mother. She loved it! I was a little smug, too, because I was one up on my brother Cliff, who was supposed to be the smart and successful one in the family. He's a dentist, and I'm a lowly athlete.

Money changes some people for the worse, but after I signed my pro contract later on, I became a very generous person after pinching pennies all my life. My mother once said I would give a friend my last dime, and I think my financial success prompted me to be that way.

The day I was finally drafted I was at a celebrity tennis tournament at the Riviera Hotel in Las Vegas. I had always wanted to play in this event, and Dick Schaap was able to get me invited in 1980.

The tournament was sponsored by Dewar's, the liquor company, and every year they would bring in athletes like football greats Franco Harris, Phil Simms, Ottis Anderson, and Roy Green and basketball standouts like Julius Erving, Calvin Murphy, and Rick Barry. I couldn't believe Dick had finally gotten me into the tournament. I knew there was a long waiting list of people hoping to be invited.

I brought Rhonda with me as my guest. I thought after dragging me out on all those late-night forays to Atlantic City while we were in college, she ought to get to see Vegas. She took advantage of every minute, gambling in the casinos all night. I had been given some spending money and $500 to gamble.

"Nancy, I'll double your $500," Rhonda told me as she disappeared into the casino. In the morning I'd look over at her bed, and it hadn't been touched. When I'd finally run into her, she' d tell me stories of gambling all night with Deacon Jones or Franco Harris.

During the day, we would sit by the pool. Every few minutes someone would be paged. "Mr. Julius Erving, please pick-up the hotel courtesy phone. Mr. Julius Erving." As a joke, I told Rhonda to have me paged. One day, they paged me and I thought it was Rhonda fooling around. When the page persisted, I finally went to a phone.

"This is Nancy Lieberman," I answered, half expecting to hear Rhonda laughing on the other end.

"Nancy, my name is Dave Armstead. I am the president of the Dallas Diamonds and you are the No. 1 pick of the Women's Professional Basketball League."

Part of me was excited, and part of me wanted to scream. Dallas was the worst team in the league. I would be starting from scratch again just like I did when I signed with unheralded Old Dominion University four years earlier.

Still, I knew that the WBL was young, and there were some strong franchises developing. I had heard about the good owners and support in cities like Dallas, Chicago, St.Louis, San Francisco, and Omaha. Apparently $12 million had been infused into the league and everyone involved was working hard to make it a success. Even the weak sister teams got support from the league to help them survive.

I was looking forward to playing 40 games a season in the United States instead of Europe or Japan, which had once been the only options for a woman pro. I wanted to travel around the country and sell my sport to fans who didn't have strong collegiate women's teams to follow. And it was going to be a lot of fun playing in the big arenas.

I couldn't wait to get back to Norfolk to talk to my lawyer, Mr. Howard, and start negotiating my contract. I didn't know anything about negotiating a contract, but I knew I had to learn. This would be my first big step into the business world. I called as many professional athletes as I knew, asking for their advice. I asked a million questions—What should I look for? How much should I ask for? How do I know what I am worth?

Julius Erving talked to me for a long time, then sent me a copy of his old American Basketball Association contract. Mr. Howard and I used the framework of Julius' contract to set up my contract with Dallas.

I found out that Anne Meyers had made $50,000 playing in the league the year before with the team from New Jersey. I figured that I was younger and twice as good, so I was worth

$100,000. There was one catch. You just don't march in to someone's office and say, "Pay me this," unless you can back up your claim. The old Muhammad Ali principle again.

Mr. Howard and I sat down and came up with a game plan to prove to the Dallas Diamonds that I was worth that kind of money. First we got the attendance figures, won-lost record, and sponsorship for Dallas' 1979-80 season. I knew I could help improve on the 6-20 record they had posted. The Diamonds had averaged only about 600 fans per game, and with an improved product, I saw the potential to quadruple the attendance. When I multiplied the difference in numbers with me on the team times the $7 ticket price times 15 or so home games, I suddenly saw signing Nancy Lieberman meant a substantial payoff for the Dallas Diamonds.

I also took into account the likelihood that the team would pick up more endorsements and a few other deals here and there with a marquee player on the team. When all the potential dollars were lumped together, it made sense to ask for $100,000. In the back of my mind, I thought about all my sports heroes who made $100,000—Mickey Mantle, Walt Frazier, Willis Reed. Ever since I was a kid, it was a personal goal of mine to earn "six figures."

At first, naturally, the club didn't bite, but while the people in Dallas were sitting tight, I was getting into the best shape possible. I played with men in the New York City Summer Pro League and the Rutger League. We played at Xavier High School on 13th Street, and the league was full of former and hopeful NBA players. It became a media extravaganza for me.

Former CCNY coach Floyd Lane was coaching, and I was playing with Nate "Tiny" Archibald and Charlie Criss, formerly of the Atlanta Hawks. I had grown up playing with guys so it really wasn't that big a deal for me to be playing in a men's league. The press thought differently. Jane Pauley interviewed me for the "Today Show," and soon everyone was getting into the act, *Sports Illustrated*, *Time*, and the *New York Post* all running features about me playing in the league. The gym only held 600 people, and every time I played, it became a sweat box, crammed with fans and reporters.

After the N.Y. League ended, I got a call from the commissioner of the Southern California Pro League. He said the Lakers were interested in my playing for them and asked if I would talk to Jerry West. I grew up watching West play for the Lakers, and now he was calling me to play.

"Nancy, come on out to our summer league. You'll enjoy the competition and the coach. His name is Pat Riley," West said.

I was giggling. It was incredible. Jerry West had called me to play for the Lakers in a summer league. I had barely arrived and gotten situated in Los Angeles when it was time for our first practice at Loyola Marymount. I reported to the head trainer, Jack Curren. "You Nancy?" he asked, as if he was expecting two or three other women players. He tossed me my purple Lakers gym bag and gear, nodding in the direction of the locker room. I could tell by the look on his face that he didn't approve.

"Uh, Jack. Where do you want me to change?" I asked.

"In the locker room with the rest of the team," he said. I figured this was my first test and I couldn't act afraid. I took a deep breath and walked in the locker room with my eyes straight ahead. I was in the men's domain.

I quickly found a place out of the way and opened up my purple Laker gym bag. My hands were shaking as I pulled out my socks, my purple and gold Lakers mesh jersey and shorts, and my official Lakers jock.

"Yo, Jack! What do you want me to do with this thing? It's way too small for me," I called out to the head trainer.

As I was waving the jock in the air, the guys in the locker room looked over in my direction and started laughing. They realized I had a sense of humor and could take a joke. That incident really broke the ice for all of us.

I know a lot of them probably resented the fact that I was playing in their league. Most of them were great college players trying to earn a spot with the Lakers or hoping to catch on somewhere else in the NBA. The four, five, or six minutes a game I was getting took away from their time to shine. These guys were trying to make it in the NBA, and every minute is precious to the player who is trying to prove himself.

I made the most of my experience playing for the Lakers. This was Magic's team, and I was part of it. At the time, Paul Westhead was the head coach and Pat Riley was his assistant. Usually I found myself on Riley's team, and a lot of the time was spent on the bench. I still learned so much from being around those people.

Coach Riley took me aside early on and told me, "They're going to play hard against you because it's a no-win situation for them. If they beat you, people will say, 'Oh he got by her because she's a girl.' If you stop them, it's going to be embarrassing for them. They're not going to say, 'She's a good player,' they're going to say, 'A girl stopped you?'"

The crowds usually packed the gyms we played in, and any time I would do something well they would go nuts. One time I was going to the hoop and pump-faked this guy so he wouldn't block my shot. He flew past me, but a 7-footer came out of nowhere and swatted my shot out of bounds.

The NBA referee, Darell Garretson, turned to me and said, "Don't bring that weak shit in here."

I just stared at him in disbelief. "Weak shit? Haven't you seen any other shots get blocked today? What game have you been watching?" I asked him.

"He didn't block my shot because I was a girl. He blocked my shot because he was seven feet tall. Do you think the ball knew I was a girl when I shot it? It was just a good block by a good player," I yelled at the ref. I shouldn't have been mouthing back, but his comment was ridiculous.

We played and practiced hard but we had a lot of fun, too, and the guys were just great to me. A lot of times in pick-up games teams will play shirts and skins. It had been hot in the gym, but because of me the guys had just been flipping jerseys to another color instead of playing skins. One day I decided to play a little joke on everyone.

It came time to flip jerseys one day and I stood up and said, "You guys have been great to me. Our team will play skins today," and with that I whipped off my jersey. I heard a collective gasp that broke into laughter when they realized I had on my bathing suit top.

Whenever I would joke around with them, I felt like it helped break a little more ice. I wanted to show them that I could play hard, but that I also had some personality and emotion and could laugh at myself. More than anything, I think my attitude helped earn their respect.

My summer league experience in New York and Los Angeles taught me more about the game, and it was great exposure for me to be around so many outstanding professional players. We all had one thing in common, a love for the game. It didn't matter that they were faster or better; we were all performing to the best of our abilities. More than anything, I think they accepted me as a real player, not just a gimmick, and appreciated my competitive spirit.

I still hadn't signed with Dallas when former New York Knicks great Dean "The Dream" Meminger took me aside one day. I got to know Dean pretty well when I played in the New York Summer League. Dean had coached one of the WBL teams in 1979-80.

"Nancy, when are you planning to go to Dallas?" he asked me. I told him that we hadn't reached an agreement on a contract and I was waiting to hear a better offer than $45,000. He shook his head and proceeded to give me some solid advice.

"Nancy, book a flight and get down there. Show those people that you care about the league and want to play. If you have to call your own press conference, then do it. If you want to sell tickets and convince them to tie your salary into ticket sales, then go down there and get involved in the community right now. Don't let the public think that you are the bad guy by holding out."

Chapter 12

Shining as a Diamond

 Mr. Howard and I flew to Dallas and met with Dave Armstead and team owner Mike Staver. We sat down and went over the numbers again. I think they finally saw my marketability after I had signed several endorsements with the products Matt Merola had lined up for me. Matt, who worked with Reggie Jackson, Tommy John, Cathy Rigby, and Tom Seaver, was serving as my agent. Matt is the guy who had gotten me into the SuperStars competition the previous year— he's a real hustler.

I became the first female to have a contract for an autographed basketball when Matt lined up a deal for me with Spalding. He also negotiated a book deal for me, *Basketball My Way*, landed a nationwide Johnson & Johnson baby powder commercial, and signed me to a shoe contract with Jordache. Just like that, I had lucrative endorsements and contracts. Before I even got to Dallas, I had $40,000 in the bank, and that gave me a better bargaining position with the Diamond owners.

I was honest with them. I told the Diamonds that all I was asking for was what I was worth. I knew I would have to produce and do all that I could to benefit the team and the community. After looking at the numbers again, they agreed to pay me the

$100,000 contract, $65,000 up front, and the rest after the season. As a signing bonus, the Diamonds purchased the furnishings for my new condominium.

I had found a condo in the south part of Dallas about a mile from downtown. Mr. Howard was worried about my spending money so fast, but I had some dreams that my new-found wealth could fulfill. The condo was bigger than my home in Far Rockaway, brand new, in a beautiful setting. I had never had anything like that before and I was so excited to be setting up my own home.

It was hard to believe that people were going to pay me very good money to do something I loved. I had never looked at basketball as a business and at myself as a tool to market products, but now the bottom line at 22 years of age looked very good to Nancy Lieberman.

When I got to Dallas I had a car deal with a Lincoln dealership in Hurst, Texas. I also started doing a lot of speaking engagements with local businesses and had my face out in the community. Matt started preparing me for the business world without my even realizing it. He persuaded me to diversify and to always have my hand in something that could be an alternative to my playing career. He suggested broadcasting and helped me line up some television jobs with ESPN and NBC-TV. That summer, I even did some broadcasting of games from the N.Y. Rutger League when I wasn't playing.

When I met Martina Navratilova, I realized that I had more endorsements than she did. It took me about six months to figure out why no one was interested in Martina for a product endorsement. Part of it was her image. What she needed was to win and to get good advice about marketing herself.

Marketing and athlete endorsements became a whole new world for me. I was curious about how someone would sell Martina. I applied the knowledge that Matt had given me and coupled it with Martina's agents at the International Management Group. Be creative, show a company your value, and show loyalty—that was Matt's method. It would spell endorsement success for Martina just as it had for me.

I was on top of the world. I had my contract, my endorsements, my home, my cars, and recognition from the community as a top professional women's basketball player. There were mornings when I would wake up and not believe that I was making a six-figure salary to play the game I loved. I would get up late, go to practice for two or three hours, and then come home and take a nap. Later, I would call my college friends in Norfolk and just chat for hours.

This was a job? I was a highly paid professional athlete, and all my daily energies were geared to being the best player I could be. Usually, two or three hours of practice weren't enough for me and I was constantly getting people to open the gym so I could shoot and work on my game.

Early in my season with the Diamonds I tore cartilage in my left knee. I went through rehabilitation like crazy and worked my way back into the lineup. When I first starting playing with the Diamonds, I would average 16 or 17 points a game and pass the ball to my teammates a lot. After the injury, I had a horrible game in the Superdome in New Orleans when nothing seemed to go right. In trying to blend in with the team and not be a ball hog, I was passing the ball into the hands of defeat.

I felt horrible. I was the highest paid player on the team, and I was concerned with passing the ball and not shooting. After the game, my coach, Greg Williams, called me over. "Nancy we signed you to shoot and score in this league. Don't worry about it. You can score. Just relax. I have confidence in you, " he said.

After I talked to Greg, I went through an incredible transformation. I ended up averaging 28 points per game and was the second-leading scorer in the league. My averages soared to 55 percent from the floor and over 90 percent from the line. My game was reaching new levels.

The Diamonds organization had to be pleased with the 1980-81 season. We turned the team around into contenders with over 30 wins. We averaged around 3,400 spectators per game, over 8,000 in the playoffs. One home playoff game outdrew the Milwaukee Bucks' seventh game of their NBA championship series that year.

It seemed more like fantasy than reality, and unfortunately, that was about right. The league was having financial problems, and the future of the Diamonds and owner Mike Staver was dismal. But for a year, playing professional basketball in Dallas was my Camelot. When I presented my $100,000 salary plan to the Dallas owners, I was confident that we could produce the numbers, exposure, and wins. We did.

Armchair basketball players enjoyed watching us play because they could physically identify with some of our moves. Women are big on fundamentals and finesse. The guys forego fundamentals for physical ability. How many people can actually duplicate a Michael Jordan move in their own backyard? Our game showed people that there were all levels of play, and there were pro moves they could actually duplicate.

We earned a lot of recognition and it was not unusual for us to share headlines with the Mavericks or the Dallas Cowboys. I was proud of the endorsements I was able to generate because there were very few female athletes able to do that in 1980. I felt I had opened the door for the rest.

It was such a great time for me to play basketball. There were a lot of talented players in the league and we had some really exciting games. We always wanted to put on a good show because there might be one person out there seeing his or her first women's game. I hated to disappoint anyone, so I played hard every game and implored my teammates to do the same. The last thing I wanted was for someone to leave the arena and say, "Oh, they're terrible." I worried about what people thought because I wanted to give them an entertaining experience.

We built a great fan following in Dallas and enjoyed celebrity status. When we'd walk around town, people would come up to us and ask for autographs. Kids would drag their parents to the locker room and wait outside for us. Some nights there would be 200 kids looking for our autographs. I always made sure that I took the time to sign something for everyone who took the time to wait for me.

It was important for me to be a role model. You always play to win, but you play to your audience and for your audience, too. Our fan and media following was great in Dallas and I think we came along at the right time. People were constantly approaching me to speak to their kids, school assemblies, and business groups. I was used to this type of treatment from my years at Old Dominion. Athletes are performers and we can never get too much attention. I had walked into another great situation in Dallas and I hoped to leave my mark there, too.

We had so many little boys and girls turned on to basketball in Dallas. The media loved our electric brand of basketball and we offered great entertainment. I remember Mitch Kupchak, then with the Washington Bullets, coming to town one day to play the Mavericks. He had some time to kill so he caught our game and visited with me afterward. He was amazed at how much the women's game had progressed since he watched me play in the 1976 Olympics when we were USA teammates. Michael Jordan, Julius Erving, and Magic Johnson, among others, have said that about the women's game through the years. They are now big fans of women's hoops.

My success with the Diamonds led in a roundabout way to a 1982 guest appearance on the "Happy Days" spinoff, "Joanie Loves Chachi." Martina and I were in Los Angeles with her close friends Al and Mumsey Nemeroff. We were talking basketball, and either Martina or Mumsey said to her son, "Nancy can beat a lot of guys at one-on-one." "No way," said her son. "She can't beat my friend Larry." "Larry" turned out to be Larry Levinson, a writer for the show.

We set up a day and time and played on the Nemeroffs' tennis court, which has a hoop. Larry, mind you, played college ball at St. Mary's College in San Antonio, also the alma mater of former Houston Rockets star Robert Reid. Larry's about 6-2, strong, with a quick first step. He finally beat me in a fairly close game, 11-7, I think, but not before I won his respect. A couple of months later he called me with an idea for a script.

"Nancy, we want you to play yourself and challenge Chachi to a game of one-on-one. He's kind of a macho guy in the series, and I think we could have fun with it," Larry said. I had always watched "Happy Days," so I thought I'd give it a try. It was the first time I had tried acting and it was the most nervous I've ever been in my life. I had read the script and memorized my lines, but when I got on the set I found out that everything is practically rewritten every day.

They had transformed a studio to look like a basketball court, with bleachers and everything. The work was some of the hardest I've ever had to do: the constant repetition, hitting your marks, rehearsals until everything is perfect. Scott Baio was great to work with, and the whole cast of characters was like one big family.

We filmed the show in front of a live audience, another scary part. Girls were constantly screaming for Scott. At one point he took off his shirt and I thought they were going to have to give oxygen to some of those squealing girls.

Between takes and on breaks I would just hang out and shoot around with the cast and crew. A couple of little boys showed up every day and wanted me to spin the ball on my finger, play one-on-one, or do a few tricks. One day Henry Winkler came by and thanked me for taking an interest in his sons.

"They think the world of you," he said. "Somehow they just couldn't believe that a girl could play basketball and you've changed their opinions."

It was nice knowing that you could be yourself and have an effect on someone. I wonder today if Henry's sons take women in sport more seriously now.

As the season progressed and the attendance continued to soar, we positioned ourselves for a spot in the playoffs. In fact, we were on the verge of winning the championship, jumping out to a 2-0 lead on the road in the best of five series with the Omaha Wranglers.

We came home to Dallas for Game 3 and had a 12-point lead in the fourth quarter, minutes away from winning the title. Then we started playing not to lose instead of playing to win.

I kept looking at the clock, praying it would wind down. It didn't wind down fast enough, and we gave Game 3 away.

I had severely sprained ligaments in my left ankle the game before in Nebraska. I got tangled up with Susan Taylor of the Wranglers, and my ankle was pulled the wrong way. That injury was the end of my effectiveness for the series, but we only needed to win one game in Dallas to sweep and take the title. They put me in a lightweight cast, and I was heavily taped for the game.

I could only play sporadically, and I eventually watched from the bench as our Game 3 lead dwindled.

It was so disappointing to have a 2-0 lead and not win the deciding game on our home court. *Sports Illustrated* had sent a writer to the game to report on our sweep over Omaha. Needless to say, that story never ran. Then the Wranglers took the next game in Dallas and knotted the series at 2-2.

It had come down to a one-game series, at their place. Bragging rights again: the Wranglers had Rosie Walker and Holly Warlick, my former teammates. We all lived to one-up each other. With my limited mobility, though, I wasn't very effective at either end of the court. And having squandered a chance at home to wrap up the series was a major blow to our confidence.

We had played the first two games in Omaha at the Civic Auditorium. The scene for the final game, though, would be the University of Nebraska at Omaha. It's funny, I now visit Omaha regularly. My company, Pro Motion Events, Inc., is located there. My partner, Tom Thompson, graduated from UNO, playing basketball there, along with his brother Dean. But back then, it was just another foreign court.

We played for the championship on Easter Sunday. Boy, did we stink up the joint. We never got into a rhythm, and the Wranglers had their fans pulling hard for them. Rosie Walker was unstoppable on the inside, and my old pal Holly ran the show and played great open-court defense. I was never a factor—I could hardly walk, much less run.

You had to admire the Wranglers. They hung tough after falling behind 2-0. My injury might have given them extra confidence, but you still have to give them credit. And in a way, I was happy for Holly. Mostly, though, I was disappointed for myself and for my team. I was so used to winning titles that I was kind of shocked when we didn't win this one too. I wanted to give the Diamonds fans another championship team in a town of champions.

I was disappointed, tired, and hurt. I needed some time off to regroup and relax. I went home to Dallas and wondered what my next move might be.

"Baby Magic"

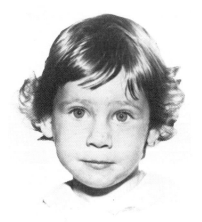

❖

My mom, Renee, with my brother, Cliff, and niece, Melissa

❖

One of the few photos of me and my dad, Jerry

❖
1980 Old Dominion
University National
Championship Team

❖
Team Captain, Sue
Richardson presenting
Inge Nissen and me
with plaques at our
last home game

❖
With close friend
and teammate,
Rhonda Rompola

❖
My mentor, LaVoiser Lamar early on in the AAU League

❖
Dear friend Wes Lockard as Burnie, the Miami Heat mascot, clowning with Charles Barkley

❖
Mr. Howard, my attorney, Mr. Wilkins, and Harry Lozon

❖
The 1981 Dallas Diamonds

❖
"Shining as a Diamond"

❖
Guarding Tyrone "Mugsy" Bogues in a men's pro league - I am still the only woman ever to play in a men's league

❖
Going one-on-one with
Martina before the 1982
SuperStars Competition

❖
Martina, me, and my
best friend growing up,
Barbara Wood, at our
1983 Wimbledon
celebration party

❖
My working relationship
continued with Martina
through the 1980s

❖ Through basketball, I've met many interesting people . . .

❖
John "Junior" McEnroe

❖
One of my
childhood idols,
Walt Frazier

❖
One of the biggest
inspirations in my life
and a great man, "Dr.
J." —Julius Erving

❖
With my husband, Tim Cline

❖
Tim and I with Tonya and Dave Winfield and Meadowlark Lemon on a promotional cruise to Mexico

❖
I had a great time meeting Bill Cosby and playing ball on *The Cosby Show*

❖
1989 World
Championship
Qualifying
Tournament
Team

❖
New York
Knick Fantasy
Camp, Atlantic
City

❖
Tim and I
playing flag
football at
Martina's with
Robin Givens
and her sister
Stephanie, and
Judy Nelson's
sons, Eddie
and Bales
(back row)

❖
My right hand, secretary
Vicki Arnold

❖
I guess when your husband
works for "Hoop-it-Up"—you
play!

❖
Me with Maureen
Curren-Maksuti, who
got me in shape for
'89 USA National
Team Trials

❖
Me with Senator Bill Bradley and Lyn St. James, President of the Women's Sport Foundation at National Girls and Women's Sports Day

Photo by Nancy Ploeger

❖
National Women in Sports Day, 1990, at the White House

❖
I was a guest speaker at Working Woman's Night

❖
Tim and I with New York
City Mayor David Dinkins

❖
Tim and I with Don
Drysdale and his wife
Anne Meyers-
Drysdale, one of my
fiercest competitors

❖
Business partner
and best friend
Tom Thompson
and I with Oscar
Robertson and his
wife at 1990
Legends and Fans
dinner, Chicago

❖
My new promotional poster for Bike Athletic Wear Co.

❖
I've always felt that when one door closes another door opens

Chapter 13

Meeting Martina

 I didn't wake up one day and decide to have a relationship with Martina Navratilova. People tell me that's the part of my life story they don't understand. Well, I've thought about my time with Martina a lot, and I don't understand it completely, either. I can't answer why I had the relationship with her, but I can say I felt comfortable around her, felt I could trust her with things that were very sacred to me. I know, too, that I have no regrets about it. I learned a lot about myself. I grew up quite a bit. Why was it Martina? I don't know. But there was an instant attraction, an instant comfort level I had never experienced with anybody else. Maybe for that particular time in my life, that's what God wanted me to experience. I honestly don't know.

Anne Smith, a professional tennis player who lived in Dallas, had watched a few Diamond games, and she and her family had become fans. For weeks, Annie had talked to me about going to watch her play. I had never really liked tennis. I had no desire to sit indoors through a lot of boring baseline to baseline points. I liked sports with a lot of action.

Then, too, the Diamonds had been moved off of our home floor at Moody Coliseum when the women's tennis tour came to

Dallas that March. We had to move to Fort Worth for a week, and I resented the fact that we couldn't be on our home floor before the playoffs. So I turned down the tickets the Avon Tour offered us to watch the tennis event in Dallas.

But after the playoffs, I was mentally and physically drained, beat-up, tired, and in desperate need of some time off. She knew how grueling the season had been and asked if I wanted to go with her to watch the Women's Tennis Association Championships in Amelia Island, Florida. Now tennis sounded like just the ticket for some rest and relaxation. It would be a good chance to take it easy and watch someone else work for a change. If I got bored I could always go to the pool or the beach.

Since I had never been to a pro tennis event before, I really didn't know what to expect. For the first day or two I just wandered around, watching matches and chatting with friends I happened to run into. A lot of reporters were surprised to see me and approached me wanting to know what I was doing there.

"It's a good question," I answered. I wasn't being evasive; I wasn't sure myself why I was there.

The first day I was there I was walking around the grounds and saw Chris Evert. At the time, I was in a national television commercial for Johnson & Johnson Baby Powder, "Take a powder." I bumped into Chris when I was going into the players' area. "Hey! Aren't you Nancy Lieberman? I saw your shampoo commercial," she said.

"Shampoo commercial? It's baby powder," I explained to her. Chris was just being smart with me, but I didn't know her well enough then to get the joke.

As we spoke, I saw Martina Navratilova for the first time. She was about 50 yards away, heading out to a match. She turned around to see who Chris and the other players were talking to, and we kind of locked eyes for a second. From the expression on her face, she seemed to recognize me.

Later I found out that she was calling all over the place trying to find out if I was there, who I was there with, and why I was at a women's tennis event. I was walking around the grounds later when Martina had finished her match. She was standing under a tree, checking up on her doubles partner, Pam Shriver. I saw her from a distance. She was wearing a white Tacchini skirt and shirt, and she looked so small. She was like a little kid, sneaking around, trying to peek in. I remember thinking she looked so innocent.

The second day a couple of the reporters approached me and asked if I knew any of the players. I told them that Tracy Austin and I had met at some benefit dinners and that was about it. Bud Collins, the *Boston Globe* columnist and NBC commentator, asked if I knew Martina Navratilova.

"No, I've never met her," I told him. He asked if I would like to meet her. She had left the court and was walking directly by us on her way to the press room after her match. "No, I really don't think so," I said. But he and Mel DiGiacomo, a photographer, insisted, and I followed them into the press tent. Martina didn't have the same look on her face as the day before when she saw me talking to Chris. I wondered if she had put Bud and Mel up to introducing us.

When we met, everything I knew or vaguely knew about her flooded through my head. When we shook hands, I was surprised how small she appeared to be. Reporters always described her as big.

The first words out of my mouth were pretty awkward. "I can't believe how small you are," I said. "The way people talked about you I was expecting an Amazon. Like, 'Hi Nancy,' and with your handshake you'd throw me across the room."

She laughed and we immediately struck up a conversation. I was so comfortable and at ease with her from the very start. She seemed to take a genuine interest in those brief moments in the press tent.

After a while I started to leave, but she asked me to stay around. "Give me five minutes to take a shower and I'll be right out," Martina said. Then we went outside the player's area to some off courts and just sat in the bleachers and talked for hours. Her Japanese Shiba dogs, Tets and Ruby, were running around as we talked about all the pro sport teams in Dallas, the playoffs, what so-and-so does on third-down-and-four when he calls an audible.

I had never had that kind of conversation with another female before. I usually reserve talking about the sports world for hours on end with men who are tuned in to what is going on, the kind of guys who read the agate and have all the box scores memorized.

Finally, here was a woman who knew as much about sports as I did. That is how our friendship initially started, talking about sports and athletes and our careers. We hit it off immediately, and it was like we had known each other for years instead of hours. It was immediate chemistry. She was just so nice, and so different from what I expected.

The next night Martina asked me to go with her to a big WTA Western-style gathering for the players and sponsors, complete with an electronic bull and a Western buffet. We sat next to each other at dinner and talked about everything. It was like we were alone in our own little world laughing and giggling like a pair of little kids. She even enjoyed my trademark sarcastic sense of humor.

Martina had won her semifinal match that day and we sat and talked about her final the next day. After the dinner, we went to her villa and talked and watched television late into the night. Much to Martina's chagrin, she found that Tets had chewed up a new Gucci shoe, the latest in a series of items that had not-so-mysteriously disappeared or been destroyed.

We were like two hens cackling away, enjoying each other's company. The more we talked, the more we realized how much we had in common. It's a special bond when you can meet someone like that and realize that so many experiences in your lives are similar.

Martina talked to me for a long time about her relationship with Rita Mae Brown, the lesbian author and her lover. Apparently, they were going through a rough time, and Martina was frustrated. She and Rita Mae usually traveled on the tennis tour together, but these days Martina was often alone. She said Rita Mae was in the middle of a manuscript, and it was taking precedence over their relationship.

She seemed to be really hurt by the lack of attention from Rita Mae. My first instincts as a friend have always been to protect people from being hurt. In some ways she was like a helpless baby who needed somebody strong to take care of her. The more we talked the clearer it became that I could be the person in Martina's life to protect her and be strong for her.

Then Rita Mae called the villa, and I thought, "Boy, I ought to go. This can only be trouble." But Martina was so nice and calm on the phone. After she hung up, we just went on with our conversation and with learning about each other.

I was so curious about Martina. How did she defect, and why? Was she scared? How'd she meet Rita? Why wasn't her family allowed to leave Czechoslovakia? And most of all, if I took off my shoes, would Tets eat them? I shared my family hurts, the lack of attention from my dad, why my basketball was so important to me. I felt like I was revealing some of my deepest, darkest inner thoughts, things I had wanted to tell someone for years, but had never felt comfortable enough with anyone to say, never believed they'd understand.

By the time either of us looked at a clock it was 6 a.m. We were so tired, but all we could do was laugh when we saw how early it was. I felt bad because Martina had a championship match at noon and here she was falling into bed at 7 in the morning. As I left, I wished her luck in the match and told her I'd be watching and pulling for her against Chris Evert.

The match was a disaster. Martina was in slow motion. I'm not sure she won ten points in the whole match. Final score: Evert, 6-0, 6-0.

The reporters asked, "Martina, you didn't look like yourself today. What happened? You and Chris never dominate each other."

It was all I could do not to laugh looking at a grinning Martina as she tried to explain her goose egg loss. She may have lost the match, but she gained a companion who was going to help her reshape her life and women's tennis for the next three years.

In just the few days I had known Martina, we had already begun to grow close. She was a fun-loving person and the feeling was contagious. I saw both her strengths and her weaknesses. She gave me a little peek into her soul, and I opened up to her about myself, too.

The following day Martina drove me to the airport, and I headed home to Dallas. Martina took off for the next stop on the tour, the Tournament of Champions at Greenleaf, Florida.

Our parting was one of the most emotional things I've ever been through in my life. It was almost like leaving my new best friend from summer camp when I was a youngster. Over the next week we kept in touch as Martina breezed through the field beating Andrea Jaeger in the final. I kept asking Martina to pull on her ear or something so I'd know she was thinking of me.

After Greenleaf, Martina asked me to do some running around with her. First on her agenda was her hearing at the Immigration and Naturalization Service in Los Angeles, the last step before the swearing-in process of becoming a U.S. citizen. Months later, after the French Open and Wimbledon, on July 20, 1981, I was in the courtroom the day she was sworn in as a citizen. She was so happy, and you couldn't help but share her excitement when they pronounced her a citizen of the United States. She told me how lucky I was to be born in this country, with citizenship a right of birth. She told me how hard it was to leave her family in a Communist country and how much she had wanted to be an American.

After the hearing in L.A., she asked me to go to the French Open with her. "Nancy, it would mean a lot to me," she said. I had mixed feelings, knowing that the French and then Wimbledon were two huge events for her. I was flattered that she really wanted to share her experiences with me, but I wondered why Rita Mae was no longer included on Martina's travel itinerary.

We had been spending a lot of time together, getting to know each other through our long conversations. I enjoyed being around her because she represented a whole different culture to me. She opened my eyes to art, fine restaurants, and wines. She was worldly and had been exposed to so many things in her life. My life had always revolved around basketball, basketball, and basketball. Now I felt like I was being given the chance to grow as a person and I relished the opportunity.

Just before we were to leave for France, Martina called me one afternoon at home in Dallas from Charlottesville, Virginia. She was crying hysterically.

"Nancy, Rita Mae shot me. Rita Mae shot me," Martina said.

I was stunned. I had talked to Martina just a little before at her office at the Boar's Head Inn and she was fine.

"Rita Mae heard us on the phone talking and we ended up going back to the house and got into a terrible fight," Martina told me.

Rita Mae had been peppering Martina with questions about us for weeks, and now it had come to a head. She demanded to know what was going on between Martina and me.

"Are you lovers?" Rita Mae asked. Martina told her it was none of her business. Rita Mae persisted, "What is your relationship with Nancy? What were you talking about with her? Why did you leave the house to call?"

Martina told her that we were friends and that what she did was her own business. Trying to avoid a confrontation, Martina walked out of the kitchen. As she did, Rita Mae grabbed her by the shirt and said, "We're going to talk about it right now." They went upstairs. Rita Mae went into the bathroom and got a gun off of the window sill and confronted Martina. "You're not going anywhere. We're going to talk about you and Nancy right now."

Martina pushed Rita Mae out of her way and took off running. On a nine-acre estate with 20 rooms, there are plenty of places to go and hide. Martina got a big enough lead on Rita Mae to jump in the BMW 733i parked in her circular driveway. She always left the keys in the car, but when she tried to get it in gear and gas it, it died. At this point, Rita Mae caught up with her and pulled open the back door just as Martina finally got the car in gear.

As Martina was driving away, the gun went off as Rita Mae followed her out the driveway. The bullet went through the passenger's side head rest and out the corner of the windshield where the inspection sticker normally is placed. The windshield shattered in Martina's face, and pieces of the glass cut her face. As she tells it, she took off out the driveway, got on the highway hysterically crying, and drove like hell away from the house.

She went directly to her coach's house and called me. There wasn't much I could do but calm her down. I couldn't believe that someone would try to hurt her like that, and the overwhelming urge to protect her came over me.

I think a lot of our closeness was cemented that night. I felt like I was stronger and able to protect her from the people who might try to hurt her. That much I knew about Martina already. She always needed someone around to take care of her, to be there for her, to say no to people who would take advantage of her. I was beginning to fill that need.

When we left for the French Open, I was nervous and scared. I really didn't know what to expect because I was still learning a lot of things about her. I knew that even after the incident with the gun, Rita Mae was still living in their home in Charlottesville. I knew, too, that Rita Mae was convinced I was ruining her life by becoming Martina's friend.

"Martina, how could you live with someone and love someone who would try to hurt you?" I asked her. "It's just too destructive to be in that kind of situation and you are both going to end up getting very hurt."

When I asked her what she was going to do about the situation, all she could say was, "I don't know; we'll talk about it after the French Open."

When we got to Paris in 1981, I think I was accepted by the other players on the tour because I was a professional athlete. They didn't make the snide comment, "Martina's got *another* one of those friends on the tour with her." Players befriended me and made me feel comfortable in their world. I think they genuinely liked me.

Some of the "old guard" of women's tennis like Paula Smith, Billie Jean King, and Rosie Casals told me I was a refreshing and good influence on Martina. Our conversations made it clear that some of the players had problems with Rita Mae's being around on the tour. Some of the players told me Rita Mae had made Martina quit playing doubles with Billie Jean after a number of years. Rita Mae thought Martina should play with Pam Shriver instead. They confided in me and told me a lot about Martina's past. "Nancy, so and so really hurt Martina," or "Martina shouldn't be doing such-and-such."

Paula Smith and I jogged and talked quite a bit together in Paris and she helped me get a handle on Martina's life. Martina trusted and relied on me from the beginning and I wanted to make sure that I was doing everything I could to help her. I also wanted to know what I was getting myself into, and Paula really gave me insight into the wonderful world of Martina. I tried to figure out where I fit in the scheme of things.

Until I was actually at a major tournament, I didn't fully understand the magnitude of Martina Navratilova because I had never lived in that fast lane. I had lived in my own little basketball world. All of a sudden I was in the company of Billie Jean King, Tracy Austin, and Chris Evert and I realized I was involved with a major participant, someone who was really important.

Little by little, the others helped me piece Martina together. I didn't have a full insight into her until they came to me with little dribs and drabs of information. As I pulled everything together, I was able to get a better picture of Martina, and I began to understand who I was dealing with.

Martina never took the French Open very seriously. The first time she took me to practice with her, she was proud and excited that I would take the time to go watch. So we went out to the practice courts and she warmed up a little. She hit some baseline shots, a few volleys, came to the net, talked to Billie Jean and Betsy Nagelsen, stretched, hit a few more volleys, went to the service line, talked to Billie and Betsy again, stretched some more, and was then ready to go home.

On the way home, we spotted some basketball courts adjacent to the practice tennis courts. We got out and shot some hoops. Martina wanted to learn how to shoot a layup off the correct foot. I'm thinking, "She barely broke a sweat at practice, and now she is working her tail off to learn how to shoot a layup." A hundred times she tried "right foot, left hand." I even held her leg down as she tried to master the shot.

"Nancy, I did it. I really did it!" Martina was ecstatic that she could shoot a layup correctly.

I was astonished. How could shooting a layup be more important than preparing to play at Roland Garros Stadium in the French Open? We had probably spent more time driving to and from practice than she had practicing. Back at the hotel I finally had to say something.

"Martina, when are you going to practice?" I asked her.

"Nancy, I just practiced," she replied.

"Martina," I said, "your practice habits stink. I've never seen anyone who is such a champion and who's made millions of dollars take practice so lightly. There was not one bit of intensity in your practice. You spent more time on the layup than you did your overhead."

She gave me a wide-eyed stare of disbelief as I continued with my harangue.

"You have no discipline and your priorities are all wrong. I would give my right arm to be in the position you are in, and you just blow it off."

As a professional athlete I was shocked by her lack of preparation. There was little chance that she would be able to win the French. I couldn't imagine putting myself on the line in front of the world practically set up to fail. Martina didn't see it that way. I knew I had hurt her feelings, but there was one more thing I had to say.

"Just think of how good you could be if you really worked at it."

When the tournament began, I tried to drop my criticism and just sit back and watch. It drove me crazy. My stomach churned on every point. I was so used to playing and winning and having control. This was a new experience.

Martina got through her first three matches with ease and I was thinking that even without a lot of practice she might win the Open. She still puzzled me, though.

"Martina are you excited to play today? Are you going to win?" I'd ask her.

"Oh, I hope so," she'd say.

"You *hope* so?" I blurted. "This is the quarterfinals of the French Open and you just *hope* you'll win? Martina, how can you compete if you don't *know* that you're going to win? You are one of the greatest players ever. Every time you step on the court you need to believe without a doubt that you will win. But that confidence comes from hard work and practice."

So much for lecturing. Martina went out and lost the first set to Sylvia Hanika, 6-2, and was ranting and raving the entire time. Darkness postponed the completion of the match until the next day, but it didn't get any better: She lost 6-4 and was out of the tournament. All I could think of was how untouchable she would be if she trained hard. I wished I could help her, but at that point I didn't know what to do.

Her cure for defeat was to go shopping. "Martina, you just got knocked out of the French Open and you want to go shopping and reward yourself? You've got it all wrong," I tried to explain.

All my criticism fell on deaf ears. To make matters worse, she took everything literally. We were window shopping and I made an observation. "That's a pretty bracelet," I commented.

"Do you want it?" she asked.

"No, Martina. I was just making an observation. You don't have to buy this stuff for me. I like you for you, not what you can do for me or give me. I have my own money. It's OK."

Martina was so used to giving people things, it was hard for her to understand that I would like her and be her friend without any fancy gifts. We made it home from her shopping spree after dropping about $15,000. She bought herself a Piaget watch and gave me the bracelet I had made the comment about. I couldn't believe her.

"Martina, I like you. You don't have to buy me anything and I'll still like you. And you've got to stop rewarding yourself when you lose. Save it for a win!" I said.

She couldn't picture the way I would take a loss growing up. When we lost a basketball game we'd go in the locker room and get chewed out from here to there. Lockers would be slammed and there would be a lot of emotion because of the loss. She loses and rewards herself. I knew that would have to change.

I guess I'm a protector by nature. I am always trying to help people and I find that a lot of people get stranded with me and I'm always saving them. I think that's my biggest problem in life. Because I have a strong personality, I try to protect and save people from being hurt. Martina didn't need to be saved, but she needed direction as an athlete and discipline as a person.

After the French I went back to Dallas and left Martina in England to play two tune-up tournaments before Wimbledon. She ended up losing in the semifinals in three sets in both tournaments and was a little dejected by the time I got to Wimbledon. Still, Martina looked much more confident on the quick grass courts than she had on the slow red clay of Roland Garros. I had only heard of Wimbledon, and of fans queuing up for days for standing-room-only tickets. Surrounded by green, I had a chance to soak up the world's most prestigious tennis tournament as an insider. We had rented a flat two blocks from the front gate of Wimbledon. As I took in the historic venue, the ivy scaling the walls, club members milling about, I realized the importance of the event.

Former champions are extended privileges that others don't receive. Martina had won the event in 1978 and '79, which confirmed my theory that when she was on her game, there was no tournament she couldn't win; when she wasn't, she was only near the top. And just as there was no consistency to her life, there was no consistency in her game.

Martina played well throughout the first week, her serves biting, her volleys crisp. The more she played, the more confident she became, and I tried to provide a relaxed and fun atmosphere for her off the court. Shopping, lifting weights, eating out, soaking up the culture—it was a different life for me.

People were always fond of Martina, but Chrissie was their favorite. She had married Briton John Lloyd, a solid player himself, and good-looking. Chris was the toast of the town.

The only time I sensed Martina was nervous was when she had to play Hana Mandlikova, a fellow Czech. Hana didn't talk to Martina very much, perhaps because of Martina's defection. But Martina's decision helped all the Czech athletes because the Czech government became more lenient toward them so they wouldn't be so tempted to leave.

Hana's game was always inconsistent and not well thought out, but she had incredible talent and athletic ability, and that worried Martina and lessened her confidence. Hana played well this time, and she gave Martina a disappointing exit from Wimbledon, 7-5, 4-6, 6-1.

Still, I could see the loss made it a good time to return home, to get Martina to move to Dallas and get a new start. A training program would be the beginning.

As we were walking through the Wimbledon grounds we passed the wall with all of the former champions listed on it.

"Look Martina, this lady won a lot of these plates," I said, awed. The history buff told me about Helen Wills Moody. "And Billie Jean has done pretty well for herself too," I said.

Martina told me about Billie's singles, doubles, and mixed doubles championships.

I was so naive I ended up saying, "Oh, it's all right. You'll probably end up winning ten of these things."

She looked at me and said, "But I've only won two." My unflinching optimism was in full stride. I told her she was only 24 years old and there was no question that she would win more titles. At last count she had nine Wimbledon titles under her belt. Maybe I wasn't so naive after all.

Chapter 14

With A
Little Work

 The first six months I was around Martina, she never won a tournament. The stretch from the French through Wimbledon was tough for her because she couldn't get over the hump, losing time and again in the semifinals. I really didn't know enough about tennis to help her at that point, but I knew we had to do something to get her past the gray area and into tournament finals. It was time we had a talk.

Before we came home from Wimbledon, Martina and I had made some decisions. First, she was going to begin really training when we got home. She had six weeks before her next tournament, and I was determined that she was going to be in better mental and physical shape by then. I had contacted Ken Johnson, a personal fitness trainer from New Canaan, Connecticut, who had helped me get ready for the SuperStars.

Second, we decided to move in together. The only way we were going to be able to make the training effective was to live together and make it a daily priority. Martina was going to move into my modest Dallas condo from her 20-room mansion in Charlottesville. I wondered where everything would go.

I had a two-car garage and a lot of "No parking" signs around my house. Martina had eight cars. I didn't major in math at Old Dominion, but I knew we had too many wheels. We had a Mercedes convertible, a BMW 733i, a Pontiac J-car, a Jeep Renegade, a Rolls-Royce Corniche, a Porsche 928 in Minerva blue with bug eyes, and later a BMW boat that we kept in Virginia. At my mother's house in New York was a brand new Toyota Supra. The Rolls-Royce Silver Cloud was still at the mansion in Charlottesville.

I tried to convince her that she needed to save her money. "Martina, just because you make millions of dollars doesn't mean you have to go right out and spend it," I said. "Does it?"

I wanted to help Martina get a handle on her finances as well as her tennis and sock some money away to fall back on. Little by little we started selling off the cars and putting the money in the bank. When my attic and garage were full of her belongings, we had a garage sale. She told me what we could get rid of, and I got a bunch of my trashy treasures together. We waited until she went out of town for a tournament, then held the sale at Nancy Nichols's garage. "Nick" was the general manager/public relations director for the Dallas Diamonds and a neighbor of mine.

Once word got out it was a Navratilova-Lieberman garage sale, it became an event. There were old wooden rackets, Wimbledon ball gowns, basketball sneakers, gym bags, tennis clothes, and shoes that had never been worn. Our big joke to Martina was that we'd found a $20,000 check in the pocket of one warm-up jacket. She almost believed us. Almost as astonishing — but true — was that she'd made a couple of thousand dollars one Saturday afternoon just selling some stuff she'd never use.

Then there were Martina's children, the Japanese Shiba dogs, Tets and Ruby. The first time Martina left for a tournament, the dogs, already upset because they were in a new environment, went berserk. They chewed the carpet. They scratched down the door. They pooped and peed all over the house. They ran wild in the neighborhood.

Martina had trouble abiding by condo bylaws. "Please observe all no parking signs or be towed." We had the whole row of spaces, plus the fire lane. "Dogs must be on leashes at all times." Martina was accustomed to opening the door and letting them out. Then the phone would ring: "Your dogs are loose." Not my dogs, I'd explain, my roommate's.

"Tell her if she'd move her cars, maybe she'd be able to see that they're running through the neighborhood," the caller said.

I knew it would be a big transition for both of us, and I told Martina it would be different from anything she had been through. She went from the manicured lawns of Wimbledon to community courts with a chain-link net. My house is next to a creek, and a balance-beam width of concrete connects the two sides, with a 15-foot drop into the creek bed. The tennis courts were on the other side of the creek so we'd usually cut across the beam rather than walk a half-mile around.

People driving by couldn't believe they were seeing Martina and Renee Richards hitting a basket of balls. Some people stopped and watched and would applaud shots. They got a big kick out of seeing one of the world's greatest athletes hanging out on public courts with a metal net.

It had to be a big transition for Martina to move from a 20-room estate into a three-bedroom condo with two roommates. "I don't have a mansion or a $75,000 pea gravel driveway or leaded and unleaded gas tanks next to my garage," I told her. "What I can promise is that you'll be comfortable and have a great environment to workout and train. Plus, we'll have fun."

That seemed to appeal to her.

We went to Charlottesville and picked out the things she wanted to take with her. Martina and Rita Mae walked through the house and decided what each of them would keep. I had just had gum surgery at the dentist's office in Norfolk. I had been out during the drive to Charlottesville and was still groggy and a little spacey. So I sat in the kitchen, out of the way, while they decided how to divvy up the belongings.

Rita Mae was not happy having to deal with the reality that her relationship with Martina was over and that Martina had moved away from her to Dallas. When that reality sank in, I think it was too much for Rita Mae to take. It seemed inevitable that she would try to retaliate against Martina or me.

But before Rita Mae could drop a bombshell, a New York *Daily News* writer ran a story about Martina's sexual preference. Martina kept apologizing to me. "I'm sorry you're having to be dragged into this thing," she said.

I told her I didn't care what people said or wrote about me. "Look Martina, I'm your friend," I said. "I care about you. And I'm behind you 100 percent. It'll blow over and be replaced by tomorrow's headlines."

Martina left for the Canadian Open, and I stayed behind in Dallas to take care of some business. A few days later Rita Mae called Martina in Canada and threatened to go public with her thoughts about our relationship. She was convinced that Martina and I were having an affair, and unless Martina gave her the Rolls-Royce and some cash, Rita Mae was going to the *Washington Post*.

I got a call from Martina in Canada, and she was crying as she related her conversation with Rita Mae. I told her not to let Rita Mae blackmail her because if she did it once she would do it again.

"Martina, just put your foot down and don't allow it to happen," I said. "She can get on the morning news for all I care and tell people what she wants. I don't care."

I guess when Martina realized I meant what I said, it gave her the strength to pick up the phone and tell Rita Mae to do what she wanted. "Go write an article or a book," she told her. "Knock yourself out — it won't bother Nancy or me."

In the end, a big article appeared in August in the *Washington Post*, with Rita Mae coming across as the "love scorned." Eventually Martina gave Rita Mae some money anyway. In fact, the two have been friends over the years, and on occasion they still visit with one another. I guess time does heal lots of things.

I eventually flew to Canada to calm Martina down. The press was hounding her and she needed some support. Besides, I wanted to see how she was doing with her training. It was a sunny 90 degrees on the hardcourts when Martina played Tracy Austin in the semis. Martina just wilted, ran out of gas; Tracy could have pounded balls all day long, and she won, 7-6, 6-4. I vowed to myself that Martina would never lose another match because she wasn't in shape.

By the time the U.S. Open rolled around in late August, we had worked together for two months, and Martina was showing improvement in all areas of her game and her life. We moved into my mother's house in Far Rockaway. I had called home some time before to tell mom I had a new friend who was a professional tennis player.

"Mom, I'm coming home and bringing Martina with me," I said to her. The name meant nothing to her. "Martina Navratilova," I explained.

"Nancy, the only name I pay attention to in tennis is that little Chrissie Evert," she explained to me.

She turned it into a twenty-questions quiz show. "So who is she? Where did you meet her? What kind of name is Nav-ra-ti-lova?" she asked.

I explained that I met Martina at Amelia Island in Florida through another friend. I told her that she loved sports just about as much as I did and we had struck up a friendship. Later I told her that Martina was moving in with me, and I gave her a little bit of the background before she could read about it in the papers. She told me to be careful, then asked, "What will people think?" There was that question again, the same line I heard in the sixth grade when I brought a houseload of the black guys home from the playground.

"What will the neighbors say? What will people think about you playing ball and bringing all these guys home?" And now, "What will people think about you and Martina?"

Eventually, she and Martina developed a good relationship. I had told Martina all about my childhood and how tough things were when I was growing up. She asked my mother about all of these things. "How could you not want to see your daughter play basketball?" Martina asked.

She was really frank with my mom.

In turn, my mother really liked Martina. The two of them shared a passion for food, anytime, all the time, and my mom gave our new friend the nickname "Tini." Martina ate so much pasta that my mother started calling her "Tini linguini." It kind of stuck.

One thing my mother never really adjusted to was Martina's habit of walking around the house without a stitch of clothing on. Martina would go to the front door to let the dogs in and my mother would panic.

"Martina, put some clothes on — my neighbors are out there! You should like it if I went to the door without a stitch?" my Jenny Craig-sized mother would ask. We all got a big laugh out of those times. My mother really enjoyed having us around, even if it made life crazy. She liked going to the Open and to dinners in the city.

Before the Open started, I gave Martina a special necklace. My mother had given me a diamond "NANCY" necklace in 1979, which Martina really admired. So as a surprise I had a sapphire "TINI" necklace made for her by some jewelers in Los Angeles. It was beautiful and she really loved it.

Soon most of her close friends were calling her Tini. People in the stands might be shouting encouragement to her, "Come on, Martina," but she wouldn't necessarily look up and see who was yelling. If she heard someone yelling for Tini, though, she would always whip her head around. John McEnroe is the same way. People might be yelling for "John," but he'll only pay attention when he hears someone yelling for "Junior," his nickname with family and friends.

We had a pretty good cheering section in the stands for Martina. She played hard over the two weeks of the Open and didn't drop a set en route to her semifinal match with Chris Evert. The match would be a big test for Martina and a great way to gauge the progress we had made in her game. I could help Martina with training, but I didn't know enough about tennis to serve as a real coach. That's where Renee Richards came in. Renee, a former player on the tour who gained notoriety as a transsexual, approached Martina and offered to help coach her before the match with Chris. Martina had befriended Renee years before when Renee came on the tour and not many people wanted to talk to her. That's Martina at her best — sharing, caring, eager to make people feel good about themselves. Renee's strategy was to pin Chris behind the baseline with looping forehand shots to Chris's backhand. She didn't want Martina to give her anything to hit with authority.

"Let her send moonballs back, and then put the volley away," Renee advised.

She also advised Martina to change the pace on the ball because Chris likes to hit hard balls. Change it up and make her create the pace, Renee said, and pull her wide with your serve to her backhand.

Chris had always known what Martina would do in certain situations, when she'd come to the net, what sort of shot she'd hit. Now there was a difference — Martina picked her spots, came in only on short balls, and served wide, pulling Chris off the court. It was textbook tennis, a beautiful thing to see.

Chris is a great strategist, but I think Martina and Renee caught her by surprise. Martina was nervous as she took the court with Chris, but she pulled out the first set 7-5. She dropped the second set 6-4, but returned the favor in the third, winning 6-4. I was so excited. Martina had advanced to her first U.S. Open final.

Martina had other things on her mind before she was to face Tracy Austin in the final. On our way into the match from Far Rockaway, Martina decided that she wanted to stop and look at some rings at Marvin & Sons Jewelers. My mother and I had shopped there often, and I knew quite a few people when we went in. I told Martina to hurry because we would be hitting traffic on the Grand Central.

Martina picked out two rings and gave the salesman a credit card to pay for them. "Could you please hurry," Martina implored.

The salesman went to the back of the store to charge up the sale. I overheard part of the conversation. "This credit card says it's Martina Navratilova. It can't be. She's playing in the finals of the U.S. Open in just a little while," the salesman said.

A few minutes later Bobby Zuckerman, the owner of the store and a friend of mine, came out from the back. "Hey, what are you two doing here?" he asked. "I'm getting ready to leave to watch you play in the finals in a little while, and you're buying jewelry now?"

It was so typical of Martina.

We were piled up in traffic going to the Open, and I started to get really nervous. On the radio, "We are the Champions" started playing; Martina and I just looked at each other like it was an omen.

She took the court full of confidence and really relaxed. She looked fit in her pretty white outfit with the orange and yellow stripes, and her hair was braided with ribbons in it. I thought, "She looks like a champion today."

When she breezed through the first set, 6-1, she kept looking to Renee and me with a look on her face like, "I have it. I have it." Martina kept pounding away at the ball and was in control. She was serving for the match at 5-4, up 30-15, that close to being the champion, when it got away.

Maybe she was too anxious, I don't know, but she dumped two consecutive forehand volleys into the bottom of the net. She went on to lose that game and wound up dropping a tiebreaker for the set. All day Tracy had been going crosscourt in the rallies, but during the tiebreaker she suddenly went down the line twice for winners. Afterward, we were convinced that someone in the stands was coaching her, which is illegal.

The final set went to a tiebreaker, too, and Tracy came out on top. It was a great display of tennis by both players, Martina coming to the net, Tracy hitting pinpoint passing shots, great rallies that had the crowd on its feet.

Martina was devastated. She'd had her first U.S. Open title in the bag and let it get away. She just put her head in her hands and started to cry. I wanted to take the pain away, but I knew there was nothing I could do. When Martina got up to speak, the crowds were cheering her and I had tears in my eyes and a huge lump in my throat.

Martina started to speak and then just got all choked up. All she ever wanted was to be liked and accepted. All of a sudden, the crowd just stood up and kept clapping and cheering and clapping. A standing ovation. I remember watching Martina finally pick her head up and the astonished look on her face when she realized they were cheering for her. There could be no doubt: She was liked, she was accepted.

My New Yorkers were giving her her due, and I was overcome with the warmth and consideration they were showing her in defeat. She had given the crowd everything; she had left her blood, sweat, and tears on the court, and they were telling her how much they appreciated it. In that brief moment of defeat a new Martina emerged, one who had won the hearts of her new countrymen.

Three weeks later, at the U.S. Indoors in Minneapolis, Martina won her first tournament in the six months since we'd met. She was beginning to wonder if all the training would ever pay off, and I was wondering if I was a bad luck charm. It was especially sweet, since she beat Tracy Austin 6-0, 6-2 in the final.

Martina closed out the year making it to the finals in every tournament and winning four of the seven events she played. In the string of wins was an incredible 6-7, 6-4, 7-5 championship win over Chris Evert at the Australian Open. Renee was working as her coach now, and the conditioning was getting easier as she found out how much fun it was to be in shape and win.

I learned a lot in the first year I was on the tour with Martina. There were clearly defined groups of older players and younger players, but the groups were pretty friendly with each other, more like teammates than opponents.

Billie Jean King, Rosie Casals, Betty Stove, Virginia Wade, Paula Smith, Anne Smith, Candy Reynolds, Wendy Turnbull, and Chris Evert were some of the mainstays on the tour. Lee Jackson, the touring umpire, was in the chair for most of the championship matches in the United States. Anna Laird, a high-school friend of Chris Evert's, was the public relations director for the tour. It was a very tight, close-knit group.

The younger players then were Tracy Austin, Andrea Jaeger, Pam Shriver and Hana Mandlikova. Tracy and Andrea traveled with parents, but they weren't giggling teenagers. They were very mature, and I think that came from traveling all the time.

I remember walking into the locker room one time and a few of the players were sitting around playing Scrabble. I couldn't believe it. They were sitting around cutting up and laughing. I couldn't imagine playing cards with my basketball rivals, then going out and playing them in a big game. The mentality of the women's tennis tour was just foreign to me. They liked and respected each other, but they could still compete on a very high level.

Wimbledon is famous for rain delays, and it's not unusual for the players to be stuck for a couple of hours waiting out the rain. One minute Chris and Martina would be out on Center Court, fighting it out for the greatest crown in tennis, and the next minute they would be in the "Ladies Changing Room," chit-chatting during a delay.

"What's going on? How's your mother? Have you called Czechoslovakia?" Chris might ask. Martina would jabber about Chris's family, husband, or sister Claire. It was just all so homespun.

Sometimes I would go nuts because I couldn't understand that mentality. Looking back, I realize it's just a special bond these athletes have. They travel the long tour and circuit and they don't have teammates. The only people they have city-in, city-out are each other. The legends of the game, the pioneers, developed this feeling of camaraderie among both the older and younger groups.

Even Lee Jackson was able to distinguish between her time in the chair as the head lineswoman and her role as friend to the players off the court. She could be giggling and conversing with them in the locker room before the match, then go out and make some tough calls. Sometimes you would see a player look at her and say, "Come on, Lee, you know the ball was out." Lee would look at her in a motherly kind of way and say, "I saw it good." And that was it.

In some ways, the professional tennis tour is like a merry-go-round. All of a sudden your expectations change. Things you never had growing up suddenly become necessities. It's so easy to get caught up in that attitude. Growing up, I never really wanted a lot besides a good pair of sneakers and a basketball. Suddenly, I was looking at things other people had, and thinking, "Boy, that is really nice."

In 1981, Martina and I were going to visit a friend of hers, Linda Dozoretz, at the public relations firm of Rogers and Cowan in Los Angeles. Tini and I were walking down Wilshire Boulevard when a hot car blew by, and I asked Martina what kind it was. She told me it was a Ferrari. I said something like, "That is really a hot-looking car."

Her response was typical Martina. "Nancy, here is my credit card. The Ferrari place is two blocks down the street on the right. Go down there and test drive one, and if you like it, just go ahead and get it."

I was like, sure, uh, really? She said, "Yeah, I'll be up with Linda, see what you think," and so I walked down to the dealership and asked one of the salesmen for a test drive. He gave me a look and said they didn't allow test drives of Ferraris. He looked at me like I was nuts or something.

Since I had the credit card he finally let me test it out. I was wild — taking a Ferrari out for a test drive and having a credit card with a credit line on it that would cover it. The funny thing is that after I drove it, I really didn't like it. It was too low to the ground and the ride was too bumpy for my taste.

We got special treatment everywhere we went. We were at a New York Yankees game one day when someone came over to us and introduced himself as Al Frohman, Dave Winfield's agent. Dave had just signed the most lucrative contract in all of sports to date. As the game progressed, Frohman asked me to meet with him in his office in Fort Lee, New Jersey, home of the Dave Winfield Foundation. He wanted to do some endorsement work for Martina, and I saw he had great ideas.

We ended up meeting Dave and going to see him in the 1981 World Series. My mom, never one to miss a major sporting event, came along and wound up spending the game talking to Dave's mom and his brother Steve. Every once in a while we'd see Dave at a game. He even came to see Martina play at the Toyota Championships in New Jersey in December of '81.

While we were at that tournament, I was in the room one day while Martina was doing "Good Morning, America." It's pretty early, but the phone rings, and this very British voice says, "Hi, this is Elton John, and I'm in New York. I just saw Martina on the show — is she there?"

I stammered something like, "Elton John . . . uh, she's not back . . . can she call you?" What I wanted to say was, "Can you come over and sing to me?" More benefits of being around Martina.

Also during that tournament, Martina's beloved Dallas Cowboys were playing the Giants the next day at noon, and of course she wanted to go to the game. Her championship match started at 3 or 4, but she wanted to see the Cowboys. "Are you crazy?" I asked her. "Get some rest," I said. "Be prepared to concentrate on your match — you could be No. 1 this year. Martina, would Tom Landry allow his guys to watch you play tennis two hours before their game? Go to sleep." She won the tournament, but Tracy and Chris were Nos. 1 and 2; Martina was still No. 3, but climbing.

Of course, a player who is in the top ten on the tour and making hundreds of thousands, even millions, of dollars, has one lifestyle, and a player ranked No. 50 and barely getting by has another. There are no fat endorsement contracts for No. 50. Most of these players rely on housing with people in the community, hitting all the SuperSaver flights or driving. They have their whole schedule mapped out in advance. It's really difficult. When I traveled with Martina, I knew we'd be in a city until the finals. We would see the sights, eat in some great restaurants, and maybe go home with the championship trophy. I used to look at the low-ranked players and wonder how they did it week after week. Their bags were always packed ready to go to the next site. Most didn't get past a round or two in singles or doubles and — boom! — they'd be gone to the next city. You have to admire them for hanging in there.

Chapter 15

Team Navratilova

The hard work was finally paying Martina in big dividends. Beginning in 1982, she started winning consistently and the other players on the tour soon realized they were up against a different Martina. The Martina who would lose in the third or fourth round once in a while was gone. This Martina was a consistent, razor-sharp athlete, well-conditioned, full of stamina, physically strong. I think Martina raised the consciousness of the other players on the tour.

Players like Tracy Austin and Andrea Jaeger would go out and hit tennis balls for four or five hours a day and think that was all they had to do. Our new regimen with Martina included hitting for three hours but it also featured a lot of off-the-court workouts — running, lifting, basketball, and agility drills. We were making her a better tennis player, but also a better athlete. And on top of her physical prowess, Renee gave her the strategy to go out and outsmart her opponent.

The plan was one I learned from my old teammate and coach, Pat Head Summitt. In training camp, Pat would push us past the point where we didn't think we had anything left. She taught us that our bodies wouldn't quit if our minds didn't quit.

Pat's practices were so tough that the games seemed like cake. That was the concept I was trying to get through to Martina. Great athletes are the ones who can step up to another plateau with their minds and bodies when it looks like they have nothing left.

Martina is as bright a person as I've ever met in my whole life. We used to call her "mastermind" because she was so smart. She's a great game player. She'll beat you every time in Scrabble, playing in her second language against your first. She had a tremendous amount of knowledge about world affairs. She could speak in different languages and travel anywhere in the world and be comfortable.

When she learned to translate that intelligence to her sport and began to take it seriously, she was untouchable. It also marked the first time that two high-profile women had come together to help each other train for their sports. I think that had a significant impact not only with women's tennis but with women's athletics as a whole.

The tennis tour was not accustomed to a female player traveling with a huge entourage. Initially, it was just me out there helping Martina. My focus was getting her in top mental and physical shape. I realized that I could not help her with the technical side of her game, so Renee Richards came on board to coach Martina. Later, Dr. Robert Haas joined us as our nutritionist. Pam Derderian handled some of my business dealings, securing endorsements and assisting with logistics at some of the tournaments. In one *Sports Illustrated* article, Pam was referred to as the "dog walker" of our group, an unfair suggestion that she wasn't really doing anything important. Before long, our group was dubbed "Team Navratilova."

I guess having so many different people around to share so many duties was a throwback to my basketball days. We had an administrator, coaches, assistant coaches, managers, trainers, public relations directors, and statisticians. People just had certain responsibilities to make life easier, especially on the road.

I learned a lot about myself while helping to train Martina and give some direction to her career. Martina wanted to be known as the best shotmaker in the world. I wanted Martina to be known as the greatest tennis player of all time. Maybe that was asking too much, but I wanted her at least to have that vision. It was the same vision I'd had, wanting to be the best women's basketball player in the world.

Pretty soon, all the top players were following her lead trying to get a better balance in their games. Chris Evert hired aerobics guru Cathy Smith to help her with movement, flexibility, speed, and quickness. The players found out what Martina had learned: You can hit all day, but if you don't have the stamina, strength, and mental toughness to get to a ball during the match, then you're not going to get the results.

In the minds of some of the players and officials, I had gone in six months from being a "nice guy" on the tour to Martina's slavedriver. I think they saw me as a threat because I was driving Martina to be the best, and in turn she was forcing them to elevate their games to try to keep up. Some people thought I was making Martina meaner. I called it more focused and competitive. They didn't quite know how to take it because they had never seen that side of her before.

When I first met Martina, she told me about her great friendship with Chris Evert and I thought it was fantastic. Of all Martina's friendships off the court, I think the new competitiveness affected her relationship with Chris most of all. Between 1982 and 1983, they met each other in 10 championship matches. Martina walked away with nine titles.

Chris may have outwardly given the appearance of being buddy-buddy, but she was shrewd and mentally tough, and she never forgot she was out there to beat Martina. Chris and I came from the same mental school of thought. She knew that she could psychologically beat Martina because their friendship was more important to Martina than winning a tennis match.

Chris would go into a press conference and say, "Well, Martina's great when she's a front runner. If it's three-all in the second set and the score is 40-15, Martina will choke." Then they would get in a match and Martina's muscle memory would kick in at three-all in the second set. She would start getting tight and tense because Chris had said she was supposed to choke.

When Martina started getting mentally tougher, Chris came up with a different approach, refusing to give her much credit in a win. "Martina played the big points better than me," Chris would say. "If I could have gotten her to three-all and put the pressure on her, then I think I would have won."

It bothered me that Martina considered Chris such a good friend and then Chris would play mental games with her. "If Chris is such a good friend, how could she say these things about you?" I'd ask Martina. Martina didn't want to believe that Chris was saying negative things about her. Finally, enough was enough.

I just started cutting out the comments that Chris had made in the newspaper and taping them to the bathroom mirror. "Martina, this is what your friend had to say about you today," I'd tell her. Pretty soon, I had a file full of negative clippings.

The last straw was a *Newsweek* article in September 1982, during the U.S. Open. Chris was quoted as saying about Martina, "She's not the kind of person you'd go to with marital problems."

I was outraged. We had spent so much time on Martina's image, trying to get people to focus on Martina the athlete, not Martina the bisexual. Here was Chris, Martina's "friend," saying that she wouldn't go to her with her problems because she was gay. Like, what the heck would a gay woman know? It was a low blow, and I wondered how a friend could do such a thing. I wondered how she could deliver a low blow like that to Martina. Chris had the media in the palm of her hand. If she had said Martina was a great gal, everyone would have believed it. Instead, she reconfirmed the negative perceptions that we were trying to counteract.

I decided two could play the mental game. I knew it bothered Chris for people to ignore her, so I went into my act. My goal was to get Chris too concerned with my snubbing her to play mind games with Martina. I'd be sitting in the lobby or by the locker room and Chris would walk by. I wouldn't say boo. She'd flick my newspaper with her racket to get my attention. "Oh, hi Chris. I didn't notice you," I'd say. The more I ignored her, the more she tried to get my attention.

Chris even mentioned something to *Sports Illustrated* about the three of us not getting along in December 1982 at the Toyota Championships. A reporter asked Martina what was going on because Chris had mentioned that I wouldn't let Martina talk to her.

I knew we had it made if Chris had started complaining about the brush-off to other people. Eventually, Martina got mentally tougher, especially when she played Chris. No longer was Martina just going out to play tennis while Chris was going out to win the match.

"Martina, you want to go out and beat Chris 7-5, 7-5 so she doesn't feel bad," I told her. "She wants to kick your butt and beat you love and love. When you get on the court with her, she is faceless. Play to win, then worry about where the two of you will have dinner."

I finally got through to her: Martina wanted to win the war and gain the prestige, money, titles, a place in history. When she finally realized it, she was on her way to some of the most successful years in her career.

At that point in Martina's career I was a bad influence on their friendship, I admit it. I tried to use Chris's comments as a wedge between them. But the fact of the matter is that I really have always liked and respected Chris. What we were doing was gamesmanship and maybe I carried it too far, but Chris, Martina, and I are much more congenial now because we are not on a collision course. After I stopped working with Martina, they became comfortable around each other again. Martina even introduced Chris to Andy Mills, who became her husband, at a Christmas party in Aspen.

In 1988, when I started training Martina again, I ran into Chris at the U.N. Plaza in New York City. We sat down and talked and both kind of apologized to each other. I told her I was sorry that I let the animosity get out of hand. We both got our feelings out in the open and talked about all the things that had happened over the years. It was good to have the opportunity to clear the air and get back our mutual respect.

Whether her opponent happened to be Chris or Andrea or Tracy, we knew we had to have all the parts of Martina's game clicking to be successful. "Team Navratilova" was developing all phases of her physical and mental game. The last piece of the puzzle was her diet. When she first joined the tour Martina proclaimed that she was on a "see food" diet — if she saw food, she ate it. That soon changed when we met Dr. Robert Haas.

We met Robert after Martina's bout with toxoplasmosis at the 1982 U.S. Open. He was at the Open helping a friend of mine, Italy's Sabina Simmons. Robert developed a diet for both of us, and we could see and feel the results almost immediately. His diet was mostly just good sense, and we both lost weight and felt great. Soon he was traveling with us and monitoring our diets throughout the year.

Martina had won six of seven tournaments going into the 1982 French Open. It almost was getting too easy, as the level of her play and her bank balance both continued to rise.

She had a fairly easy time getting to the finals with the exception of a second-set lapse against Kathy Rinaldi in the round of 16. Martina beat her 6-0 in the first, lost the second 6-2, and closed out the match 6-0. She breezed through her semifinal match with Hana Mandlikova, 6-0, 6-2, to set up the final with Andrea Jaeger.

I was nervous the whole time sitting in the Friends' Box at the French. I wanted so badly for Martina to win, to have the French Open title to go along with the No. 1 world ranking she had attained on May 4, 1982. But of course all I could do was be a cheerleader and shout encouragement to Martina.

"Come on, Tini. Don't quit on any point. Just hang in there!" I'd shout. There is no doubt in my mind that encouragement is vital in any sport you play. It gets the adrenalin flowing and that's what I tried to do for Martina during a match.

I could tell when she would get scared during a point. If she was on the offensive, on the attack, nobody in the world could touch her. But if she was attacked and got scared she would hide on the baseline with her head up and back and hit chip shots instead of driving the ball over the net. She was so tentative and iffy when she got like that.

In the final against Andrea, the first set went down to a tiebreaker. I could sense Martina getting tight, even though I knew she was in control of the match. So I tried shouting buzz words like, "Come on, let's go, Martina, don't worry about it, just hit it."

She took the tiebreaker, then completely dominated the second set 6-1. She had won her first French Open. I couldn't wait to congratulate her, and I headed toward the press area.

The loser enters the press room first, and apparently Andrea's father, Roland, had told his daughter that I had been giving Martina signals during the match, which is illegal. In the press conference, the first thing out of Andrea's mouth was that Nancy Lieberman was coaching Martina from the stands. When Martina went in for her half of the press conference she couldn't believe the allegations. Who could believe them? I can teach her a few moves on the basketball court, but I'd never be so bold as to coach her in tennis.

Our next stop was the Wimbledon tuneup at Eastbourne, and the issue still hadn't died down. At one of the matches, Candy Reynolds' mother was in the stands, and there was some discussion about my coaching Martina. Roland Jaeger turned around and spit in Candy's mother's face. I guess he just wanted his daughter to be so good that he had a hard time with any kind of failure.

About the same time we were having a falling out with Renee. Initially, Renee and Martina had agreed on a salary. A few months later Renee asked for a raise and Martina gave her one. Then six months later Renee would be back for even more money. And while she was working full-time with Martina, she was earning every penny of it. But then she cut back on her weeks, coming to the tournament the week of the finals. I didn't like that arrangement, especially with Wimbledon coming up and Martina in the hunt for the Grand Slam.

Renee had gone back to the States after the French Open to look into an ophthalmology practice in New York City, planning to be back for the second week of Wimbledon. Her business manager called Martina one day and said Renee wouldn't be back to coach Martina unless she got a raise. Renee also wanted Martina to give her some money to open her practice.

The demands made no sense. Renee was only spending the second week of the major tournaments with Martina. She was getting back into her ophthalmology practice and wanted to devote more time to setting that up. While I thought Martina really needed Renee full-time, I also understood Renee's desire to get back into her profession. But you shouldn't ask for more and give less, and that's what she was doing. She was already the highest-paid coach on the tour and she was coming to the well again. But Martina agreed to pay her more, and Renee was back on the team.

Now it was time to get down to the business of winning Wimbledon. Martina had stayed focused in winning at Eastbourne, beating Hana Mandlikova 6-4, 6-3 in the final. She felt ready for Wimbledon and was eager to get started in her favorite tournament. She waltzed through her first five matches in straight sets, setting up a championship date with Chris Evert.

When we were packing for Wimbledon I had asked Martina if she planned to pack a gown for the Wimbledon Ball.

"Nancy, it's bad luck to show up at the tournament with a gown," Martina warned me.

I had a feeling that she was going to win. She had been playing too well and working too hard not to win. After her semifinal victory over Bettina Bunge, I just knew she would need that gown. And since the women's final is played on a Saturday afternoon, it would be impossible for her to find a shop in London open after the match.

I came up with a plan with the help of several friends who had come over to watch Martina. Four of us went downtown to find Martina's gown while she was busy practicing with Renee. She had no idea what we were up to as we all disappeared for a couple of hours.

No one was an exact match for Martina, so we all took turns trying on dresses. One person checked for length, another for the shoulders, someone else for the waist. We drove the salespeople nuts, all of us taking turns trying on dresses. After an exhaustive search, we found the perfect gown, and all agreed it would be a perfect fit. Best of all, there was a parasol to match the dress; after two weeks of rain we thought it might come in handy. Ball gown in hand, the only thing left was a win over Chris Evert.

While I was getting ready to surprise Martina with her gown, my friends from the States were preparing a surprise for me. My birthday, July 1, always falls during Wimbledon, and they had gotten together with Martina to plan a party, inviting a dozen people or so. I was off playing basketball and when I came back to the house everyone jumped out and yelled, "Happy Birthday."

I was livid. I hated surprises. I stormed through the house to my room. I wanted to leave and go back to the basketball courts. The party continued as best it could without its guest of honor. I stayed in my room, mad as hell. My friends were shocked at my reaction, and I was too emotional to talk to them about it. Martina didn't really know what to do and it was a very awkward situation. To this day, I don't know if I was embarrassed by the party or mad because I wasn't in control of it.

I wasn't the only one upset by the party. Through an oversight, Renee wasn't invited. She thought I had purposely snubbed her, though I didn't even know about it. She was clearly unhappy during the rest of Wimbledon, and there was no convincing her that my friends just hadn't thought to invite her.

All the off-court happenings might have been distracting, but Martina didn't let it affect her. She sprinted out of the gate against Chris in the finals, winning the first set 6-1. It seemed too easy. When both players settled down, it became a game of nerves and strategy, each player placing her shots and hitting winners. Chris took the second set 6-3 and I began to squirm.

There was no need to be nervous. Martina took the third set 6-2 and was crowned the Wimbledon champion. We were so excited for her. It was like a dream come true for her to follow the French title with the Wimbledon crown. I remember turning to Debby Jennings, a friend of mine in the Players' Box, and saying, "We're rich!" Martina had won the $500,000 bonus for winning three legs of the Playtex Challenge, a bonus for winning designated tournaments on three different surfaces.

When Martina showed me the silver plate they presented her after the match, her name was already engraved on it. Apparently, there is a gentleman who engraves the winner's name right before it's presented. The champion gets to keep a smaller version of the championship plate the winners always hold over their heads for the photographers.

Martina came back to our flat and we were all ecstatic with her win. She was really tired and wanted a hot soak in the tub before we went out for her victory dinner. Somehow we got her to take a bubble bath, and while she was busy my shopping partners helped me lay out her Wimbledon Ball gown. Next, we opened a magnum of champagne I had brought from France, and with glasses in hand we invaded Martina's bath.

We all took our shoes and socks off and stood in the tub to toast her win. We were drinking champagne and pouring it over Martina's head when the phone rang. It was Frank Deford of *Sports Illustrated*. "Martina," he said, "you've finally made the cover. Congratulations!" I can't remember ever seeing Martina happier about a phone call. When everything finally calmed down we took Martina to see her dress.

She loved it. Then she tried it on. It was too long and the waist was too big. A million pins later we had the dress under control and it didn't look that bad. The next night we all went to the Wimbledon Ball with her at the Savoy Hotel in London.

Secretly I was pulling for John McEnroe to win the men's title so he could have the first dance at the ball with Martina, but he lost to Jimmy Connors.

When it came time for Martina to make her speech, she walked up to the microphone and opened up her parasol. "The weather has been so bad this fortnight, I just didn't want to take any chances." Everyone loved it and she was the hit of the ball.

In the month we had been away from home, Martina had won two legs of the Grand Slam. We were both on an emotional high, but I knew the toughest part was ahead. Getting to the top is one thing; staying there is another. We both needed a break, so we decided to go to Quayside, Florida, to get away from tennis.

But almost as soon as we arrived, Martina got a phone call from Renee, and the subject, again, was money. After that, it just seemed that everything fell apart between the two of them. Renee said that she wouldn't coach Martina any more unless Martina agreed to pay her 15 percent of the Playtex Challenge money if Martina won the U.S. Open. Martina was in line for another $500,000 bonus if she won the Open. Renee was demanding 15 percent to go along with the salary, expenses, and bonuses Martina had already paid her.

Finally, Martina put her foot down. "No more money," she said. "I am paying you a salary and bonuses and that is it." The timing was bad because it was so close to the start of the U.S. Open. Martina ended up contacting Peter Marmureanu to coach her.

We were both pretty busy that summer between my basketball camps and speaking engagements and Martina's playing in the Federation Cup. Our workouts were geared to getting Martina ready to win the U.S. Open, the third leg of the Grand Slam.

When we came home from my basketball camp in the Poconos, Rupert Murdoch, the publishing tycoon, was trying to locate Martina to play in an upcoming exhibition in Australia. Usually Martina enjoys playing in exhibitions but she wasn't interested, and I couldn't figure out why.

"Martina, they are going to pay you $200,000 and all you have to do is play for three days," I tried to explain. They upped the ante. "Martina, you really should consider their offer. They will also do a commercial for another $50,000 and give us plane tickets for the Australian Open in December. You should really start thinking about this," I told her.

She really didn't want to go or even discuss the matter. I was getting upset. There was no way in my mind to justify turning down that kind of money with no real reason.

"Nancy, I don't know why, but I just don't want to do this," Martina kept saying.

I had noticed that she was listless, sleeping and reading a lot more than usual, but I just chalked it up to a busy summer. Eventually, they got her on the plane to Australia, but she called me from Hawaii, crying. She was so tired she had stopped there to sleep for half a day before continuing on to Australia.

She played two matches in Australia, then had to default. When she came home, she spent a lot of time lying around my mom's house, sleeping. The U.S. Open was right around the corner and I couldn't understand what was wrong with her.

She finally went to Dr. Gary Wadler, who diagnosed her with toxoplasmosis. He told Martina that the disease can be transmitted by eating undercooked meat or by exposure to cat feces where the parasite might be present. Naturally, the press later picked on that and dubbed her condition the "cat disease." Dr. Wadler tried to discourage her from playing, warning her that the parasite associated with the disease just keeps weakening the body. If she did play, he advised, she should get on and off the court as quickly as possible.

We were crushed by the news. I told Martina she ought to pull out of the doubles to save her strength, but she didn't want to let down her doubles partner, Pam Shriver. Her other option was to limit practices and try to get on and off the courts in two sets.

Martina managed to win her first four matches in straight sets, leading to a quarterfinal meeting with Pam Shriver. Martina won the first set 6-1, and I kept telling her to hang in there. But as the second set dragged on, I could see Martina's energy was being sapped. She led 5-4 but just couldn't close out the match, losing the second set in a tiebreaker. I knew the third set would be a killer. She looked like a zombie during the third set changeovers and lost 6-2.

Martina was devastated by the loss, and there was no way I could console her. "They'll say I choked again," Martina sobbed. "They'll say that I can't win the big one here in New York."

"Martina, tell them about the toxo. You didn't choke, you were sick," I said. She wasn't going to say anything about the disease. I told her if she didn't say anything then I would. People just had to know that she didn't choke. I told her Dr. Wadler had the lab reports if anyone doubted her. A few minutes into the interview someone asked her how she felt physically and she told them.

Afterward, we hid out at my mother's house, the phone ringing off the wall as everyone called to say how sorry they were. Martina didn't want to talk to anybody. Before we left New York, Dr. Wadler advised her to take some time off and skip the next tournament in Philadelphia, which meant Martina wouldn't be eligible for another $500,000 bonus from the Playtex Challenge. Instead of earning half a million dollars, I helped Martina find a way to spend it.

We had been talking about buying a house for quite a while when a woman approached me at the U.S. Open about one for sale in Virginia Beach. She showed me some pictures of a beautiful home on the water.

"You just have to see it. I know that it is what you are looking for," she said.

The house was named Shibui, which is Japanese for serenity. When we saw it we knew we had found a home. It was situated on a little peninsula and was surrounded by water. It was modern and beautiful and exactly what we had in mind. Martina used the $500,000 Playtex Challenge money from Wimbledon to buy the house.

We had some friends come down and do the interior design work. Later I called my father and asked the professional builder to take a look. He knocked down some walls, put in light soffits and new furniture. The house had tennis courts and a basketball court so Martina and I couldn't have been happier. Since it was on the water, we also had our own boat dock. When she won the next tournament in Eastbourne, she bypassed the cash and car and took the BMW speedboat. It was a great addition to the house.

Sometimes we put out crab nets and just sat on the deck waiting to haul in our catch. We always had friends over and it was a fabulous house for entertaining. It's too bad we were on the road so much that we didn't have more time to enjoy it.

We were traveling as much as ever once Martina started feeling better. In late October she played in her first event since the U.S. Open, beating Tracy Austin 6-3, 6-3 to win the Porsche Tournament in Germany. A week later she recorded a 6-1, 6-4 win over Chris Evert in Brighton, England. To close out the year, she had back-to-back meetings with Chris in the finals of the Australian Open and the Toyota Championships. Chris prevailed in Australia 6-3, 2-6, 6-3, but Martina won the Toyota 4-6, 6-1, 6-2.

Martina enjoyed not only 16 tournament titles in 1982, but also a much healthier bank account. Before she signed her contract with International Management Group at the beginning of 1982, I had sat down and looked at it with her.

"Martina, it says here that IMG gets 25 percent of your bonus money, 25 percent of your exhibitions, and 25 percent of any endorsements. Did you realize that?" I asked her. She just shook her head.

I couldn't understand the 25 percent cut they were taking out of Martina's earnings. I thought the better you were and the more money you made, the lower the percentage should be because of the big dollars you were bringing in for everyone.

Martina's affairs were handled by IMG's Peter Johnson. I could tell as I looked over the new contract that Peter and I were going to have a battle. I wasn't wrong. The negotiations put a strain on all of our business dealings with him until I left the scene in 1984.

Peter told me that IMG clients paid a standard 25 percent. I did my homework and asked some people like Jimmy Connors and Larry King, Billie Jean's husband, what kind of percentages should be taken out, and they gave me a different story. I confronted Peter with my findings.

He got mad that Martina and I had been checking on what he'd told us and insisted that he thought the percentage was standard. I didn't believe him and asked him to provide us with some real information instead of lies. The episode really soured me on Peter, and in turn he wasn't pleased that he would have to renegotiate the whole contract, item by item.

We took each item, one at a time, and debated the percentage. Was it on the court or off? What if she secured her own

endorsement? How much should she get for tools of the trade —
shoes, rackets, clothing? Eventually, we decided on the percentages for each of the items, ranging from 10 to 20 percent. It may
not sound like a lot of money, but figure out how much 5 percent
of five million dollars a year is over five years and you'll see why
I made a big deal of it.

Next I asked to see the marketing proposal IMG used to
promote Martina for endorsements. Peter was insulted that we
would ask him about it, but I insisted that she was entitled to
know how people sell her. This added fuel to our feud.

In retrospect, maybe I was too hard on Peter. He was just
doing his job, and I realize now that he had Martina's best
interests at heart. Some of the problems Martina and I had later
stemmed from the fact that I was being too protective of her and
her dealings with Peter. I regret forcing Martina into a position
of having to choose between trusting Peter or me.

What was 1982 like? It was incredible. Martina was on a roll
never before seen in tennis. Steffi Graf has come close in recent
years, but look at the competition Martina faced in 1982. It was
one big match after another.

Martina was not only winning, but she was also finally
confident and had peace of mind. Personally and professionally,
we had a blast that year. Check the record. She won over 90
matches and only dropped two.

The critics had said that she would never win the French
Open because that surface was not suited to her style of play. In
1982, she went in and beat Andrea Jaeger in straight sets. Next
she took Wimbledon by storm and beat Chris Evert in the finals.

And after a slow and difficult start, product endorsements
were beginning to fall in line. We couldn't understand at first
why she didn't have more endorsements when she was No. 1 and
undeniably the best. Peter thought companies wouldn't sign her
because they still doubted whether her image was positive.
Martina took it personally; she thought she wasn't wanted.

"Nancy," she told me, "I'm not a bad person, I'm hard-
working. Why don't they want me?"

From that point on, my goal was to get Martina as many
endorsements as possible. I had to be creative, sell her winning
ways, identify her with companies that were far and away No. 1
in their fields.

First, there was an image to create. After seeing the Winfield Foundation, we told Peter we wanted to start the Martina Youth Foundation to give needy kids Christmas parties, toys, and food. Then we signed her as playing editor with *World Tennis* and did endorsements for Thorlo socks and Future weight equipment. True, these weren't $100,000 deals, but 15 or 20 thousand a year adds up after a two- or three-year contract.

I had always liked Puma sneakers growing up because Walt Frazier had endorsed them. I asked Peter to try to get Martina a contract with them, but he said they weren't interested because of her image.

We had completed a deal with Porsche, Martina getting a free car a year. When Porsche sponsored a tour in Germany, she got a Porsche to drive in each city. She did a photo session and wore a Porsche patch at each tournament on the tour. In this business, you even learn which shoulder is worth more — which one, that is, catches the TV cameras more.

I asked Ed Peter, a Porsche executive and a close friend of Martina's, if he knew any execs at Puma. He set up a meeting for us, and the company's president, Hans During, met Martina and wanted to do a deal. We started talking at $200,000, and Peter, impressed by our getting a foot in the door, wound up completing the contract — nearly $500,000 a year for five years.

At the French Open, Hans and I talked about Martina wearing Puma clothes as well as shoes, like Lendl did for Adidas. He agreed, and we put another agreement together, Peter working out a five-year deal and extending the shoe contract to run concurrently. All told, we were talking about five years endorsing Puma shoes and clothes for nearly a million dollars a year.

When Robert Haas started working as our dietician and had such magnificent results, we started charting Martina's matches on paper; then we worked up to his laptop computer. We sat front row at Wimbledon in '83, and the press went crazy over this new technology they thought we were bringing to her game. Headlines: "Bionic Woman," "Sci-Fi Martina," "Computerized Champ" — it was great publicity. Robert and I were creating a new image for Martina, and where better to do it than front row at Wimbledon, with the world's eyes on us? In 1984, Peter was able to secure a very lucrative endorsement for Martina with Computerland. We even had the house in Virginia Beach carpeted through an endorsement I worked out with David Brand, president of Haynes Furniture. Martina did print ads and commercials for them in exchange. I had known David during my days at ODU, and he and his wife, Bonnie, became good friends of ours.

This was big business, and I was handling a lot of everyday work for Martina, from endorsements and requests for appearances to tournament fees and making sure money she won was sent and in the correct amount. I even did her instructional book, *Tennis My Way*, and put the deal together with Rich Elstein for "Tennis Kinetics," a workout video for improvement of footwork and agility, not to mention keeping Martina in one place long enough for George Vecsey to co-write her autobiography, *Martina*.

Martina Navratilova had become the most visible female athlete in the world, and I was glad to be a part of history.

Chapter 16

The Team Disbands

 If 1982 was the dream year for Martina, then 1983 was the beginning of the nightmare for me.

Martina obviously was the No. 1 player on the computer to start out 1983, and she was putting together an awesome streak of tournament titles. It seemed more and more that even Chris Evert was becoming an easy win every time.

It was rewarding for me, too, because everything I had told Martina was coming true. The hard work, practice, discipline, and diet were paying big dividends in victories. We started to set goals to make all the pieces of the puzzle fit tighter together. I told her not to play tournaments just to be playing. Don't play 20, 22 a year and win seven; instead, play 15 or 16 and win them all. By now, Martina's confidence and attitude had become an aura of invincibility.

The plan was working to perfection when we went to Paris for the 1983 French Open. Martina had played in seven tournaments and won them all to start the year. I was feeling pretty good on my own account, too, because I had put together an all-star basketball tour, Ladies Over America, with promoter Steve Corey.

Steve was the genius behind John McEnroe's Tennis Over America exhibition tour. He applied a one-night-stand approach to John's exhibitions and probably made him millions of dollars. Steve was interested in doing a similar tour with Martina, and one of his lures during negotiations was to piggyback a basketball tour for me. It was a smart move on his part because it gave me an outlet to play, and he knew that would make it more attractive to Martina. It's pretty typical in that line of business: If you want the big guy, you have to take the little guy, too.

I got some of my friends from the pro league to play, and we split ourselves up into two teams. We had a lot of fun going from city to city playing glorified pickup games. I was so happy to play in front of an audience again, and we usually had a couple of thousand people show up to see us. The media picked up on the tour, and I kept thinking maybe the pro league could make it with consistent media attention.

We had planned to play 18 cities, but the tour was tied into my participation. I tore cartilage in my knee again and couldn't continue, so we ended up playing games in Dallas, San Antonio, Chicago, Louisville, and Norfolk. Even with the shortened tour, we all had a lot of fun. For a couple of weeks I was in my own spotlight, not Martina's. I had forgotten how good it felt when the crowd was cheering for me.

More and more Martina and I were doing business together. We formed a corporation called Tini-Magic and used it to save "fun money" from endorsement earnings I had created. We also talked about long-range business prospects and decided to open a sporting goods store. We had a great offer from the Rouse Company, a leading mall developer, to open our first store in Philadelphia. After a lot of discussion with Pam Derderian, who helped package the deal, Sports Impressions was created. What a great feeling, to walk into a mall and see your store selling merchandise like crazy. We had official licensed apparel, t-shirts and novelty items. It was doing great business, and plans to expand were in the works.

We also wanted an apartment in New York City, so after Martina won her semifinal match at the 1983 U.S. Open, I said, "When they are handing you your winner's check, say something like, '$120,000 is hardly enough for a down payment in New York.'" Donald Trump was there, and shortly afterward we got together and worked out a deal for an apartment in Trump Plaza.

Donald has always been very kind to me the few times I've seen him. At a dinner in New York in 1985, he was behind me on the dais, and he said, "Everyone knows you were the best thing to happen to Martina — you did a great job." I saw him in 1988 at a Roberto Duran fight and introduced him to Tim. A good choice, Donald advised me: "A very handsome guy you've got there."

I continued my business developments and interests even after Martina and I parted ways in 1984. But at this point, tennis was always the focal point, and it was time for me to climb back into Martina's spotlight as she began her defense of the French Open.

The on-again, off-again coaching relationship with Renee was back on. She and Martina had patched things up after the disappointment of the U.S. Open. As they had agreed, Renee wouldn't be at the French until the second week, so she gave me the instructions to go over with Martina. The instructions were so specific that Renee had Martina's practice partner, Andrea Leand, hit certain kinds of balls to Martina in warm-ups. Renee told me to keep Martina's intensity level up and that she'd join us in time for Saturday's match. Martina's practices with Andrea were intense and aggressive, and I had the feeling she was going to dominate the tournament.

In her first three matches she allowed her opponents to win a total of only seven games. Martina was on a roll, and her punishing style of play was leaving the opposition in the red dust of Roland Garros.

That Saturday, Renee arrived at the courts just before Martina's match with Kathleen Horvath and changed the game plan. As we watched Martina drop the first set 6-4, I asked Renee what was wrong with her. "I can't believe how passive she's playing today after blowing people away all week," I said. Renee then told me how she had instructed Martina to approach the match. Instead of being aggressive, she had told Martina to lay back, play it safe, and wait for Horvath to make the mistakes. Renee had not seen Martina play all week, and now she had taken away the aggressive game that had served Martina so well through her first three matches.

I was furious.

"Renee, she's been playing great all week," I said. "You're sending her mixed messages. There's a difference between playing it safe and playing to win. Martina has obviously taken what you said literally because she is not attacking. Horvath has been at the net all day, and Martina is trapped at the baseline."

While we were arguing how Martina should play the match, she beat Kathleen 6-0 in the second set. I got up to go to the bathroom, and when I returned I moved closer to the court and stood near one of the portals. I knew I had to be a cheerleader for Martina and encourage her as best I could.

"Stay up, Martina, stay up," I yelled to her. I motioned to her to hit through the ball. I clapped. I smiled. In the end, nothing worked. She never got the rhythm in her game and lost the third set 6-3, one of the biggest upsets ever. The defending champion was bounced out in the fourth round.

When Martina came off the court, I could tell she was mad and disappointed. Not only had she lost the match, but she was also wondering what had gone on between Renee and me. We both offered our explanations. Renee felt I was undermining her by moving closer to the court and attempting to coach Martina. Martina was mad at Renee for changing the game plan at the last minute.

It was a mess. I thought Renee should have been there for both weeks of the tournament coaching Martina. When she stepped in at the last minute before the match with Horvath, she had no idea how Martina had been playing all week. Martina was paying Renee good money to be her coach, and I felt like Martina wasn't getting the return on her investment. When it came to the Grand Slam events, Renee should have been working 100 percent with Martina.

That night, Martina got a letter from Renee. Renee told Martina she was quitting her position as Martina's coach and that I was the primary reason. She told Martina I was interfering with her coaching and that the whole "Team Navratilova" concept was getting out of hand. Renee wanted Martina's full attention and didn't feel like she could get it while I was around.

It was very cut and dried: Renee flies in, Martina loses, Renee quits, and I'm the reason. But I never once presumed that I could coach Martina. I'm not stupid enough to think that I could ever tell Martina what to do on the tennis court, but according to Renee, I was undermining her coaching.

My biggest problem, as would become more apparent, was being too protective of Martina. I didn't want people jerking her around because of the money. I guess I resented Renee because of the money. I liked Renee and I respected the coaching job she did with Martina. I had learned a lot about the game of tennis just being around her at Martina's practices. I felt like I was doing my part by having Martina in great mental and physical shape to execute Renee's game plan on the court. I just thought Renee should work harder to earn her pay.

After a while the firing and rehiring of Renee became like George Steinbrenner vs. Billy Martin. Renee was probably hired and fired as often as Billy was as manager of the New York Yankees. We knew we needed Renee, but we also knew that we would butt heads. Mine just happened to be the head getting butted.

As the summer of 1983 started, my relationship with Martina was showing signs of strain. After Renee resigned at the French, Martina hired Mike Estep to coach her before Wimbledon. Mike and his wife, Barbara, arrived on the scene full of ideas and opinions. I guess I was a little wary and protective of Martina with Mike and Barbara around.

Martina was still at the top of her game, but we were nearing the bottom of our friendship and working relationship. It was exciting to know that I could help somebody with her career and dreams, and I truly enjoyed the experience. But I knew, too, that I was missing my own identity. I was missing basketball and my freedom to achieve on my own.

I sadly realized that I was living my life vicariously through Martina's achievements, and it was a bitter pill to swallow. I felt I was getting less and less secure in myself, just hanging on while she became more secure and was standing on her own. Martina was getting to the point where she knew how to be disciplined and train hard. She was playing every match like a great champion. I felt like I had put Frankenstein together and now Frankenstein was at the point where she didn't need the doctor anymore.

It was threatening, and when you're threatened, it's natural to overreact. That's what I did. She didn't need me in some areas any more, so I overcompensated in other areas, like the business end of things, and it was my downfall. I tried to do too much, and my role became too consuming, suffocating our friendship. How we ever made it through Wimbledon in 1983 without killing each other I'll never know.

I arrived at Wimbledon later than usual. I had been at home, tying up some loose ends, and the London tabloids picked up on my absence. Fortunately, they didn't pick up on what was going on behind the closed doors of our flat after I arrived. From the minute I arrived we were at each other's throats, mostly over the business dealings and my overprotective nature.

It was constant torment. We were always arguing, always fighting, always having horrendous battles. Martina would go out on the court with tears in her eyes in many a match that fortnight. I respect what she was able to do, staying focused, playing hard, and winning. She should never have been subjected to doing her job under those conditions. Maybe Martina played so well because she used the court as her refuge from me. She had a great capacity to block things out, and I think once she zapped me out of her mind and focused on the match, she was unbeatable.

Despite all the turmoil, Martina didn't drop a set in the tournament, defeating Andrea Jaeger in the final 6-0, 6-3. The night before she took the court with Andrea, we had a literal knock-down, drag-out fight until the early hours of the morning. Fighting didn't stop the winning, and winning didn't stop the fighting. I'll always regret that we had a terrible fight right before one of her shining moments, the Wimbledon Ball.

I'll readily admit it was all my fault at that point. I was pushing her too much in tennis and business. I was acting selfishly because I was frustrated with my label, "Martina's trainer." In the back of my mind all I could think about was my recognition and identity. I had worked very hard to become one of the best basketball players in the world, and I resented that my only identity was through Martina. My self-esteem and confidence were just going down the tubes.

Still, it was hard to break away because it was my job. It's hard to bite the hand that feeds you. I was so removed from basketball that her life had become mine, too. After growing up without having much, I was living the good life, in material terms, and it's easier to accept your lot in that kind of environment.

All around us, people were beginning to sense that "Team Navratilova" was having problems. Peter Johnson of IMG saw cracks in the armor and tried to solidify his hold on Martina. It became a tug-of-war between Peter and me, with Martina in the center as the prize. It seems that the more you try to maintain control, the more you lose it. I was going about things all wrong, but I was too stubborn to change.

It got to the point that people were taking sides. Martina was a commodity and people were trying to jockey for position. Loyalty went out the window because everyone was trying to improve his or her own lot. Martina finally got to the point where she said, "I don't want to do this anymore."

After Wimbledon '83, everything was shaky with the exception of Martina's tennis game. When we got home, our relationship improved for a little while. I guess being at home in Norfolk in my own element gave me some confidence or peace of mind. Martina was able to work out on the courts at home and visit with her family. It was a break that we all needed before the U.S. Open.

Martina's streak of wins was phenomenal. From Wimbledon in June until the Australian Open in December, Martina won 52 consecutive matches and ten tournaments, including her first U.S. Open title.

I wanted everything to be perfect for Martina during the Open. We decided if we didn't stay at my mom's, we'd have more privacy and the chance to just relax and be ready for the matches. Instead of entertaining a constant stream of friends, we were secluded and only visited with people when we felt like it. The furies and the fighting that surrounded Wimbledon took a back seat during the Open. I didn't want to spoil anything for Martina.

She raced through the Open, winning her matches in less than an hour each. Her game was honed to a machine-like precision when she met Chris Evert in the finals. The first set was over in the blink of an eye as Martina won 6-1, but "Team Navratilova" still sat tensely in the corner of the Stadium. The second set took 40 minutes before Martina prevailed, 6-3, and dashed out to us with high fives in celebration of her first U.S. Open title. It was incredible. In the 2 and 1/2 years I had been with Martina, she had won all the major titles at least once. The sense of accomplishment I felt for her was overwhelming. The sense of despair I felt for myself was just as intense.

By December and the Australian Open, our working relationship was still like a yo-yo. For days, even weeks at a time, things would seem to improve and we had a nice time in Australia before Christmas. But I kept a constant strain on the relationship because I still had basketball on my mind.

That December, I received a letter from Bill Wall, the executive director of what is now USA Basketball. He was trying to form a training squad of former greats to play the 1984 USA women's Olympic basketball team in a series of tuneups for the Olympic Games. The exhibition games would be in Colorado, Iowa, and Indiana, and most would be doubleheaders with the USA men's Olympic team coached by Bobby Knight. I was excited about the opportunity to play again until I looked at the dates of competition. I would have to miss the last week of Wimbledon.

I kept looking at the application as I packed to leave for the Australian Open. The decision tugged at my heartstrings. Wimbledon was Martina's tournament, an event I always enjoyed because she was so successful. But as I packed, I kept telling myself I needed to be thinking of me. I was so accustomed to training all week with Martina, working out to get ready for Martina's tennis championship, and then seeing Martina go out and play and experience the reward, be it winning or losing. I think a lot of my frustrations came from the fact that there was nothing for me to win or lose, except through Martina, and I took a lot of that anguish out on her. Now I was being given an opportunity to play, to put myself on the line and do something for Nancy.

The more I looked at the application, the more I knew I had to do it — for me. A few weeks later I completed the application and mailed it off to Bill Wall. I never mentioned to Martina that I was going to play. Deep down I knew I had to do it even if it interfered with Wimbledon. Little did I know that Wimbledon wouldn't be an issue a few months down the road.

After the Australian Open we had a wonderful Christmas together. For a while, I thought we were going to work through all of the problems. Martina showered me with gifts. She had earned over six million dollars in prize money, bonuses, and endorsements, and I guess she was showing her appreciation with the gifts she gave me. I got a shiny new black Mercedes 380SL, a fur coat, a beautiful ring, and Wayne Gretzky's hockey jersey, one of my most treasured gifts.

In 1982, we had met Gretzky when he was playing for the Edmonton Oilers. Martina and I were both great hockey fans, and we had been trying to catch Wayne on the ice in between traveling around to her tournaments.

We were in Chicago for the Virginia Slims tournament that February when we heard that the Oilers were in town to play the Blackhawks. Martina had an opening-round match scheduled against Yvonne Vermaak, and I pleaded with her to win in straight sets so we could go to the hockey game. We called all over town looking for tickets and finally ended up with a couple of press box passes.

I didn't care. I just wanted Martina to have the opportunity to see the "Great Gretzky" on the ice. Somehow Wayne heard that Martina was scouring the city for tickets, so he offered us two of his. Now our only problem was polishing Yvonne off in straight sets, which shouldn't have been too difficult for Martina the way she was playing then.

Martina won the first set with ease, 6-3, and I was thinking that we wouldn't have to rush to Chicago Stadium. We might even get there early enough for warm-ups. The second set was moving along in good time when the umpire called a ball out that Martina hit. She debated the call and swore that it was good. The call stood, and it broke Martina's concentration.

I yelled at Martina to hurry up because we were going to miss the game, but the quickie match turned into a three-setter before Martina could pull it out. Still, we reached the Stadium in time to see a great hockey game. We went to the locker room after the game to thank Wayne for the tickets, and he invited us to go out with him and a few teammates to celebrate his birthday. Martina had a 5 p.m. match the next afternoon, but we ended up staying out dancing on Rush Street until 4 o'clock in the morning. All the while I was thinking, "Boy, Martina is going to be punished and lose to Candy Reynolds." She beat Candy 6-2, 6-1.

I still stay in touch with Wayne and catch him in a game whenever I can. I admire what he has done for his sport and people in general. He is a very kind and giving man who has kept his head no matter how much money he has made and notoriety he has received. When Martina gave me his jersey for Christmas in 1983, it was one of the most special gifts I've ever received.

She gave me all these beautiful gifts, and I thought, "Well, maybe things will get better." But not long after we had a horrible time at the tournament in Mawah, New Jersey, in February. I was such a jerk, and the people around us could see how I was acting and reacting to her. I was really unfair, and I know our friends voiced their opinions to Martina.

They gave her the bottom line: "If you can't work together, be friends, and be happy, then get away from her if she's so destructive in your life." They were right. My behavior was horrific. Still, things got better one more time, and Martina made an unexpected contribution to my finding myself as an athlete again. I had been in great shape when I finished second in the SuperStars in early 1983, but by July I had put on 20 pounds. My third year at SuperStars, 1982, I had also finished second, and then I lost to Anne Meyers the next year. After losing to Annie, I vowed to come back in '84. I said, "This is it." I not only wanted to win it, I wanted to break every record. I trained my butt off for about four months.

Mark Block, an old friend from Old Dominion, helped train me for the competition. Mark's background was in track, and I knew if anyone could help me get ready, it was he. He was relentless, training me in much the same style I trained Martina. In my last months before SuperStars, we trained in Palm Springs, staying in Martina's condo.

By the time I went to SuperStars, I had bowled over 200 frames. We taped my running and did a lot of visualization. And my best preparation for the quarter-mile run was the rabbit I had training with me, Martina.

Yes, after all those years of helping her, Martina was showing her appreciation by helping me with *my* training. "Help me," I asked her. "Run with me. Do this with me, and maybe you can schedule a couple of tournaments around my schedule. Leave a block of time open for me." And she was great about it.

This was during her 70-match winning streak, and Mike Estep was upset that she would take time out to work out with me. She would go bowling, hit tennis balls, and run with me. In three years, it was one of the few things I had asked her to do for me athletically, and I didn't think it would be bad for her, but Mike was afraid it would upset her focus.

When the SuperStars finally rolled around, I was set on winning it all; I had trained hard, I deserved it. I was really nervous because this was my only way of proving that I was still a great athlete in my own right. On a personal level, this was one of the most important events during the three years I spent with Martina, both psychologically and for my self-esteem.

There were a lot of great athletes at the SuperStars in 1984, people like high jumper Louise Ritter and Olympic speedskater and cyclist Beth Heiden. I got through the bowling and the tennis in great shape. I bowled 212, a SuperStars record, and I won the tennis hands down. I also broke the rowing record. With each record, my euphoria swelled.

In the 60-yard dash, I ran neck-and-neck with Ritter, who would be a high-jump medalist in the 1988 Games, and she nipped me at the tape. I planned my revenge in the quarter-mile.

It may sound funny, but this event was more important to me than anything I had done in sports. The night before, I had gone to sleep thinking about that race. In the middle of the night, I heard Martina say to me, "Nancy, what's the matter?" I guess I had started hyperventilating in my sleep, dreaming that I was running the quarter-mile.

My strategy was to stay on Louise Ritter's shoulder. I was supposed to stay with her no matter what anyone else did. At the 300-yard mark, we were fourth and fifth in the pack, and I started thinking, "You have to be in the front to win." That's just my mentality.

I stuck with my strategy, though, and sure enough, the front-runners burned out as Louise and I picked up the space down the stretch. I kicked past her and beat her to the tape in 60 seconds. I was overcome by euphoria once again: It was the greatest thing that had ever happened to me in sports.

When SuperStars was over, I was standing on the victory stand's top step. Martina had come in second and was standing next to me, but a little lower. I was so happy I had won, so happy I had beaten Martina; this once, that was my most important goal.

I stayed in Palm Springs when Martina went to Oakland for her next tournament, and as luck would have it, she lost in the finals to Helena Sukova, snapping her long winning streak. I flew up that night and we had a huge fight because Mike Estep's prophecy had come true. I had gone up to surprise her and console her for her loss, but it just turned into a nightmarish confrontation. Our relationship just went downhill from there. It was inevitable: It had to end.

I had burned a lot of bridges along the way. Martina was my job, and I hadn't done much in the basketball world for three years. I got caught up in a routine, the power and the money and the prestige, and I fell into a trap. Now I had the cars, furs, and jewels, but I didn't have what it took to take care of Nancy. Martina had footed most of the bills, and I had become accustomed to a very expensive lifestyle. Suddenly I had to shift gears and figure out what to do. I still had my condo in Dallas and about $30,000 in the bank, but I had no basketball career and no financial support.

Suddenly it was time to reorganize my life, and I was foundering. I had brought a lot of it on myself, but when the end finally came I was stunned. My mother had seen it coming. She could see the Nancy that kept pushing and smothering and making deals. She could see her "Tini linguini" pulling away from me as things became more destuctive in our relationship.

It sounds funny to say, but it's the first time in my life my mother became my mother. I was hurt. I was devastated and I had lost my job and my best friend all in one motion. I really didn't know what to do. My mom knew what to do; she became my best friend. She stepped in and helped me take control of my life, my business, and my finances. She came through like a trouper.

She didn't baby me, but she was there when I needed someone to talk to and confide in, someone who wouldn't pass judgment. My mother took care of my books and correspondence. She helped me write some letters and get reorganized.

"Honey," my mother said, "don't worry about it. We'll take care of everything."

My secretary, Tina, went with Martina. A lot of our mutual friends sided with Martina. But my mom came through like an MVP when it seemed like everyone else was abandoning me. I never knew she had it in her to step up like a champion. All the negative that was happening with Martina became a positive with my mom and me.

The only thing I wanted from Martina when we parted ways was a little security. I had worked very hard over three years and I felt I was due some compensation for her success both on and off the court. It's funny, everything Martina admires you for at the start of a relationship is what tears you apart at the end. In the beginning she wants to be smothered and manipulated, and at the end it's the kiss of death if you smother and manipulate her. Yes, I made some serious mistakes and got involved too much in her business dealings, but I always had her best interests at heart.

I didn't have a career in basketball or broadcasting at the time. My career had been making Martina a champion. I had given her time and effort and helped her career. I wasn't asking for the moon. But when I asked her for a little financial security to get my feet back on the ground when we split, she looked at me like I was extorting money from her. She took my request for compensation all wrong.

When Martina has enough of something, she is like, "That's it. I'm out of here. Period." She doesn't realize that she is hurting people, tearing them apart. It's not that she means to hurt people, but she can hurt them unwittingly and then go on with her life without skipping a beat.

Meanwhile, everybody's life is falling apart behind her. The strong of heart find a way to survive, and you go on with your life and reorganize. Then the dreaded phone call comes from the accountant telling you the credit cards no longer work and the checking account has been closed. I was stunned. I didn't have any money because Martina was my job.

It must seem like I'm terribly bitter, but in fact I'll always consider Martina one of my best friends. I guess our relationship just sort of goes in cycles. For three years Martina treated me like gold. She was very kind, very generous, very caring—I could do no wrong. From 1981 through early '84, I couldn't tell you one thing that upset me about Martina.

But when we split, she was like a different person. She treated me so poorly that it was like culture shock. The change was so severe there was no room for forgiving. I don't mean forgiving as in "Let's continue this thing," but there was no "You know, you're a pretty good person, and you really helped me a lot." It was just severed.

I don't think she's malicious at all, but Martina wants to be the eye of the hurricane. While everything is going crazy around her, she wants to be right in the middle and not have to deal with anything. The reality is she should just face it, deal with it, and move on with her life, because while she doesn't want to deal with it, she's destroying other people's lives. But she doesn't see that because she's right there in the eye of the storm.

I see the same kind of thing happening now to Judy Nelson, Martina's traveling companion for the seven years following me. Our situations are very different. Judy did travel plans and organized Martina's days and, like me, she was with her every step of the way. But for the most part, Martina did it on her own, or with the help of IMG's Peter Johnson, who has hung in there and made a lot of money and good decisions for Martina. I think I misjudged Peter while I was too close to the situation. He's one of the brightest agents in the business, extremely protective of Martina and loyal to her. Still, Judy helped Martina with her career and in several business dealings. Now she's on the "outs," going through some of the financial horrors that I did. I just hope she did a better job of socking away money than I did.

I went from making nearly $150,000 a year — $68,000 from Martina, $30,000 from my Puma clothing contract, $35,000 from my Puma shoe contract, and $15,000 from Rick Elstein for a Tennis Kinetics video — to next to nothing. Martina and I had agreed to a salary instead of a percentage from any endorsements I might bring her, and I helped bring her a ton of them. When I was no longer working with Martina, my salary from her was gone along with my sources of income that had depended on our association.

Peter Johnson notified Puma and Rick Elstein that I was no longer employed. I had a flashback to the tournament when Peter had approached Martina and me with the contract. Peter said Puma Germany wanted a clause in the contract stating that it would be immediately canceled if I was no longer working with Martina.

I remembered how adamant I had been that the clause not be included. My shoe contract wasn't tied to Martina, but my clothing deal was, and I couldn't understand the inconsistency. I told Martina that it wasn't right and I didn't want the clause in the contract. But she assured me it really didn't mean anything. She promised me she wouldn't tell them if we stopped working together. She said I had done so much for her that she would take care of it. "Nancy, it doesn't mean anything," she said.

But it wasn't a week after I stopped working with her that I was cut off from my Puma clothing money. Peter Johnson faxed Puma Germany and —boom! —I was out $30,000. Suddenly my $35,000 Puma shoe contract was my sole source of income. I can't explain the devastation I felt as my financial world was thrown into chaos. I was very used to living a certain lifestyle while helping to make Martina successful. All of a sudden I was cut out, unconditionally.

Martina and I haggled and haggled and finally decided on a settlement of $120,000. This seemed like a fair sum after I had helped her with so many endorsements that would continue to make her money. It took Martina almost two years to pay me, and even then I didn't get the full amount.

Martina really put me through a lot of mental anguish after our relationship. I put her through a lot of mental anguish during our relationship, but I think I got the worst of it.

I had taken myself out of the basketball mainstream to concentrate on Martina's career, and now I had to humble myself to people in the basketball world and ask to speak at camps or make an appearance at the Final Four. I wrote a lot of letters and made a lot of phone calls, getting on my knees and crawling to these people, begging for an opportunity again to advance my sport.

One of the toughest things I had to overcome was the image some people in basketball still had of me. During my three years of traveling with Martina, people never really got to know me beyond the kid who played basketball at Old Dominion. I was an adult now, trying to enter their world and asking them for a chance to pursue broadcasting or to make appearances. I had to establish credible relationships as an adult to enjoy the success I wanted. By the end of 1984, I felt I was really foundering. I had to take the little things in my life and get them on the right track before I could tackle anything bigger.

Now when I look back at those years, my feelings about Martina are a little softer. I think of all the positives about our time together. Martina was like the big sister I never had growing up. She was fun, caring, affectionate, and generous. We trusted each other completely and shared all of our innermost secrets and dreams. I think about all the good times we shared, the laughter.

We had a special bond as friends and athletes. Some of the times I miss the most with Martina are the times we played like kids. We played stickball, threw the football, and enjoyed endless games of one-on-one. Sometimes we would just hang around the house and play with the dogs or watch the movie "Arthur" for the millionth time. More than anything I missed her friendship.

Chapter 17

Looking for Nancy

The plug was finally pulled on my relationship with Martina in March of 1984. For the next six months I was sleepwalking through life, trying to regroup and find Nancy again. The toughest part was keeping our split out of the news and the tabloids. When something like that happens, the last thing you want to do is talk about it to the public. As it turned out, they didn't make a big deal of it. It was just stuff like, "Judy Nelson is at Wimbledon, replacing Nancy Lieberman." I could live with that.

Still, to keep my mind off of it, I tried to stay as busy as possible. In late March I was invited to a celebrity fitness week at the Houstonian in Houston. I looked anything but fit. My face was gaunt and I had dropped to a rail-thin 138 pounds. I couldn't eat and my stomach stayed upset almost all of the time. Emotionally, I was wrestling with the perception that people were jumping out of my life into Martina's. I had a sick, empty feeling in the pit of my stomach almost constantly.

At the Houstonian, I was around a lot of athletes, able to find some common ground. One day while I was talking to Calvin Murphy, someone came up and introduced me to Chris Kneifel, an Indy car driver. Chris knew I played basketball but I knew nothing about Indy cars.

We visited quite a bit while in Houston, then stayed in touch. One day, Chris called me and asked if I'd like to go see him drive in the Indianapolis 500. Would I? The Indy 500 was one of the fantastic sporting events I'd always wanted to see.

Going to Indianapolis when a guy is racing may not be the best way to start up a relationship, but despite the pressure, Chris was great to be around. More than anything, he took my mind off my hurt for a while. Chris and I had a great time. I had the time of my life being behind the scenes and on gasoline alley and pit row. Most of the time I sat on the retaining wall with the timing people recording how fast the laps were as all these guys whizzed by in some incredible machines. At 6-foot-6, Chris had to be the tallest of all Indy drivers.

Chris had been adopted as a young boy. When I spent Christmas with him in Chicago in 1984, he took me to meet his family and his grandfather, millionaire W. Clement Stone. Mr. Stone lived in a gorgeous mansion with servants and strolling violinists. It was one of the most impressive homes I've ever seen. Even more impressive was the devotion, love, and caring he displayed for his wife of many, many years. I told Chris they reminded me of newlyweds.

By May, I was training in earnest for the Olympic summer tour. For so long my focus had been diet, training, winning, earning money, and cutting deals. After Martina and I split, I didn't have to be a role model for her anymore. It was no longer, "Well, if I can do it then you can do it too." Now I wanted a steak. I wanted doughnuts. I wanted to put my face in a barrel of Häagen-Dazs. My weight ballooned by 15 pounds.

I needed to get rid of that extra weight and get back in shape, and I needed to do it fast. I had scheduled arthroscopic surgery to remove some particles that were bothering my knee, and I knew that would put me out of commission for a while. A couple of weeks before the surgery, I was doing a lot of conditioning and playing pickup ball at Old Dominion.

One day while I was playing, I stepped on somebody's foot and rolled my ankle. The pain was so intense I thought I had broken it. The X-rays said no, but apparently I had severely stretched the ligaments. That slowed my training, and even after my knee surgery I couldn't do anything with the ankle. I was anxious to begin rehabilitating my knee, but my ankle was still hurting weeks later.

The doctors couldn't find anything wrong, so I just taped it up and resumed my training. I knew I had to be in great shape for five days of training at high altitude at the U.S. Olympic Training Center in Colorado Springs and then the three-city tour with the Olympic team. I also knew that ABAUSA was giving me a chance after I had walked away from the Olympic team four years earlier. I didn't want to let anyone down.

The Olympic team trainers worked on my ankle, but there wasn't much they could do. I was taped so tight I felt like I was just dragging my left leg around with me. I was happy to be playing again, but I knew I wasn't into the games 100 percent mentally or physically.

It was the first time that there had been enough former Olympians available to field a team to scrimmage the current Olympians. There were 15 of us who had accepted the invitation. They brought us into Colorado Springs the week before we were leaving to play the first game, the second week of July. We trained for four days. Of course, the Olympic team had been training for four months; I guess they thought we didn't need as much time because of all our experience, or maybe they didn't want to wear out us old folks.

We played in Denver, Iowa City, and Indianapolis, double-headers with the men's Olympic team. There were 17,000 at Iowa, a sellout, and then we went to Indy, and somebody said, "Oh, yeah, Bobby Knight says there's gonna be 68,000 people." I'm saying, "Gimme a break — who is he, God?" Well, as it turned out, we walk in the next day and look up and say, "Are those people up there?" I was just in awe.

The tour was great, but what sticks out most in my mind was sitting in my hotel room in Indianapolis and watching the Wimbledon finals. I sat glued to the television set, watching the finals with Lea Henry, point guard on the 1984 women's Olympic team. I probably didn't say two words to Lea because I was so involved watching the match. My mind flashed back to the Wimbledon finals when I sat in the Friends' Box. Now the television cameras zoomed in on Judy Nelson, and it made me very sad. It was as if Judy was my replacement, not as Martina's trainer, but as a person, as Martina's friend. Seeing that on television and picking up the paper and reading about Martina and Judy at Wimbledon probably hurt me more than anything.

I was also being quizzed by a lot of people: "Why aren't you at Wimbledon with Martina? Are you still working with her? I thought you went to all the tournaments." It's an embarrassing situation, and the truth is your only explanation. Judy must have gone through the same thing later. When you have been identified with somebody and you're no longer around, everyone takes notice. Suddenly you're not her pal anymore and you have to explain yourself. You feel like what everyone's really asking is, "How come you failed?"

Everything was fine for them then. Judy was happy and excited to be at Wimbledon. Martina was playing well. Meanwhile, I was sitting in the Hyatt Regency watching them having the time of their lives while mine was in shambles. I had so many mixed emotions as I watched Martina beat Steffi Graf for another Wimbledon singles crown. I was trying to come to grips with the pain and the hurt I was still feeling. I got all the usual knots and the butterflies as I watched the match. Then I thought back to December 1983, when I was invited to play against the Olympic team and had planned on missing the last week of Wimbledon anyway. The hardest part was realizing that after being such an important player in her success for so long, now I was just like a million other people around the world watching the match. That made me sadder than I can express.

After the tour with the Olympic team I went to Los Angeles for the Games. While I was there, I went to see Dr. Stephen Lombardo for the pain in my ankle. It didn't take long for him to find that bone chips had been the source of my constant pain. He gave me a shot of cortisone and told me that the bone chips should dissolve in a matter of days. He was right. Within the week, I was pain-free for the first time in three months.

I started working out again while I was in Los Angeles. I enjoyed playing, seeing old basketball friends and attending the Games, but I knew I was just putting off the inevitable. Most of my belongings were still at our house in Virginia Beach, and I knew I needed to face reality and move back to Dallas. Martina and Judy were living in Fort Worth, but strange things were happening at the house in Virginia Beach — locks being changed and moving people carting things off in the middle of the night. Things started happening so fast with no rhyme or reason. Suddenly it became very hard to read people's motives for doing things. Martina was getting bad information from people in

Norfolk: I was supposedly reckless with the cars and destroying the house. Nothing could have been further from the truth.

The house had always been in good hands while Martina and I lived there. Harry's nephew, John "J.P." Fitzgerald, was a student at Old Dominion at the time and was living in the house with us. He took care of the house, the dogs, and the cars when we were away. He handled a lot of our day-to-day dealings in Norfolk and was both a right-hand man and a good friend to both Martina and me.

J.P. was alone most of the summer of 1984; Martina was gone and living in Fort Worth, and I was in and out of Virginia Beach. It was a difficult position for him, trying to remain neutral and maintain friendships with both Martina and me. I leaned on him a lot, using him as an emotional sounding board. All through that time, he was a good friend and a great listener. It was a big disappointment for J.P. and me the way some people, particularly his Aunt Pam, treated us.

One of the things that hurt me the most was how some of our mutual friends were abandoning my friendship for Martina's. When people split up a business, a friendship, or a marriage, their friends usually take sides. Often it is with the person who has the power, influence, or money. In our relationship, people sided with Martina, and it was devastating to me.

One couple in particular whose behavior surprised me was the Lozons. Instead of stepping back and letting Martina and me deal with our situation, they managed to get themselves in the middle of it. Pam Lozon, the woman who opened her house to me when I was in college, came over and started packing my things one day.

"Martina told me to come over here and do this," she explained.

I told her to get out of the house and let me do my own packing. Pam had no business being in the house and putting herself between us. I told her if she had been a friend to me, she would have told Martina that she wanted to stay neutral. The Lozons' actions destroyed all the trust and love and caring we had felt for each other for so many years. I felt like I was being kicked when I was down.

By August, I had moved out of our house in Virginia Beach and back into my condo in Dallas. The Women's Professional Basketball League was going to make a go of it again after the exposure of the Olympic Games in Los Angeles and the gold medal the USA women's team had won. I was going to be playing for the Diamonds again and it made sense to get back to Dallas. I was so glad I had hung on to my house. Martina was always telling me to sell it, that we didn't need it. But it was almost paid for and it was my first home, and I wanted to keep it.

It was good to be back there and back to focusing on basketball and on Nancy again. Ed Dubaj was the owner, and he was adamant that if he was going to take over the Dallas team, he wanted the name Diamonds because the earlier franchise had been so successful. Otherwise there was no connection between the earlier team and the later one. We were going to play a 22-game schedule. I think we had six cities.

When we started playing, I was grossly overweight at 158 pounds. I was fortunate that I still had the game of basketball to go back to at this point. I was struggling with my self-esteem, but I still had basketball. It was a security blanket. I couldn't wait to play in front of a crowd, to nail a big bucket, to hit my teammates with high-fives going back down the court.

It didn't matter to me that the league was unstable and that it was probably going to be another one-shot year. The owners in the league this time around didn't have deep pockets, but the owner of our franchise, Ed Dubaj, was a great guy who really wanted the league to succeed. The important thing to me was getting to play again.

We had a great team that was centered around myself and a pair of 6-foot-3 twin towers from the University of Southern California, Pam and Paula McGee. The twins were an awesome addition to our team, and we were practically unbeatable with them in the lineup. We always got a kick out of watching them dunk in practice. If they could have done it in a game, we would have been turning fans away at the door.

Too bad the league itself wasn't in as good a shape as our team. Halfway through the season, the whole operation was going to fold, and Ed Dubaj ended up funding the whole league to keep it afloat to the end of the season. He lost $600,000 cash in six months, but we got through the season.

This time we did win the championship, defeating Chicago for the title. I was named Most Valuable Player in my sport. It was a far cry from my three previous years as MVP — Most Valuable Partner to Martina.

One game sticks out in my mind. It wasn't a championship game or a record scoring night. It was the time Martina came to see me play for the first time as a professional basketball player. One day, out of the blue, Judy Nelson called me up and said Martina was in town and wanted to come see the Diamonds play. We hadn't talked in a couple of months, and now she was coming to see me play for the first time.

Martina sat right behind the bench and cheered for me the whole game. "Come on Nancy. Come on. Take it to the hoop," she yelled. It felt strange to have her cheering for me, our long-time roles reversed. The whole thing was like an out-of-body experience, and I had a hard time concentrating on the game.

I was always the last one to shower and dress because I went to the press conference and spent some time signing autographs. That night, I was taking more time than usual when one of my teammates stuck her head back inside the door. "Hey, Martina is waiting on you," she called to me. "She said to hurry up and get out of here."

I didn't want to leave the security of the locker room. I didn't know what to say to Martina. I knew Judy was with her, and it would be the first time I would meet her face-to-face. I was a little mad and a little scared at the same time. Finally, Martina came into the locker room and I told her I wasn't ready to talk to her or meet Judy. The time just wasn't right for me. "I don't really think this is the time for a family reunion," I said.

I packed up my stuff and walked out of the locker room, and I heard behind me, "Nancy?" I kept walking. "Nancy?" Finally I reached the door and left the arena.

"Nancy, Nancy! I want you to meet Judy!" They came outside, and Martina said, "Nancy, why won't you meet Judy?" I didn't want to make a scene, but it just didn't dawn on Martina that maybe I wasn't ready to deal with her yet, that I needed more time. Since it was OK with her, she assumed it was OK with everybody. She's like a little kid — she just forgot there were problems.

I would hear from Judy off and on after that, inviting me to Fort Worth to visit them. I declined each time, usually tossing in a cutting comment: "What's her motive for inviting me?"

After a few months I finally accepted an invitation to visit them. We all sat around a table, Martina and I on each end and Judy in the middle. All she needed was a referee's striped shirt. Martina and I sat staring at each other, arms crossed, stiff-lipped.

Judy turned to Martina and gave her a hard stare. "Hi, Nancy. How are you?" Martina said. "Fine," I replied. It was my turn for Judy's stare. "Hi, Martina. Are you doing OK?" I asked. "I'm fine, too," she replied.

Judy smiled at us. "OK, you guys have broken the ice and I know you have a lot to talk to each other about. There's been a lot bottled up inside, and you two have to get it out. I know you both love and care about each other as friends and you need to talk about it," Judy advised us.

She looked at me. "Nancy, you have been very instrumental in Martina's career, and I want you two to be friends," she said. "You have to tell each other what is still bothering and hurting you." So I told Martina what bothered me and what my hurts were, and she did the same. It was a big relief, and before long we were both laughing.

"Why don't you guys go out and play," Judy told us. So Martina and I went to the North Dallas Athletic Club and played basketball for a couple of hours. It felt good to be in her company again, and this time we were at ease with each other.

I have to thank Judy Nelson for taking two stubborn women and bringing them back together as friends. Still, everything with Martina goes in cycles. Sometimes I'll feel like I've gotten back to where I know her and can trust her, and then she'll pull the rug out from under our friendship again. While Martina and Judy lived in Fort Worth, we would get together from time to time to work out, shoot hoops, or play some golf. Little by little we got to know each other again under less stressful conditions. Sometimes I would approach things with a wary eye, but most of the time it was just two good friends enjoying each other's company.

One day before the Australian Open in 1984, Judy and I were sitting around discussing business. Judy commented that she was surprised Martina and I hadn't fully capitalized on our training. I told her there had been people asking about a fitness video, but we had never gotten around to it. Judy suggested that I put some feelers out and see if there was still interest in it.

I spent two weeks in New York at my own expense pitching a "Train to Win" video and book. I set up several meetings with publishers and learned there was a great deal of interest in a fitness and training video by Martina and me. After the meetings, I started getting bids from the various publishing houses.

By now, Martina was back from Australia, and I went over our options and the money that was being offered. "I don't want to do it," Martina said. I was stunned.

"Martina, you gave me your word. I've been in New York for two weeks out of my own pocket pitching this. What is going on?" I asked her.

"Nancy, I changed my mind," Martina said. "There's not enough money to get me to do this. Wait a minute. I'd do it for $800,000."

So I go slinking back to the publishers, embarrassed to tell them the deal with Martina was off. To my surprise, one publisher, Holt, was still interested. They offered $130,000 for a video with just me. I'm wondering what the catch is: Just get Martina to do a foreword and a 60-second intro, they tell me.

"Oh, she'll do that," I thought. "She did the same thing for Robert Haas for nothing, and I taught her everything I'm talking about in the video. She's making millions of dollars off what I taught her."

I approached Martina again. "Listen, they still want to do it with me if you'll do the introduction. They'll come to Fort Worth and film it. Will you do it for me?" I asked her. She told me she would — for $50,000.

This was around the time we were working on the $120,000 business settlement we had agreed on after I'd stopped working for her. She told me she'd give me $70,000 and charge me $50,000 for the video. With the $130,000 the publishers were offering for the fitness video at stake, I accepted Martina's offer.

We wrote the script and filmed the video, and before it could hit the stores, Martina came out with "Martina's Fitness Workout." Holt canned my project after one payment, so I lost not only most of the $130,000, but the $50,000 I had paid Martina for the introduction. I vowed it would be a long time before I trusted another business deal with Judy and Martina.

I was soured on business dealings for a while and spent a lot of time trying to land some broadcasting jobs. I silently was thanking my agent, Matt Merola, for suggesting that to me four years earlier. I provided color commentary for ESPN on a few women's basketball playoff games and bounced around doing some appearances. There wasn't anything I really enjoyed or anything steady at that point, and I just wasn't sure what to do.

After the pro league ended, I had a hard time getting motivated. By 1985, my sole business interest was the two Sports Impressions sporting goods stores I owned in Philadelphia. The stores were doing well, but I was undecided as to whether to hang on to the business or sell it. I didn't know whether I was ready to handle the ups and downs of a business just yet. Finally a local competitor made a great offer to purchase both stores, and I was out of the retail business.

I wasn't giving up on business, though. I knew if I could find a really efficient secretary, someone to help with the business and handle my mountain of correspondence, it would free me to go out, make appearances, do charity work, and secure endorsements for myself. If you're going to train, broadcast, and be in fifty places at once, you have to have an assistant. Vicki Arnold, the most reliable person I've ever dealt with, filled that role. She handled everything from my store accounts to doing my taxes for the accountants to handling my schedule of speaking engagements, camps, and drug education assemblies. It wasn't your normal 9-to-5 job; she could switch gears in a heartbeat and never lose track of other projects. She took care of details so I could do what I do best: sell Nancy.

Chapter 18

No Business Like
Show Business

 "Professional women's basketball player" was looking like a more improbable career all the time, and the more improbable it got, the harder it was to keep training for it. I would get up every day and go to the Dallas Athletic Club to work out, play hoops, and train.

One day I got a call from someone who wanted to take that improbable notion a step further, into pure Hollywood fantasy. Jim Harris, who was bankrolling the project, wanted to know if I'd be interested in doing a movie called "Perfect Profile," which called for a professional women's basketball player in one of the lead roles. Except for my spot on "Joanie Loves Chachi," I had never acted before, but I figured the role of a women's basketball player wouldn't be much of a stretch.

I met with Jim, who was also casting the characters. He told me the story line, and it sounded like it would be interesting. Best of all, he would be shooting it in Dallas, making it easier for me to juggle 2 and 1/2 months of my schedule to fit the production schedule.

We had our ups and downs during the filming. I had some appearances I was locked into and had to leave town a few times. Jim ran into some financial problems. I received one paycheck and that was it. We finished most of the scenes, and then he stopped paying me. I didn't want to finish the movie without being paid.

It's too bad we ran into so many problems because it was a good movie with a fun story line. It centered around a fictitious millionaire owner of the Dallas Mavericks who had made all of his money in computers. He swore by his computers because the computers were never wrong.

He asks his top computer nerd to find the "perfect profile player." His team has never won the championship, and he thinks if he plugs in the name of every NBA player he'll find a championship lineup.

The computer determines that the perfect player will be a point guard, so a bunch of other lists are programmed into the computer, which then decides that the perfect profile player is Terry Williams.

The owner has to have Terry Williams signed to a contract at any cost. He dispatches the assistant coach to find this Terry Williams and sign him. Except, of course, "he" turns out to be me. The coach tries to explain to the front office that Terry Williams is a woman, but no one will listen, so he signs her to a five-year multimillion-dollar contract.

Everyone connected with the team is astonished that they've signed a girl. The coach won't play her, but the owner will never admit that his computers could be wrong. In the end, the owner falls in love with the player. She gets into the title game against the Lakers and the Mavericks win. The owner asks Terry to marry him at center court in the midst of the celebration as the film fades to black.

I have a copy of the film at home, and I understand that it has been shown at the Los Angeles Film Festival. Later it was purchased by Arista and released in Europe. That's about the last I've heard of it.

I had another brush with show biz about that time, though. One day I got a call from a trainer at the Dallas Athletic Club. He said the Jackson brothers were in town and wanted to play some pickup basketball. Would I be interested in getting a few other players together and coming up to play with them? I was going to meet Tito, Jermaine, and Jackie of the famous Jackson family.

We played ball all day, and it was all I could do not to ask them about Michael. I quickly realized that they were all unique and talented individuals in their own right. After we played ball, I invited everybody over to my house for dinner and to watch the Lakers game on television.

My house was filled with the singing idols of my youth. The guys were so nice, so down-to-earth. Jackie was looking at some of my Old Dominion memorabilia and told me that he had been a fan of mine since my college days. He had been a fan of *mine*?

After their appearance in Dallas, we kept in touch off and on. I talked to Jackie on the phone quite a bit, and he'd tell me about his girlfriend, Paula. After they had broken up a few years later, I found out that the person that I would talk to when I called his house was Paula Abdul.

Around the same time I met the Jacksons, I was introduced to Ralph Sampson, who was playing for the Houston Rockets. Ralph and I were both under contract to Puma for our basketball footwear, and when Houston played in Dallas, we went out to eat after the game. Ralph and I started seeing each other during the playoffs and the filming of "Perfect Profile."

Ralph and I had some things in common besides our Puma shoes, and we really hit it off. He had gone to school at the University of Virginia and I was across the way at Old Dominion. We were really good company for each other, and I enjoyed flying around and watching him play. The Rockets were rolling in the playoffs that year, beating Sacramento and then Denver.

I called the Jacksons when we came out to Los Angeles for the next round. Jackie picked me up at the airport, I stayed at his house, and we went to the Forum together. He took me with him to Jermaine's jam session and we had a great time. Jermaine had a basketball court set up in the studio so we could shoot around during breaks.

I was with Jackie Jackson in the Forum the night the Rockets beat the Lakers to win the Western Conference title and advance to the NBA Finals against the Boston Celtics. That was the game when Ralph turned and shot the ball all in one motion with just a tick or two left on the clock. When the shot went in, the Forum was as quiet as a tomb. I'll never forget that eerie silence.

Later that night back at the hotel, Ralph received a hero's welcome. It was fun to be sitting with the hottest basketball newsmaker in the country that night, talking about the winning basket again and again. After the playoffs and as my movie was winding down, I received an offer to play in the United States

Basketball League. For whatever reasons, my relationship with Ralph died down. I was cramming a lot of different things into my life at once, and I guess the timing just wasn't right for Ralph and me.

The timing of the USBL offer, on the other hand, was really amazing. All I wanted to do was play again. I had just finished filming the movie; Ralph and I had pretty much ended. One day I was lying in my room in Dallas, and I just started crying. "Please, God," I said, "I just want to play ball, have teammates." I missed the camaraderie, that atmosphere, being in the locker room talking to people. I wanted to play so bad. Three days later the phone rings and, "Hi, this is Andy Eckman, I'm with the Springfield Fame . . . ." and that's how it happened. I would be the first female to play in a men's professional league, and I realized I would be making history. What I didn't realize was just how much it would change my career and give me more basketball credibility than I had ever dreamed of.

I went to Springfield, Massachusetts, for the press conference to announce my signing with the Fame. I was so excited to be playing basketball again it never dawned on me the kind of media attention I was about to receive. I would be doing over 600 interviews over the next two months, not to mention signing more autographs than I could imagine. Every time we went into another city for a game, the media response was overwhelming. I was featured in all the national publications, radio and television talk shows, cable shows, and magazines. I was a gimmick at first, the token girl in the league. But my objective in the USBL was self-improvement, and everyone benefited from the experiment: me, the Fame, and the league. I would have felt like a gimmick if I had come in for one year, gotten the exposure, and gotten out. But you know what? The second year they wanted to sign me to a three-year contract.

My teammates were great during all this crazy media frenzy. I developed a really close relationship with one of my Fame teammates, Michael Adams, now of the Washington Bullets. We'd work out together and talk about our dreams. When Michael made it to the NBA, he called me and couldn't stop thanking me for supporting him. He was one of the kindest, hardest-working guys in the league, and he was my pal and confidant that summer.

It's funny because I didn't even know Michael for my first two or three weeks with the team. He was always polite and he was always sweet, but he'd never really talk to me. Meanwhile I was getting to know all the other guys on the team. They'd all take turns asking me out to dinner because having a woman with the team was new for them, too. Then one day in Tampa Michael came into my room and said, "I think the smoke has cleared. Want to have dinner tonight?"

We went to Benihana in the hotel, and I said, "You're the only guy who hadn't had dinner with me." He said, "I was just waiting for you to clear out, you know, sift through all the guys on the team. I was gonna be patient. I wanted to get to know you, but not when you were confused with all the other people." From that point on we became the closest friends.

To this day I kid Michael about beating him in a game of one-on-one. I don't think he took the game seriously at first, and I beat him, 11-9. He'll never live it down because every time I see him I make a point of asking him in front of a group of people, "Michael, what's your one-on-one record against me?"

Chapter 19

Making History

 The USBL opening game in Springfield was going to be a big night in history and a big night for me, the first woman to play in a men's pro league. Out of the blue, I got a phone call.

"Nancy, this is your father. I'm coming to see you play in your USBL debut."

I couldn't believe it. My father wanting to see me play, now? After all of these years? He had never been to a single one of my games. And if I was shocked, my mother was mad as hell. She resented the fact that my father was going to show up, and she didn't want him to have any of the attention. In her mind, he didn't deserve a damn bit of attention after all his years of neglect to his family.

The last thing I wanted was to have a fight with my mother over this. She tried to put me in a position of making a choice of one parent over another. I wouldn't do it.

After all, it wasn't my mother's night, it wasn't my father's night. It was my night for history as an athlete. Unfortunately, I spent so much time worrying about trying to please everybody that it wasn't as enjoyable as it might have been. After a lot of disagreements and arguments, my parents finally made peace for that night and came to the game.

When I got into the locker room before the game, all my teammates knew how emotional this game was going to be for me. Coach Henry Bibby, Michael Adams, Sam Worthen, and many of the other guys were saying, "Hey, this is Nancy's night and it's history for all of us. Let's play hard and have fun."

They were incredible. As the story unfolded about my parents being there and my dad seeing me play for the first time in my life, the guys all rallied around me. Michael was there for me every step of the way and he was just tremendous.

As the game against Westchester started, I was a nervous wreck sitting on the bench, not knowing when or if Henry would play me. But the competitor inside wanted the chance, and I knew once I got out on the floor I'd be OK. All the guys wanted to sit next to me on the bench or be near me in the layup line. Trying to give me moral support? Well, not exactly: With all the media there, they knew that sticking close to me was a good way to get their picture in the newspapers and on TV. Sam Worthen and Andre Patterson were the lucky guys pictured next to me in *Sports Illustrated*.

After what seemed like hours, I got my chance with four minutes left in the first quarter. Henry calls me down to sit next to him and then gives me instructions. The crowd roars its approval when I enter the game. Michael Adams is constantly talking to me, giving me instructions and encouragement. We get into the halfcourt offense, and Michael keeps looking for me. I finally get a pass on the right wing, spot up against the Westchester 2-3 zone and — bang! — I hit my first jumper. Then a steal and a layup.

My heart was pumping, and Michael kept trying to create opportunities for me. After that first basket, I'm sure the opposition didn't know what to think or how to deal with me. My teammates, meanwhile, were as happy for me as I was for myself. I scored eight points, and we won the game. The emotions in the locker room afterward were dizzying. I told my teammates how much I appreciated their trying to make me look good, and I told them I loved them. There were tears in a lot of eyes. I met the press with USBL publicity director Mike Bovino and offered my thoughts on everything from history, family, and teammates to how I felt on this historic occasion.

My family went out to dinner together — another first — my mom on one side of me and my dad on the other. A fulfilling night for me in every way. A photographer from the *Daily News* took a picture of my mother and father and me. When it ran in the paper the next day, I realized it was the first picture I had ever seen of my parents and me together. It was one of the most emotional moments of my life.

Suddenly, when I'm 28 years old, my father is interested in seeing me play and being a part of my life. Since that time, our relationship has continued to improve over the years. When my husband Tim and I renewed our wedding vows in 1989, my father paid for the wedding. I know he cares about me, but it has been difficult for us to have that father-daughter closeness I always dreamed about. I still wish I knew him better, but these days he calls and keeps in touch. I know I have a lot of his hard-working and creative traits, and I'll always love him because he's my dad.

It was great to get my family relations back into better shape, but those guys on the team were really like my brothers that season, and I think they got along better with one another to try and make things easier on me. Michael Adams said to me once, "You know, I've played on these teams before, and everybody just kind of goes his own way. Since you've been here, I've never seen any team closer."

Of course, I'm capable of pulling some pretty dirty pranks even on the people I love. There was no one on the team closer to me than Michael, but when the USBL All-Star Game came around, I pulled a real doozy on him.

Springfield was the defending champion, and the way the game was set up, the champs played the league all-stars. It was on cable, there were 4,000, maybe 5,000, people in the arena, and my friend Wes Lockard was coming down to do the halftime show at the Springfield Coliseum.

Wes had been hanging out with Michael and me, and the night before the game, Wes says, "Let's go out, let's party," but I said, "You know how I am: We've got the all-star game tomorrow." I was like a little choir girl before a game: I'd just go to bed, never drink.

Then I pulled Wes aside and said, "Wes, you've got to take Michael. Just make sure when Michael gets home, he's plastered." Wes gives me a surprised look, and I say, "I wanna play tomorrow." These guys come staggering back into the house I'm living in — boom! — Michael passes out — boom! — Wes passes out. I'm trying to lift up Wes' hand to give him a high-five. In the morning the guys are dead.

Game time — the all-stars have guys like Lowes Moore, Hot Rod Williams, and Kevin Williams, and we're getting killed. I'm sitting on the bench and I kind of move over to Henry.

"Henry, Michael looks slow today, doesn't he? Henry, Michael's sweating a lot, isn't he? He doesn't sweat that much — is he sick? Henry, they're killing us, Henry — what's going on?"

Finally Henry sends Billy Goodwin, from St. John's, and me into the game. Michael walks by and I say, real sweet, "I hope you're feeling OK."

We were down like 16, 17 points. I played the best game of my USBL career in that all-star game; I was third runner-up for most valuable player. Spud Webb was at the game, and I hit a three-pointer, and looked over and said, "Hey, Spud's here!" I took two charges — Lowes Moore was just ready to clock me after I drew a charge. I made some good passes. I ended up with eight points, eight assists, and two steals and we won. Billy Goodwin had 47 points and was the MVP. And I'm like, "What's the matter, Michael? You jealous? I have one good game and you're jealous?" We still laugh about that stuff.

With all the travel that summer, I had an opportunity to catch up with some friends in different cities, too. When we played in Tampa, for example, Andrea Jaeger called and came to see me play. After she left the women's tennis tour she settled in Tampa and we struck up a friendship. We had both changed a lot over five years, and the accusations of my coaching Martina in the 1981 French Open were just a distant memory. Later, Andrea came up to Springfield a few times and watched us play.

Another memorable event of that USBL summer was going to the Basketball Hall of Fame in Springfield. *Sports Illustrated* was doing a story about me and my playing experience with the USBL, and the writer and I visited the area for women's hoops at the Hall. There, in a little bitty corner dedicated to women's basketball, were my jersey and picture.

It was like a flashback to see that jersey and think back to the impact that players like Cheryl Miller, Lynette Woodard, Anne Meyers, and I had had on the sport. They are in the Hall, too. It's a great feeling to realize that you've furthered women in the game. With so few women in the Hall, that's an important achievement.

After playing in the USBL, I got a call from the Utah Jazz asking me to play in their summer league. It was a great opportunity to take my game up another notch, playing with and against some really outstanding talent. There was a great deal of media attention again, and it almost felt as if I were back at Old Dominion. During the two weeks I played in Utah, I met a lot of really nice people. My teammates, Karl Malone, Tom Chambers, Danny Schayes, Mark Eaton and Danny Vranes, really showed confidence in my ability as a ballplayer.

In the midst of that hectic summer, a terrible tragedy gave me an opportunity to make a difference for some young people. Ralph Sampson called me after Lenny Bias had died and told me that a number of athletes were going to Washington, D.C., to participate in a Sports Drug Awareness Program in August. Along with Mike Tyson, Sugar Ray Leonard, Bobby Allison, Dave Winfield, and a number of others, I jumped at the opportunity to participate in the program.

We were met by John Lawn of the Drug Enforcement Agency. We attended seminars, toured the FBI Building, met with a group of senators, and got a complete indoctrination into our nation's war on drugs. They wanted to use athletes as role models for the younger kids, to show these sports heroes taking a stand for being drug-free. DEA and FBI agents were going to get off the street and take their plea into the schools, hoping to educate the kids, give them the facts about drug abuse and stop them before they even get started.

Len Bias's mother spoke in Washington, and her talk moved all of us. She told us that Lenny ingested that final killing dose of cocaine all by himself. She told us that anything we as athletes and role models could do to help maybe one kid might prevent another senseless death like Lenny's.

After that talk I had the good fortune of going to Quantico, Virginia, and participating in some of the training that FBI and DEA agents undergo. I was allowed to do this by Frankie Coates of the DEA, a no-nonsense woman who doesn't want you in the program if it's just to help you toot your own horn. She wanted people who would get involved and help the kids, pass the message on to the kids in the streets.

When I got to Quantico, I was assigned to Agent Lane Betts, and he took me through my phase of the training. We signed in and were briefed about what we were going to do. The first phase involved electronic decision-making games. Considering my background on the basketball court, I was amazed how slow I was about making a split-second decision. The games were played on big screen televisions, and I shot a gun from my holster at the scenes on the television. I think I shot a couple of innocent bystanders in one scenario and an ambassador in another one.

Next they took me to the pistol range, where I attempted to shoot a gun backward while sighting with a mirror. The instructors were hitting the target every time. I never got close and felt like I was spraying bullets everywhere.

Then I went up in a helicopter and had the treetop ride of my life. They lowered a rope and I had to shimmy down out of the chopper about 100 feet off the ground. I was scared to death and asked Lane if anyone had died doing it. Only a few, he assured me. Thanks, Lane — that made me feel a lot better.

In addition to the physical training the agents undergo, I also went through a lot of lectures and classroom work. I got an opportunity to put my training to work when I went to some drug assembly programs in Albany, New York, with a former DEA agent, Bob Stuttman. I looked out over the assembly while Bob spoke and he had the kids enthralled with all of his stories. He held the attention of every kid in the room.

I felt like I could contribute because the DEA had given me the knowledge and information to impart to these kids. I wasn't just standing up saying, "I'm Nancy Lieberman and I play basketball. I don't do drugs and you shouldn't either."

That's not getting the message to the kids at all. You have to be able to answer their questions and give them good information. That's more important than standing up on a stage as an athlete and a role model. We need to talk to them and give them the straight story about drugs, addiction, drug-dependent babies, and prison.

I had one great experience after another that summer —the USBL and the summer league, the media attention, speaking and camp engagements, and the experience with the DEA. Just about when I thought that nothing would top those experiences, I got a call from Spud Webb asking me to play in a benefit game for the Boys Club in Dallas. He had gotten commitments from Isiah Thomas, Magic Johnson, Karl Malone, Dennis Rodman, and Joe Dumars for the game, which was played in the Dallas Convention Center in front of 10,000 people.

When I got into the huddle the first time, I had a giant smile on my face. Here I was in the same huddle with Magic Johnson — Magic and Lady Magic together. Never could I have imagined it in my wildest dreams. Magic set up a play for me, bringing me off a screen to take a behind-the-back pass from him and shoot a three-pointer. The play worked to perfection just the way he drew it up. Going back down the floor he asked me who I wanted to guard — Joe Dumars or Isiah Thomas. I had the time of my life playing with these guys, and for a good cause too.

I've been involved with a lot of charities and making public service announcements since I was at Old Dominion. Whether it was the Boys and Girls Clubs of America, the Winfield Foundation, Special Olympics, or the Juvenile Diabetes Foundation, I tried to make time for these worthy causes. In 1987, I worked some clinics with Michael Jordan, who was being honored by the JDF as the North Carolina Man of the Year.

Michael and I sat down that night in his hotel room and talked about our involvement as athletes with worthy causes. Then we went out and got ice cream and hung out like a couple of friends. One time in 1988 when I was training Martina again, I called Michael because she wanted to meet him. I think it's kind of funny when famous people get excited about meeting other famous people. I guess it just goes to show that no matter what your stature is in life, people are all pretty much the same.

My schedule in 1986 had been hectic but exciting. Toward the end of the year, I felt myself burning out on the fast-paced life. One day while I was lifting at the North Dallas Athletic Club with my friend Jamie, I just put the weights down and said, "Let's go." Jamie looked at me kind of funny, as though she expected me to finish my workout.

"That's it," I said "I'm finished. I'm not going to run or lift or play until I absolutely feel like it. I've had it. I'm burned out. I'm not happy. Let's go," and with that we walked out of the gym.

A few days later I went to Campisi's restaurant in Dallas. I had known the owner, Joe Campisi, since I signed to play with the Diamonds in 1980. He came by my table and asked me what was wrong.

"Joe, I don't know what to do," I told him. "I've been working all my life to play ball. It seems like there's never going to be anything there for me. I'm tired of training because from year to year I don't know what I'm training for, and I can only compete in the men's league to a certain extent."

He smiled, told me it was going to be OK and asked me to call him the next day. When I called him, he told me all I needed was a vacation. Just get away for a while and enjoy life. He had booked me and a friend into the Golden Nugget hotel in Las Vegas for two weeks. "Go and have a good time. I'll take care of everything," he told me.

I had the Thanksgiving of my life. I took a video camera and made a video for my mother for Christmas. Mr. Campisi had set up everything from our food to the tickets for the shows. We were even there when the World Series of Poker was going on. I'll always remember Mr. Campisi giving me the opportunity to go away and try to reorganize myself.

By February of 1987, I was ready to get back into working out and playing ball. I felt good about myself when I took the time off, and now it was fun again to be back into training. I took a lot of personal time to visit old friends, going out to dinner and just taking life a little easier.

When Dean Meminger called me and asked if I wanted to play in the USBL in the summer of 1987, I was ready to go out and have a good time playing basketball. Stan Goldman, the owner of the Long Island Knights, flew to Dallas and visited with me about the team. I was excited about playing basketball again and signed a three-year contract with the Knights.

On paper, we had a really solid team, with Micheal Ray Richardson and Geoff Huston as two of our top players. Dean, who had persuaded me to go to Dallas to talk to the Diamonds owners in 1980, was the coach of the Knights.

Micheal Ray and I were real close. The only thing keeping him out of the NBA was that he'd had some drug problems, and I was his unofficial babysitter that summer. Dean made it my job to keep him away from drugs, because he was tested every week, and to keep him away from women, too.

When I got into a fight, I always knew Micheal was right there. "Baby, ain't nobody gonna hurt you." Once I got into a confrontation with Andre Turner. I have the ball, and I'm trying to pass, and he's right up in my face, so I take the ball and — boom! — I hit the ball off his forehead. He started yelling and screaming and cursing at me, and I said, "Why don't you just cut the crap and play ball and stop whining like a girl?"

"I ain't no girl," he said.

"You're 5-8, you're 160 pounds, got a high voice, and you tell me you're not like a girl?" So we get into this shoving match, and all of a sudden Micheal Ray comes in and — boom! And Micheal Ray and Geoff Huston are saying, "Are you OK, baby? Are you OK?" They were just so good to me, so protective.

The hardest thing about traveling in the USBL, which was the first time I ever had to go on the road with men, was that you never knew where your locker room was. In some arenas I'd have a locker down the road. Sometimes I had to get my own area in the shower. The guys were really good to me; they were never lewd or anything like that.

I will say, though, that all some of these guys talk about on the road is who they've slept with, groupies, maids in the room, whomever. I remember one five-hour bus ride and this one player who spent the whole trip talking about one escapade, leaving nothing to the imagination. I looked at Dean Meminger and said, "He's been talking about this for five hours. I cannot believe that is the only thing this man has thought about for five hours." And everybody listening to him was like, "Yeah!" "Right!" "Oh, yeah!" It was like everybody was trying to prove their manhood to each other.

I always enjoyed playing in the USBL because the guys in the league were steps away from a team in Europe, the Continental Basketball Association, or the NBA. Many of them had played previously in one of those leagues and were back trying to get the attention of the owners and general managers. These leagues are basketball's minors, and impressions are made and forgotten quickly.

One time we were in the locker room, getting ready to play against Tyrone Bogues' team. Tyrone's a big fan favorite, of course, because he's only 5-foot-3, but he's one of the quickest guys around. All the other players are always scared to death of getting embarrassed by someone so little.

So Micheal Ray is trying to fire up the guys in the locker room, saying stuff like, "I don't care how big he is, he comes near me, forearm to the head. I don't care how little he is." And Geoff Huston's joining in: "We'll kill the dude! He comes down the lane, boom!" All these guys are talking about what they're going to do to Bogues.

When the game starts, Micheal's saying, "I'm gonna post him up." First time Micheal gets the ball down on the post, he goes to make his move, and Tyrone strips the ball from him and takes off down the court. We're on the bench yelling, "Micheal, post him up, baby!" Next time down, he goes to post him up, and — zip! — there goes Tyrone the other way with the ball again. "Keep posting him up, Micheal Ray!" Finally Micheal just walks over to Meminger and says, "Take me out of the game, I ain't guarding that little son of a bitch!"

Everybody on the bench is just sitting there laughing and Dean says, "Nancy." "Huh?" "Go in the game for Micheal Ray." "Who am I gonna guard?" "Bogues." "Hey, I wasn't mouthing off about him before the game — I respected him!" Dean says, "Would you just shut up and get in the game?"

So I get in the game, and Tyrone is dribbling the ball, and Geoff Huston is forcing him to the sideline and we're trying to trap him before he gets to halfcourt. Tyrone goes to spin and I steal the ball from him. He is just surprised as can be. I'm coming down the left side, with my left hand to make the layup. I go up with the ball — and Tyrone can jump, he's got like a 40-plus-inch vertical leap — he goes up, and I just put the ball back behind my back and drop it off for Huston to make the layup.

The crowd goes nuts, and Tyrone just turns around to me and says, "That was a *damn* nice move!" "Thank you, Tyrone. Can I call you Mugsy?" After that, he really respected the fact that, one, I stole the ball from him and, two, he thought he had it blocked because I had held it up in front of me as long as I could, and at the last minute I dropped it off, and Geoff made the shot. Of course, Micheal's on the bench yelling, "You're so lucky!"

In order to play against guys, I always had to be mentally and physically ready. Some of those guys would come in to practice, they'd been drinking, they hadn't been asleep in two days, but they were so physically gifted that the next night they'd play and score 40 points. It would just drive me nuts. I'd drink V-8 juice and go to sleep at 10 o'clock and say my prayers and lead a clean life, and I'd go out there and these guys are bigger, quicker, faster, stronger — there's nothing that I could have done to compete on an equal footing.

So every day in practice, I'd be ready and keyed up — I couldn't afford mental lapses because I had physical shortcomings to deal with. But they knew every time I stepped on the court, I was ready to play or practice, and they respected that.

I had a great time playing in the league, the publicity was great, but it was getting old. I was staying at my Aunt Ruthie's on the Island while playing for the Knights. Staying with her gave me the opportunity to visit with both my mother and father that summer. In fact, they threw a surprise birthday party for me. I handled it a little better than my party five years earlier at Wimbledon.

The day before my birthday I was flying up to Binghamton, New York to speak at a basketball camp. There were two guys who got on the plane who looked kind of interesting. The younger one was particularly good-looking, but he looked as if he had been out camping for a couple of weeks. The younger guy, whose name was David Koffman, fell asleep and his uncle struck up a conversation with me. We discussed our business up in Binghamton and realized that we'd all be flying back that after-noon. As we deplaned, we joked about saving a good seat for each other that evening.

After a day at camp, I wasn't exactly as fresh as a daisy when I returned to the airport that afternoon. I was in the newsstand at the airport buying a paper when a good-looking guy in a suit approached me.

"Nancy? I'm David. I met you on the plane this morning," he said. He was freshly shaved and dressed in a business suit that spelled success.

"How was camp?" he inquired. Our flight was about to leave, and I said I'd tell him about it on the plane.

"Well, I'm inviting you to fly back with us on our corporate jet," he said. It sounded like a quicker trip home, and with more enjoyable company, so I accepted his invitation. We had a great time chatting on the way back to the city, and somehow the fact that my birthday was the next day got into the conversation.

"Look, I'll have my driver take you home and wait for you to get changed. I'd like to take you out for your birthday," he said. I couldn't believe it. The guy had his own plane and a driver. He asked if I had any other plans that evening, and I said I was going out with my mother to eat. "Just give her a call," he said, handing me an airphone.

The limo pulled up to my Aunt Ruthie's house and I could see all of them peering out the window to see who had arrived. When I went inside I explained that I was going to shower, change, and jump in the limo to meet my date. My Aunt Ruthie was so excited she couldn't stand it. For years, she had been trying to hook me up with young, eligible, good-looking Jewish men.

Aunt Ruthie was just beaming as I got decked out in a party dress and jumped into the limo bound for a Japanese restaurant in the city. After dinner, David took me to the China Club, and we had a wonderful evening. He had a great sense of humor and we compared notes on our hectic schedules, his in investment banking, mine with the Knights. The next day he sent me a beautiful arrangement of flowers for my birthday and thanked me for our dinner date.

After that, we would try to meet for dinner after the USBL games, and little by little we got to know each other. After my season with the Knights ended, he invited me to go to Germany with him while he conducted some business. It was a great break after the season, and I enjoyed myself playing tourist in Munich and Frankfurt.

After his business meetings were over, he told me to pick a vacation spot where neither of us had ever been. Somehow we decided on Malta and had a wonderful time relaxing and enjoying the beauty of the island. I kept an eye out for the Maltese Falcon, but no luck. When we got back from the trip, I could tell our relationship was taking a serious turn. By the end of the summer, we were spending all of our free time together. He was in the midst of moving in to his new penthouse apartment in a building at 57th and Third in Manhattan.

"Nancy, what are you going to do now that the league is over this summer?" David asked me. "Are you going home to Dallas, or would you like to stay here?" David asked me. I really didn't know the answer. David was pulling me more than Dallas, but I had received a hush-hush offer to play on the Harlem Globetrotters tour for their opponents, the Generals, and I was awaiting word about the deal. David and I talked about the possibility of his conducting some of his European business around the Globetrotter tour.

While Earl Duryea and I were working out the Globetrotters deal, I moved a few things into David's apartment. But before I had a chance to unpack, the deal was on — I was off with the Harlem Globetrotters.

Chapter 20

Wedding Bells

 When Earl Duryea, president of the Harlem Globetrotters, called me about joining the world-famous tour late in 1987, it was clear from the start what my role would be. Duryea had taken the Globetrotters over in pretty bad financial shape. The show was getting a little stale; crowd pleasers Meadowlark Lemon and Curly Neal were no longer part of the act. Earl wanted to bring in a gimmick, a new angle, so he hired former All-American and Olympian Lynette Woodard, one of the all-time leading collegiate scorers, to play for the 'Trotters.

She was the first female under contract to the Globetrotters, and Earl's idea was for me to play for the Generals opposite Lynette. Lynette had played for the 'Trotters for a year by the time I got the call. She was very successful and received tremendous publicity on the tour, but she was having contract problems.

Lynette was a popular player and there were a slew of advertisers wanting her to endorse their products. The only problem with that was that the 'Trotters don't allow outside endorsements without keeping the money themselves. Lynette had a backup plan if her contract didn't work out: She was prepared to go to Europe to play. As we both went to camp in the fall of 1987, they couldn't get anything ironed out.

I felt bad for her and the guys who were locked into their situation with the 'Trotters. The 'Trotters don't want you to have any legal representation for contract talks. They have their lawyers present, but the athlete is not allowed to have one present. Guys on the tour making anywhere between $30,000 and $60,000 must be thinking it's the best money around — "take it and keep your mouth closed."

When I played on the tour, I really thought the Generals had the better team. The Globetrotters had to rely on the Generals to execute the tricks and be the perennial patsie, but treated them like second-class citizens. I think the Generals are scraping by on about $1,000 per month. I was lucky — when they finally settled on my $40,000 contract, I was playing for the Generals, but I was actually under contract with the Globetrotters, so I received 'Trotter benefits.

The 'Trotters stayed in the top level of the double-decker buses while the Generals sat downstairs. At first, I sat in one of the front compartments, but gradually I got to know my team-mates and would sit with them. I could stay in five-star hotels and eat in all the nice restaurants, but I chose to stay at the side-of-the-road joints because I really enjoyed spending time with the Generals. In fact, there was one General I was starting to enjoy spending time with more than anyone else, a guy named Tim Cline.

In September, I had been that close to moving into David's apartment. I was comfortable with him, and I enjoyed the companionship. But while I was trying to decide, the 'Trotters called and we agreed to terms. I would miss the first part of the tour and catch up with them after their games in Spain. I called David and told him that I wasn't sure what I wanted to do, but for the next six months I would be busy Globetrotting.

Then I met Tim. Tim, who had never played in college, was a 6-foot-8 power forward for the Generals.

Since most of the 'Trotter travel in Europe is on a double-decker, there is a lot of time to get to know everybody as the bus rolls through the European countryside. Tim and I became pals right off the bat. We started talking on the bus one day in Vienna soon after I arrived on the tour. We chatted our way through Germany, which was a major portion of our tour — Hamburg, Berlin, Stuttgart, and Frankfurt. Playing, eating, riding, or walking the streets of the cities, we became closer to each other as each day passed. We recognized our closeness and were careful about getting too involved.

We talked a lot about our "significant other" back home. He listened to my excitement and doubts about David. I listened to him talk about his fiancee, Annie, whom he had been dating for seven years. Back in the States one night, after a game in Chicago, about 1 a.m., we went to have ice cream. I told him about Martina and my hurts and fears, and I had never opened up to anyone about that subject before. Tim was 24 years old, but he was very stable and secure. I was impressed by his low-key manner and his ability to handle situations around him. He was kind and had a sympathetic ear. Tim already had one year of the tour under his belt, and he encouraged me when I became disillusioned with the tour and tired of all the travel.

We talked endlessly about our lives, hopes, and dreams. It seemed that little by little we were more attracted to each other. Tim would ask me if I was happy in my life. He asked me what would make me happy. I asked him the same questions, and we found that our answers were mirror images.

After about two weeks, I realized that I really liked Tim and that my attraction to him was very strong. We had a lot in common and I enjoyed his friendship, warmth, and strength of character.

We talked a lot about his postponing his wedding with Annie so he could go on the tour. I asked him why he would do that if he really was in love. Didn't that come first? I guess deep down he knew something wasn't quite right even before he met me.

We got home from the European tour right before Christmas and had a couple of days off before we had to meet again in Louisville. The Globetrotters typically play in Louisville the day after Christmas, and that begins the North American part of the tour for another four months. Tim and I couldn't wait to see each other. On the bus around the U.S., we always sat across from one another just to share more and more time.

City after city I wondered — was I really falling in love, or was this just a "tour thing" to occupy each other's time? I was constantly spinning questions through my head — Do I really love him? Does he love me? What about the people in our lives before we met on the tour? Where do they fit now? We started communicating our feelings through the songs we heard, and the words were getting very strong.

By the end of the tour the outcome was inevitable. There were a lot of things that needed to be thought out. My relationship with David had ended, but I was still sorting things out, and there was still his fiancee to think about. In the end, there was only one thing I could say to Tim about the situation.

"Tim, I love you and care for you but you have someone at home and you need to go back and see what is there," I told him. "You owe it to Annie to talk to her and find out what your feelings really are for her. You'll know where to find me."

We'd had a great time on the Canadian trip, the last week of the tour, and on the flight home from Nova Scotia. I invited Tim to stop at my house in Dallas for a few days. In the back of my mind I guess I was trying to build up extra brownie points before he went on to Houston to see Annie. After a great time in Dallas, Tim finally drove to Houston and the waiting game began for me.

I sweated it out as I waited for Tim to call me after seeing Annie. When the phone rang at 3 o'clock in the morning, my heart started pounding and I had this terrible feeling that he had changed his mind about us. When he told me he had ended it with her, I couldn't believe it. I was happy, but I also felt bad for Annie.

Tim drove from Houston to San Antonio for a few days and then came to Dallas so we could train for the USBL summer league he was going to play in. We'd play ball at the Downtown "Y," lift and run. One day before he went to New Haven, Connecticut, to try out for the USBL Sky Hawks, we were sitting around trying to decide what to do for his birthday in May.

When I asked him what he wanted for his birthday, he replied, "You." I looked at him kind of funny and asked him exactly what that meant. "It means I want you," Tim replied. We were standing outside of the Downtown YMCA when he said something like, "Wouldn't it be strange if we were married?" We looked at each other in a funny way.

"Well, do you want to?" he asked. I told him OK, then changed my mind. I didn't know what to say. I told him that I was a little surprised and that I'd have to think about it. I had a chance to think while he was in New Haven. A million questions went through my head as I wondered if it was the right thing to do — Was I ready? Have I thought everything out? I knew that I loved him. I knew anyone I'd marry would have to be a friend first and foremost. That cinched it: The answer was yes.

The tough part would be coordinating a wedding with a summer of my camps, his USBL games, and the 1988 Summer Olympics. We decided to wait six months to plan a big wedding, but the more we thought about it, the more we decided to just go ahead and get married at City Hall and have the big wedding later on. We thought perhaps we'd wait a year and then repeat the vows at a big ceremony on our first anniversary. We went down to City Hall and got married on his birthday, May 18.

Tim and I were staying at Wes Lockard's house in New Jersey. Wes was now the mascot for the New Jersey Nets. I didn't want my mother to know yet because she had contact with most of the free world, and we wanted a very private ceremony. Wes put us up and agreed to stand up for us at the ceremony.

We drove into New York and paid $15 for the marriage license and $17 to park, typical for New York City. We got there, signed all the papers, and then sat around and waited with the other couples to be married by the justice of the peace. Finally the clerk called over to us and asked if our witness was present to sign some papers. As Wes approached the desk, I knew we were in trouble.

"Sir, please sign this form for Tim and Nancy," the clerk asked him. He looked at her kind of funny and said, "Well, they haven't known each other that long, and she is an old friend of mine. I just don't know. I'm not sure."

Murderous thoughts went through my head. "Just sign the paper," we said. "Nancy, I'm not really sure," he told me.

He then wandered over to a Chinese couple sitting quietly, minding their own business.

"Here's the situation," Wes began, "I've known her since college, and I really don't know this other guy at all." He starts working his way around the room, telling everyone his story and asking for opinions.

The clerk called out to him, "Sir, please come over here and sign this paper so these people can get married." Wes finally signed the papers and then starting walking around in distress, wringing his hands and mumbling.

When we got in to see the justice of the peace, Wes was still in his little routine. Then he put a little noisemaker in his mouth and made a "zzzzzzzz-zzzzzzzzzz" sound as the justice started the ceremony.

"Do you, Timothy, take Nancy?" Wes chirps in with a whisper, "No, don't do it. Don't do it. You made a mistake. A big mistake. Just say no, Tim." I start laughing hysterically, and the justice of the peace doesn't know what to make of the situation. Wes finally settled down, and the ceremony went on without mishap until the justice asked Wes for the ring.

Wes started pulling all of his pockets out and shaking them. "Holy cow, where is the ring?" Wes kept saying. Finally, he sat down and took off his shoes and socks and pulled the ring out of his sock. Tim put the ring on my finger, and the justice of the peace kind of raced through, "Now I pronounce you man and wife."

Wes immediately started throwing confetti and singing and dancing around the room. I'm sure the justice was never happier to see a wedding party leave. One of the fondest dreams little girls have growing up is their wedding day. So that was mine. Not typical, perhaps, but memorable.

Tim and I had decided that we would use the Olympic Games as our honeymoon while I was on the NBC broadcast team for basketball. In the meantime, we had basketball camps and clinics to run, and I was up to my ears in speaking engagements. While we were at my camp at Montclair State in New Jersey, I received a message from Martina. She had called from Wimbledon, where she had just lost to Steffi Graf.

"Nancy, please call me back. I need to talk to you. I want to talk to you about working with me again. Please call me back," Martina said.

From time to time I had talked with Judy about Martina's slip in the rankings. Judy said she knew I would be able to help Martina again. I told her that there was no doubt in my mind — I had helped her attain No. 1 before, and it stood to reason that we could do it again. But this time, if she needed me she was going to have to pay the going rate, on my terms.

It sounds vindictive of me, but I had gone through enough grief with Martina taking advantage of me. Too many things had happened to make me feel that way. There was the loss of my Puma contract, the commission off the Rick Elstein Tennis Kinetics deal, the video fiasco, and on and on.

When I talked to her, she told me she needed to start training immediately and wanted me to fly to Hot Springs, Arkansas. I just laughed.

"Martina," I said, "I can't believe that you honestly expect me to just drop everything. I'm in the middle of camp and I have obligations. I'll try to work this around my schedule, but it will cost you $15,000 for two weeks."

"Nancy! I can't believe that you are asking for $15,000," Martina said. I stuck by my price, and she paid it knowing that I could help her.

We worked most of July and August up until the U.S. Open and the time I had to go to Seoul for the Olympics. Martina wanted to sign me to a contract for the year and so we worked out the details. We sat down in her kitchen, me, Tim, Judy, and Martina.

"OK, Nancy," Judy said, "we're going to pay you $90,000 a year. We want you to train with Martina twenty weeks a year; we want you to go to the tournaments. You'll get bonuses if she gets to No. 1, bonuses if she wins a Grand Slam event."

I talked it over with Tim, and he said, "I think you should do it; you know, she really needs you." I thought it was very generous on his part to say, "Go off and do this."

"Peter will have the contract by the time we leave the U.S. Open, but it's a handshake," Judy told me. "We're on."

Over the next month we worked out in Hot Springs and Martina's home in Aspen before she went to the Canadian Open. Later, we were preparing to go to New York for the U.S. Open when we received an invitation to stay with Mike Tyson and Robin Givens at their New Jersey home. The invitation was issued through another tennis player, Lori McNeil, who was a good friend of Robin's.

Martina, her coach Tim Gullickson, Tim, and I were met at JFK Airport by a Rolls Royce limousine driven by Mike's right-hand man. When we arrived in our very casual shorts, we were met at the front door by a tuxedo-clad servant. I turned to Tim and gestured that we were severely underdressed. Not only that, but we had arrived in the middle of dinner. But Ruth Roper and her daughter Stephanie were gracious as we were seated and introduced to everyone at the table. It took a while—it was a very long table.

I felt like we were at a formal presidential reception with the variety of food, silverware, and wine. Even the sparkling water looked like it had diamonds in it. Despite the formal trappings, the atmosphere was totally relaxed, even though our host and hostess were not at home. Mike was out and about, and Robin was in Los Angeles filming "Head of the Class."

Early the next morning I awoke to someone banging on the door and ringing the doorbell. It was one of those moments when you don't know whether you're dreaming or not. The noise persisted, so I made my way downstairs and went to the door.

"Who is it?" I asked. I didn't really feel comfortable quizzing people at Mike's house, but I was the only one awake at this ungodly hour. Anyway, I didn't want to let anyone in who didn't belong there.

"It's Robin," the door banger replied.

"Robin who?" I wanted to know.

"Robin Givens. This is my house. Please open the door, whoever you are."

I was still apprehensive so I asked if she had any identification. She told me she'd been on the red-eye all night and wasn't in the mood to play games. I opened the door.

She was standing there in a hat, shorts, and cowboy boots, looking like she could use some sleep. After introductions and apologies, I explained that everyone else was still sleeping, and I went back to bed.

A couple of hours later I came back downstairs. Tim and I ventured into the kitchen, where we met Mike and Walter Berry. We had met before, but when I went to shake hands with Mike, he withdrew.

"No, no, no, don't touch my hand — it hurts," the champ said. I asked him what had happened. He told me that he had kind of gotten into a fight with Mitch Green. "I hit him in the face when he broke the mirror on my car," Mike said.

Mike told me they had just come in from shopping. "Yeah, Mike," I said. "I always do my shopping in the middle of the night. Where do you shop? You must get some really good buys."

After a while, we went to work out on the courts Mike had resurfaced for Martina and Lori. The courts were really green, made from a synthetic material that looked like grass. The U.S. Open is played on hardcourts, so Martina and Lori had to find another place to practice. Mike was really disappointed when he realized he had resurfaced the courts with the wrong material.

A little while later Mike came by the courts to watch practice on his way to a press conference in New York. He had just come from the doctor's office, and his broken hand was in a cast. The papers were just full of his street fight with Mitch Green, and it was time to tell the media what had happened.

Mike didn't have time to go to the Open with us, but Stephanie and Robin went to watch Lori and Martina play. We were clowning around and taking pictures with Robin one day when she decided to call Mike. She got off the phone looking really distressed. "Mike said that he was going to kill himself because I'm not there," she said.

"Do you think he'll be all right?" I asked. She seemed to think he would be OK, but it seemed like such a strange thing for him to say. That happened to be the same day he had the accident up at his house in the Catskills. Robin ended up rushing up there, and the rest of the drama unfolded in the tabloids, with their fight and Mike throwing chairs through the windows in Barnardsville.

It was just an incredible experience being around Mike and his family and entourage. He kept his heavyweight title belt at home, and it was a thrill just to see it. He and Robin always seemed to get along while I was around them. I think Stephanie, Robin's younger sister, regarded the whole situation from a distance and there was no question in my mind that Ruth was going to take care of her girls. She was very protective of Robin and Stephanie.

I think to this day that Ruth really loves Mike. He would call her Ma, and she treated him like a son. Yes, Mike had money. Mike was the heavyweight champion of the world. I think he also presented them with a lot of opportunities, and sometimes that's a hard adjustment to make. I know the feeling.

Later, Tim and I got to be pretty good friends with Stephanie. A couple of months later Stephanie called and said she was coming to visit us. I told her to stay as long as she liked, and she said she'd probably stay a couple of weeks. That weekend we got a late-night call from Ruth.

"Hi. Robin and I have decided to visit. We'll be coming in on the red-eye tonight and will stay a couple of days with you guys," Ruth said.

When they got to the Dallas-Fort Worth Airport, they called and I gave them directions to my house about 25 minutes away. Forty-five minutes later they still weren't at the house. They finally called again after the cabbie got lost, and I gave them the directions again. When they finally got there, Tim and I spoke to the cab driver. He was trying to charge them $40 for a ride that typically runs around $25. Ruth and Robin said, "Look, we'll pay you what Nancy says because she should know how much a cab ride to her own home costs. Besides, you're the one who got lost."

He started yelling, "Pay me my money. You damn women ruined the champ's career. I know who you are. You are not going to do the same thing by stiffing me."

Tim tried to calm him down, but he only got louder, announcing that he was just a poor African-American who was being taken by Ruth and Robin. Tim finally grabbed $30 from Ruth and told him to take the money and leave. Again the cabbie shouted, "You ruined the champ's life. I've got it right here in the *National Enquirer*." And with that he held up a copy of the paper and pulled away from the house.

We really had some fun that weekend. We all piled up in the car and drove out to Martina's house in Fort Worth and played a terrific game of touch football on the golf course behind the house. It was probably the most competitive game of touch football I've ever played. We laughed and giggled for the whole three hours we played. I guess it was so funny because we were all so serious and competitive about the game. Afterward, we had a huge cook-out and relived all our fantastic plays.

When Stephanie and I tried to work out the next day, we were both sore from head to toe. Our workout was curtailed anyway when a reporter from the Dallas *Morning News* showed up at the Downtown YMCA looking for Ruth and Robin. We got out of there in a hurry.

As we were driving back to my house, we tuned the radio to a morning call-in show. One of the callers started his spiel with, "I'm just a poor African-American cab driver. The other morning I picked up Robin and Ruth Givens from the airport and they tried to stiff me. They ruined the champ's life and now they stiffed me on my fare."

Stephanie and I just looked at each other in disbelief. "See what I mean?" she said. "We have to live with that kind of behavior all of the time. We are constantly in a no-win situation."

A win was what we were looking for while spending the two weeks before the Open at Mike's home in Barnardsville. It definitely looked like a training camp with Lori McNeil and her coach, Tim and me, and Martina and Tim Gullickson all staying with Iron Mike. He was a wonderful host and we really enjoyed getting to know Robin, Ruth, and Stephanie.

As the Open got closer, I was wondering about the contract my old friend Peter Johnson of IMG was going to draw up and have me sign.

"Martina," I said, "do you have the contract?" "Peter's putting it together," she said. We get to the U.S. Open, and I say, "I'm leaving for Seoul in a week — did you get the contract, because I want to have my attorney look it over." "Oh, yeah, Peter's gonna have it tomorrow." And tomorrow became tomorrow, and tomorrow became tomorrow, and finally I'm leaving and they say, "Uh, we'll fax it to you in Seoul."

I was only going to be able to see Martina play the first week of the Open since I had to leave for Seoul with NBC during the second week. NBC was chartering planes to go over a month early and wanted most of their people in place to get comfortable with their venues.

As the Open approached, Martina and Judy began to insist that I be at the Open for the full two weeks. They had known up front that I had obligations to NBC, and there was no way I was going to turn down the opportunity to be a broadcaster from the Games. Judy was imploring me to stay for the full two weeks of the Open.

"Nancy, you know how Martina gets," she said. "She needs her people to be around her at an event like this." She even went so far as to call NBC and ask them if I could stay and then fly over a week later at Martina's expense. NBC, understandably, turned her down.

Martina ended up losing to Zina Garrison in the quarterfinals in a great three-set match, 4-6, 7-6, 5-7. I watched it from Seoul. That night, I called Judy and she said it was one of the greatest matches she had ever seen. Martina had been down 5-1 in the second set and had battled back to win the tiebreaker before losing the third set.

Finally Peter faxed me the contract in Seoul. Or maybe I should say "*a* contract" — it certainly wasn't the one we'd shaken hands on. This one called for no tournament travel and a salary of $30,000. All I was supposed to do was train her and keep her in shape. We had some teams from the Continental Basketball Association talking to us about my being the first woman in the league, and Henry Bibby was coaching at Tulsa. I had an offer to play in Italy for $100,000 and another offer to play in Israel — I was turning down basketball offers because I had agreed to train with Martina. By the time the contract came, it was too late, the timing was all wrong. Once again I had been burned by Martina. We finally agreed to $50,000 for 20 weeks, and I tried to put it out of my mind and concentrate on the Olympics. Of course, I had no illusions about this being my last clash with Martina.

When I was given the opportunity to work as an Olympic broadcaster, I approached the assignment like I did most of my other assignments. Know your subjects as though they were your teammates. Give the viewers such a special insight into the athlete that they feel a stake in that athlete's performance and are compelled to stay tuned. Make it as interesting, as dramatic as the event itself.

I enjoy sharing my experiences with people who enjoy watching the game. It doesn't matter if the viewer is male or female. I can relate to things about the game that the average viewer cannot see. I know what is happening on the court at all times. I spend so much time with the coaches and players that I am aware of what their next move will be before we get back from commercial break.

NBC Sports believed in me, believed I could carry off my assignment. That was a refreshing change because in 1984, I wanted to provide the color for CBS-TV at the NCAA women's Final Four. I was told through an agent that my image was too controversial because of my situation with Martina. That was hard for me to swallow. It seemed a paradox that someone as open about her beliefs and lifestyle as Martina could make millions in endorsements off the court, but I was too controversial for them. Even with close friend Bob Stenner, a senior producer with CBS, going to bat for me, I couldn't get my foot in the door.

I am thankful for the people at NBC, ESPN, Sports Channel America, Prime Ticket, Home Sport Entertainment, and SportSouth for giving me the opportunity to pursue broadcasting. I remember when I took some broadcasting lessons from Bob Woolf. Bob has probably broadcast every sporting event around and is one of the best in the business. He gave me a scholarship to his broadcasting school and spent endless hours with me going over the finer points of the profession. I believe he was instrumental in helping me land the job with NBC.

Bob taught me how to prepare and organize a notebook. I learned all the finer steps of preparation from him. He gave me tips on observations, personal stories, and comments. Through him, I learned the keys to a good broadcast.

I had the skills, but my problem initially was getting NBC to hire me for the Olympics. I had written Mike Weisman at NBC and asked him to give me a chance. I told him how much I loved broadcasting and the game and that all I needed was an opportunity to show them what I could do. I think when I finally got to meet with Mike and Terry Ewert at NBC, I felt totally comfortable in the role as a network broadcaster.

I think my personality suited the people at NBC because they are light-spirited, hard-working, and innovative. When I told them that it would help me to go to North Carolina State and watch some of the workouts and the games the USA team was going to play before going to Seoul, they sent me there. They gave me the opportunity to do my homework. I wanted to repay their confidence in me.

Since the door opened wide for me to be a broadcaster in 1988, I have seized as many opportunities as possible. I've been around good people in the profession who have taught me so much. Dick Enberg at NBC can make you look like a genius. He makes it so easy to discuss a play, focus on an athlete, or do a game wrap-up because he leads you into exactly what you want to say. I have done some women's basketball play-by-play with Leandra Reilly, and she has helped me become comfortable around the cameras. There really is an art to looking into the right camera.

I started out doing color commentary for three or four women's basketball games a year from 1984 to '87. It has gradually built up to the point where I was on the broadcast team for about 25 games in 1990. This year, I broadened my horizons to the NBA, doing the television color commentary for the Cleveland Cavaliers and the radio commentary for the Washington Bullets.

In 1990 I signed with Steve Lefkowitz of N.S. Bienstock to represent me in my broadcasting career. As I wind down toward

'92, I know that is a major part of my future. Steve has been very helpful and encouraging. At a Women's Sports Foundation dinner, I introduced myself to ESPN's Robin Roberts. I had seen her on TV and thought she was fantastic — it was like I already knew her. I saw her again at the NCAA women's Final Four in New Orleans. She was doing a feature on the legends of the women's game, and I was one of four athletes she wanted to interview. We talked a bit and exchanged cards while setting up. After receiving a thank-you note, I called her, and we hit it off; she's since become a close friend and confidante. She's also helped see to it that I get my share of opportunities in broadcasting. Her opinion carries a lot of weight, and she has opened some doors for me. Like Steve and my husband, Tim, she thinks that with a break I could be a regular on the air.

There are few men and no women I know who can offer color commentary about what it's really like to play against Magic Johnson. I've been on the same floor playing with and against Isiah Thomas, Tyrone Bogues, Karl Malone, and Tom Chambers. I think there's an interesting insight I could offer to the viewers. One of my next mountains? I'd love to be the first female to be a part of a full NBA package. I don't question my ability; it's all a matter of opportunity.

My experience in Seoul was rewarding from another, unexpected, standpoint. As I sat through the U.S. women's team practices and games in Seoul, I realized that I could still compete on this level. Granted, the talent level had improved dramatically since I had been an Olympian in 1976, but I saw a role for my abilities.

After my broadcasting stint in Seoul, I started working with Martina and training myself for a spot on the national team. Meanwhile, Tim was able to get a job with the Juvenile Diabetes Foundation (JDF) through Bobby Zuckerman in New York. I had known Bobby for years through his business, Marvin and Son Jewelers. After Martina and I stopped there on the way to the 1981 U.S. Open, which nearly caused us to be late to the match, Martina signed a three-year deal to wear jewelry from Bobby's store on the court and to be involved with his Sweetheart Tennis Tournament to benefit the JDF.

Bobby is a diabetic, and through my association with him I got involved in the cause. In 1985, I was the national chairperson for the JDF Walk-a-thon. I always kept my schedule open to be available for dinners, telethons, conferences, and celebrity sporting events affiliated with JDF.

When the position came up for a JDF Sports Marketing Director in November 1988, it seemed like a good situation for Tim. It was Tim's first real involvement with sports marketing. He really enjoyed working with this group and helping to put on benefit dinners with the New York Knicks and others. So many children are affected by the disease, and Tim liked being in a position to help raise money for a worthy cause.

Chapter 21

Comeback Kid

 When Tim and I came home from Seoul, we decided to move to New York so he would be closer to his job with the JDF. The move also gave me the opportunity to work out at the Plus One Fitness Center. With my weight up to 160 pounds and my diet and overall nutrition in a slump, I needed a total overhaul.

There had been rumors that professional athletes were going to be permitted to compete in the Olympic Games, and I wanted to be ready if the call came. The ruling would mean immediate participation on USA national teams, and I was looking forward to the possibility of trying out for the team in the summer of 1989.

I was training with Martina and getting in really good shape myself. Maureen Curren took on the task of getting me mentally and physically ready to return to the court by spring 1989. She was one of Plus One's best trainers, and we hit it off right away. Maureen was extremely nice, but then again not all that nice: She reintroduced me to pain. So much of training is mental attitude. A great trainer can help you get through the pain, and she did.

We started in November, and by the first of the year I was feeling fit; I really thought I had a chance to be a world-class athlete again. Tim was wonderful, extremely supportive through all this, even though New York City was taking its toll on him.

Some days, after working out in the gym, Maureen and her fiance, Marjan, would meet me at the track near where we lived. I did 880s, 440s, 220s, and 110s in rain, snow, freezing weather. Marjan is a soccer player and knows how hard it is to get in shape. My mom just loves him and Maureen like family.

In May we backed off a bit on conditioning and began to concentrate more on basketball drills. Former Tennessee star Dawn Marsh took over at this point for two months of intense UT-style drills, running, shooting, and defensive refresher courses, five to six hours a day. All I did was eat and sleep and play ball.

In the meantime I was also working on some promotions and marketing schemes. I co-promoted a tennis exhibition called the McKenzie Challenge in Sydney, Nova Scotia, with Martina and Chris Evert. While I was trying to line up some big names for the celebrity portion of the Challenge, I had the opportunity to contact Bill Cosby. Bill had a prior engagement and wouldn't be able to play in the exhibition. However, as we chatted, he formulated an episode for "The Cosby Show." He was kind of talking through the episode: "We'll get a women's basketball team to play a group of doctors," he said. "But the doctors won't know that they are playing women until everyone shows up at the gym. I'll get real basketball players to play the doctors."

He asked me if I could come to New York to work out some details the following week. I was stunned. Here I was asking him if he would play in a celebrity match, and I end up getting on "The Cosby Show." He told me to get four other women's basketball players to go up against himself, Senator Bill Bradley, Dave DeBusschere, Walt Hazzard, and Wali Jones. He asked those former NBA stars to be in the series for a basketball episode without mentioning they'd be taking on women.

I got former Kodak All-Americans Anucha Brown-Sanders and Teresa Edwards, Stephanie Givens, and my old college roommate Rhonda Rompola to take on Bill's team with me. We went to one of my old summer league stomping grounds to film the game at Xavier High School in New York. When we arrived, the security was as tight as a papal visit, walkie-talkies everywhere.

We hid out in the locker room until it was time to start taping. Meanwhile, the guys were out on the court shooting around and getting loose. Bill's idea was for us to come out on cue for a reaction shot of the guys when they saw they were playing women.

We came out and started doing layup drills. The guys all turned around and just started cracking up. They knew they had been set up, and Bill got the reaction he wanted. We filmed a real game and ended up beating the guys by ten points or so. Those guys were tall and thick, and they still could play with authority. We had the time of our lives playing against them. I know the episode still runs occasionally because we get residual checks every time it's aired.

My exposure on NBC for the Olympics had opened up some more doors to do sports commentating on both radio and television. I began receiving a number of offers for color analyst work for several women's collegiate regular season and conference championship games. Not only was I playing a lot of basketball, but also I was getting to see and analyze the game. In the back of my mind, I knew that everything I was doing would help me prepare for the USA women's national team again. I knew the rule allowing professional players to compete in the Olympics would pass, I just didn't know when.

I was back home training in Dallas, driving north along Interstate 75 on April 7, 1989, with my friend Jon Thomas when I heard the news on the radio. It was the news that I had been waiting to hear for so long: The ban on professional athletes in the Olympic Games had been lifted. I was so excited I almost wrecked my car. I think I was the first one to get my application into the USA Basketball office for the upcoming women's team tryouts.

Iowa's coach C. Vivian Stringer coached the USA national team. I had been getting back into shape and working out for a few months. I knew I needed basketball drills to put the polish on my game. Other than that, I really believed that I could compete if given an equal opportunity with the younger players.

I talked to a lot of people, wondering whether I would get a fair chance to make the team. I was 31 years old, five to ten years older than most of the players who would make the squad. When I talked to Coach Stringer about it, she told me, "Nancy, I look at players. I look at what they can bring to a team. If you are ready to make this squad, then that's what we'll look at. I'm not biased or prejudiced. Good luck."

I knew a lot of people were curious to see what I looked like on the court after such a long layoff. I think I surprised a lot of people, including myself. My timing was not great but I didn't expect it to be. That's not something that shows improvement overnight. I also had to learn a slew of new offenses. Teams were now running the flex, overload, and short corner. The game had taken on a new language since I had played collegiately.

As a point guard, I was at a disadvantage because it had been so long since I had run a team's offense. I was on the same level as the younger players physically and athletically, but they were ahead of me when it came to knowing and running the plays. It was just a matter of me learning the new offenses.

I'll never forget when I made the cut list. It took me back to so many years ago when I first saw my name posted at Queens College for the Olympic Training team. I realized I had come a long way in 15 years and when the list was posted this time, Tim was there with tears in his eyes to share my excitement. I knew I was probably going to be a role player, but it didn't matter to me. I wanted to prove that I could still get out there and play and contribute to the success of the team.

As it turned out, I didn't play a great deal in the games at the World Championships Qualifying Tournament in Sao Paulo, Brazil, in the summer of 1989. I think my primary role was as a living piece of history for the younger players. On the flight home, Stanford University's great point guard Jennifer Azzi came up to me and said, "You know, in high school we would play this game called BEAT NANCY." She also said that she had been too nervous to talk to me because of "everything you've done."

It was that way at the tryouts, too. I was caught in a strange situation because players I was competing against would ask for my autograph. One minute they were smiling and gushing because they finally had gotten the nerve to ask me for my autograph and the next minute they were trying to blow me off the court to impress the selection committee.

I had achieved step one of my goal toward a spot on the 1992 Olympic team. Once upon a time my lack of playing time would have bothered me. This time I was a little older, wiser, and less selfish. I just hoped it wouldn't hurt me the next summer when I tried out for the 1990 Goodwill Games team. What was important to me was making a comeback and then finding out what I needed to do to become an Olympian again. I promised myself I would build off my first time back with the USA team and that I would be even better prepared for the Goodwill Games tryout.

My play on the USA national team really didn't interfere with my training of Martina. I got back from playing at the end of July, and Martina had only been back from Europe for a few weeks. But when I called her I could tell she was hem-hawing around.

"Martina, when do you want me to work out with you?" I asked her. "Well....," was all she could reply. In the back of my mind I was thinking that it was a waste of money on her part not to let me train her. After all, we had a contract; I'd get my money whether or not we worked out at all. Or so I thought.

My final payment was late, and I was about ready to call Peter Johnson when I got a call from him.

"I'm calling about the payment," he said. "Oh, great," I said, observing that I'd been wondering about the September installment. "No," he said, "I'm calling for you to send me back the July payment."

"What are you talking about?"

"We accidentally paid you for the third quarter."

I got off the phone for a second to pass this tidbit along to my husband. "Tim, Peter says they *accidentally* paid me for July." Then back on the phone. "Peter, I thought you were calling to tell me you were sending me my September payment."

"Well, according to our records, you stopped working with Martina in February."

"But Peter, I was in Aspen in February, March, and April."

"But you made the U.S. basketball team."

"What does that have to do with it?" I argued. "Martina wasn't even in the country, and I only train with her when she's in the country."

"Well, you were not working for Martina," he said. "Martina told me she fired you in February."

"Fired me? That's news to me — February, March, and April, Martina and I were training."

Then he asked me if I had a signed contract from Martina. Jeff Klein, my attorney in New York, had worked everything out with IMG. We had sent signed contracts to Peter, and he had gotten Martina to sign them back in the fall after Seoul. However, it turned out Peter had never sent us back signed contracts for our files. Without the signed contracts, I didn't have much leverage.

I immediately called Martina. "Martina, what the heck's going on?" I demanded.

"Uh, well, you know," she stammered, "I figured that after I went to Europe I wouldn't need you, and since I didn't need you, I didn't have to pay you."

"Martina, you don't do business with people like that," I said. "You know, you just can't jerk people around. I gave up things I could have done to put time aside for you, and you told me you were going to pay me for that time. Have you ever lived up to your word, ever?" We got into a huge fight over who owed whom $12,500. Martina claimed that I owed her the payment from July. I wanted my payment from September.

I've never seen a penny of that $12,500. It was Martina and her cycles again. She wants to be friends, she wants me to trust her, and my instinct is I'd *like* to trust her. I think of the Martina I was with — very kind, very giving, very honest. Honest. And then I see the Martina I deal with now, and it's very frustrating for me to try and balance the two.

I was tired of being taken advantage of by her, and I'd finally learned to step aside and let other people take over her training. I vowed I wouldn't be her salaried employee anymore. She is still trying to be the best player in the world, but I had my own goals; there wasn't enough time in the day for me to get both Nancy and Martina on track. This time, Nancy's goals would come first.

After my success in the summer of 1989, I was even more determined to focus on me and my preparation for the 1990 Goodwill Games team. I became a volunteer coach at Southern Methodist University so I could once again go through drills, run offenses, see situations, and make decisions as things were developing in front of me, not to mention getting in two hours of workouts every day. I had a personal trainer, Jay Gondek, running and lifting weights with me. He would also come to the gym and pass me the ball and put me through our drills.

The mastermind of my program was SMU strength and conditioning czar Griz Zimmerman. He had previously been at Michigan, working with men's basketball when they won the NCAA title. He was tough, but he has a big heart, especially for athletes who want to achieve and are willing to work hard. I've never seen someone as organized as Griz. I think he'll end up being an athletic director one day, and SMU is lucky to have him now.

My day was filled with five or six hours of training, from September until six weeks before the tryouts. Griz and Jay pushed me, and then Dawn Marsh took over again. We spent six weeks holed up in Colorado Springs finishing training at the Air Force Academy, where the women's assistant coach was a college teammate of mine, Sue Richardson.

I had improved on my weaknesses from the previous summer, when I was rusty with the offenses, and in my 33 years, I don't think I was ever in better shape. I've always thought the peak of my jumping ability was probably my junior year in college, but in the summer of 1990, my goal, my sole goal, just as a personal thing, was to touch the rim again. I was probably an inch or two or three away, depending on how I felt day-in and day-out. By the time I was a month out from the Goodwill Games Trials, I said, "I'm ready, Dawn, I'm ready to try."

"Try what?"

"I'm ready to try to touch the rim."

"Touch the rim?" She looked at me like I'd forgotten what we were really training for. But I made it.

After that, every day I would touch the rim before practices, just for personal satisfaction. I felt so good at the Trials because I could just get up there and put my hand up by the bottom of the square up by the rim. I'd come in, stretch out, and then touch the rim. I guess I was hoping that maybe if people could see me jump the way they remembered, it would be a positive for me. In my mind and heart, I knew that I deserved to make one of the top three teams to represent the USA.

As I went through the Trials in Colorado Springs, I felt like I was getting stronger with each round of play. Little did I know that the axe was about to fall for the first time in my career. Yes, I was a little older than most of the players at the Trials, but I had years of international experience on my side, and I felt that would be a real plus for the team. In addition, I had worked a great deal on my three-point shot. I figured I could contribute as a role player with a great deal of on-court savvy.

Unfortunately, the committee didn't see it that way. It was Friday night at the Olympic Training Center, and 60 players were left in the hunt for the 36 available spots: three teams of 12 players that would be representing the USA that summer in international women's basketball competition. The top team was the one selected to go to the Goodwill Games to defend the gold medal the USA had won in 1987.

After our last session of the afternoon, I went over to my husband's hotel to get a massage. Tim was going to hang around at the gym until the cut list for the final 36 players was posted. I wanted to be relaxed and loose for that evening's session. I knew that once the committee had selected its 36 players, they would then begin the process of actually picking the three teams. As I was getting my massage, I was allowing myself to think that I actually had a legitimate shot at the Goodwill Team. I had been playing extremely well and I knew that I deserved a spot on at least one of the three teams.

Tim returned to the hotel just as the masseuse was finishing with my massage. I felt relaxed, rejuvenated, ready to hit the court that night.

"OK," I said, picking up my note pad, "what's the list of 36?" I wanted to see who my competition would be for the rest of the Trials. "Any surprises?"

"Nancy, they cut you," Tim told me. I started laughing and cutting up with him.

"Seriously, Tim, who got cut?" I asked.

"Nancy, they really did cut you." As I looked in his eyes, I realized he wasn't kidding. Then he began to cry. "Honey, I think they made some kind of mistake," he said.

I didn't know what to do. Cut? Me? My heart was racing as I wondered how on earth they could possibly cut me. I didn't deserve it. I had busted my butt every day. I was in the best shape of my career. Certainly, I thought, they have made a mistake. I thought that I had to talk to somebody and find out what happened. I called everywhere, trying to get answers. There were none to be found.

I had to find someone on the committee, one of my old USA coaches or teammates, to find out what happened. I had been around long enough to know how the system worked, and I wanted answers. But first I had to clear out my room in the dorm at the Olympic Training Center. I dreaded doing that. I had never had to make the shamefaced "I failed" walk down the hall in front of the other players — the ones who would be staying on to make a USA team and represent our country. I had always been the player to poke my head out the door and pat the back of the departing player, encouraging them that "maybe next time" they would make it. I wondered if anyone would do that for me.

When Tim and I went back to the dorm, people were running around the halls and whooping it up. All I wanted to do was get in and out as fast as I could. When I came into the corridor, a hush came over the dorm. Players kept coming up to me and telling me how sorry they were. Some averted their eyes and wouldn't even look at me. It was a long walk down that hall, and I really didn't want to hear how sorry everyone was that I had been cut.

I ran into a few of the floor coaches, and none of them really knew what to say to me either. I asked some of them why I was cut, and they just shook their heads. Most of them told me I deserved an explanation. The only person who could give me the answers was Theresa Grentz, head coach at Rutgers University and coach of the Goodwill Games team.

When I finally found her, I told her I was hurt by the decision, but I was direct when I asked why she had cut me from the team. She told me that she didn't have any other choice. She was looking for a certain style of player, one who could execute the run-and-jump and a full-court trap on defense. She said that she was looking for players who would push the ball up the court and play transition basketball.

I heard every word she said and understood none of it. I am one of the most physical players in the game, and she was telling me I couldn't execute a full-court trapping defense? She added insult to injury when she suggested I wasn't a transition basketball player. That is the only style of basketball they play in the USBL men's pro leagues, and it was our bread and butter in the women's pro league and at Old Dominion. I was looking for answers and all I was getting was more confusion.

I've always admired Theresa Grentz as a player and coach. I think my hard-nosed, competitive style could fit in with her objectives—I've always wanted to play for her. Maybe that's one of the reasons I was so disappointed. Although she doesn't know me that well, I could be a positive role player on her team — no ego, hard-working in practice, a leader to younger players. I still have the utmost respect for Theresa and I know she will select the best team to win the gold. She treats players like adults and players love to play for her. I'm one of them who would give my heart and soul for her. I wasn't a 22-year-old hot-shot who wasn't mature enough to handle the truth. I knew I could still contribute to USA Basketball, but I was being denied the opportunity. It was like I was being forced into early retirement by a company I had given all my good working years to.

Perhaps the best explanation anyone offered me came from someone inside USA Basketball. She told me that the committee goofed. When Theresa decided she wanted a certain style of player for her team, the committee panicked and decided to cut me instead of keeping my hopes up to make the Goodwill team. All I wanted was what I deserved. I know that I was one of the 36 best players in the United States trying out for the three teams picked that summer.

I thought back to some comments I'd heard during the Trials. Various coaches had said it was a sure bet that I had to make the Goodwill Games team because that was the only team I was being considered for. I never understood why I couldn't be considered for all three teams. If I deserved to be on the third-best team, then send me out and let me prove to the committee that I could still play. Don't panic and cut me. That is a disservice to my loyalty, hard work, and dedication to the game of women's basketball.

Something else working against me in the Trials, according to some of the coaches who were working or observing, was my ghost. A lot of coaches hadn't seen me play since my senior year at Old Dominion ten years earlier. I think many people expected to see me play head and shoulders above the other players, just as I had done as a collegian. But times have changed — the players and competition have soared to new heights. I just wanted them to look at the things that were still the same about me. I still had the tenacity, determination, drive, and dedication. I was a better all-around player because so many of my skills had improved playing in the men's league.

When all was said and done after the Trials, I had spent about $25,000 out of my own pocket. I was training six hours a day, six days a week, training for nothing, as it turned out.

I realize the importance that is placed by USA Basketball on the development of younger players. I can agree with that because I was a young player who got a break in 1976. However, the USA national team should be reserved for the best players our country has to offer. I'm a player with experience who isn't going to wilt in a clutch situation. I've been through too many in my career.

I'm the first one to understand the politics and the business of the situation. All I have to offer USA Basketball is my heart and my God-given ability. All I want is to be a part of the USA team and to help them go for the gold. Still, whether I'm on the team or not, I'm always pulling for the USA.

As Tim and I drove back to Dallas, I still didn't know how to react to my devastating disappointment. At first I wanted to cry my eyes out all the way home, but then I realized I had a gym full of campers waiting for me in a few days. In the big scheme of things, I thought maybe this was God's plan for me.

I was fortunate to have my BSN Sports/Nancy Lieberman-Cline Basketball Camp for Girls to throw all my energies into instead of moping around feeling sorry for myself. I really enjoy holding my camp in Dallas and having the opportunity to teach the game of basketball. I am a national spokesperson for Foot Locker, the national athletic footwear chain, and initially they became a small sponsor for my camp. In 1990, they became a major sponsor of my camp when they became involved in a scholarship program. I happened to speak at Baldwin Junior High School on Long Island to a student assembly about self-esteem, reaching potential, and staying in school and away from drugs.

The principal and the athletic director approached me and asked me to speak to one of the students who was "destroying" the school. Her name was Tanzania Stone. I introduced myself to her and at once I read a lot of hurt and mistrust in her eyes. I managed to soften her up a little and asked her why she was being such a troublemaker and causing so many problems. She opened up to me and explained what was bothering her and why.

I offered her a deal: If she shaped up her attitude, had perfect attendance, pulled a B average in her classes, and got out of her special classes, I would pay her way to my basketball camp. She seemed like she could really be a nice girl, but she just needed a little incentive. We shook on the deal, and I was on my way.

About six months later I received a letter from her principal. Tanzy had changed her ways: She had perfect attendance and was named to the honor roll. Her disruptive behavior had stopped. She flew in for camp and stayed at my house with Tim and me. She had turned into a lovely young lady with a little encouragement, and she told me that all it took was a little incentive and someone believing in her to turn her around.

Tanzy was such a great success story that I went to Gary Warech at Foot Locker and told him about her. My idea for the 1991 campaign was to establish a Foot Locker/Nancy Lieberman-Cline Basketball Camp Scholarship program. Each applicant has to meet certain requirements for attendance, grades, and attitude. We receive applications from all over the country, and we award ten all-expenses-paid scholarships every summer to the camp. We send out a news release and a photo to each hometown paper of the recipients. It's really a wonderful opportunity for all of these young women.

Camp is especially fun when big-name NBA stars spend time with the kids. Tom Chambers came to camp in 1990 after a really hectic year with the Phoenix Suns. He's an imposing man at 6-foot-11 and a real terror in the NBA, but he was a sweetheart with my campers. He sat down and talked to them, played H-O-R-S-E, and gave each child individual attention. It didn't matter that the Suns had lost to Portland in the playoffs a week earlier. He truly enjoyed giving something back to his sport and to the kids.

Right after camp, I had the Hoop It Up competition in Dallas, which Tim works for and promotes. I had some Hoop It Up competition in other cities as well, so I was back on the court doing my thing. Hoop It Up has become a great source of enjoyment for me. It's three-on-three street-style basketball played in 35 cities nationwide. It reminds me of the games I played in the streets and on the playgrounds when I was growing up in New York.

I was contacted about a couple of television and radio jobs late in the summer with Home Sport Entertainment, SportsChannel, EPSN, CBS radio, and the Cleveland Cavaliers. Even without the USA national team, as the fall and winter of 1990 approached, I knew that I had a lot of things happening to keep me busy.

In December of 1990, Tim and I had the good fortune to go on a cruise aboard the Princess Cruise Lines with Dave Winfield, his wife Tonya, and former Harlem Globetrotter Meadowlark Lemon. Dave and Meadowlark were surprised that I had as many company and product endorsements as I had without the visibility of a league. They encouraged me to start a company to help market and promote athletes. I sat down with Dave and Tonya and went through a plan to help get endorsements for Dave. We talked about the total package — training, marketing, and promotions. Meadowlark and I kicked around the idea of a Farewell Tour of the "oldie but goodie" Globetrotters.

I love the creativity of the game of basketball, and I love the creativity that goes along with marketing and promotions. It's probably why I enjoy my association and involvement with Pro-Motion Events. The company, which I co-own with Tommy Thompson of Omaha, has kept my adrenalin pumping. We have promoted and run Hoop It Up in Omaha along with my husband Tim, have sponsored tennis exhibitions featuring Martina and Zina Garrison, and have looked at other tennis, golf, and hockey promotions.

We also work closely with Dave Winfield and have secured a national endorsement with Sports Supply Group. They will work closely with the Winfield Foundation on education and prevention workouts for area kids. Another client is ESPN's Robin Roberts. We're trying to put her with select companies that make sense for her, expand her charity work, and handle all the requests for her as a national speaker.

So life in the business and broadcasting world is busy. Oh, and I almost forgot: I'm also running around the country being Nancy Lieberman-Cline, basketball player and role model. Summer means camp, my own in June with ten Foot Locker scholarship kids in tow, plus, in 1991, visits to SMU's, former Bullet Phil Chenier's, and my old friend Ralph Sampson's camp in Virginia.

My husband has been very supportive of me both as a wife and as a business partner. He is a terrific man who has helped me take some of the New York City tough-gal edge off my business dealings. Tim is a behind-the-scenes guy who is very flexible and supportive of Tommy and me in our PME venture. Whenever we sponsor an event at PME, we make sure we give something to the community or back to charity. Another very important facet of the partnership in Omaha is the Christian community I have been exposed to since 1990.

I have been a Christian since my freshman year at Old Dominion in 1976, but I was always afraid to share my news. I first became interested in Christianity in 1975 and 1976 while playing on the Pan-Am and Olympic basketball teams. One of my teammates, Nancy Dunkle, was always reading her Bible. She told me that she was a Christian and I peppered her with questions about this Jesus Christ she was reading about. I was so curious because I had never seen anyone with such devotion to religion.

I was named Jewish Athlete of the Year in 1979, and somehow it didn't seem right. I knew in my heart that I was a Christian. After I signed with the Dallas Diamonds in 1980, a column appeared in the newspaper mentioning my Christianity. I received thousands of hate letters from Jewish people all over the country. It was hard being a closet Christian and wanting to learn but being afraid to tell anyone.

That all changed in 1990 when Tim introduced me to Tommy Thompson. Tom is a Christian, and I spent hours asking him all the questions that had bothered me for years. He exposed me to the fellowship and teachings in his church in Omaha, and I've never felt more comfortable in my life. Through the help and instruction of Pastor Lance Bingley, my eyes have been opened to Bible doctrine and the teachings of the church. This process has helped me redirect the importance of things in my life. I don't get overwhelmed by the great moments or the bad ones anymore.

Business is important, but my priorities are different now: Christ, family, career, in that exact order. I haven't mastered it all yet, and if I had to take a guess I'd say I never will. There's just so much to learn. While in Omaha, we attend class three nights a week and church on Sundays. It's like a storybook, and Lance is teaching the story. But it's not some fairy tale, it's the Lord's word. My confidence comes now from Bible doctrine, not business deals or points scored. It comes from believing.

In the fall of 1990, I had planned to serve once again as a volunteer assistant coach with the Southern Methodist University women's basketball team. I saw volunteer coaching as a way to keep my hand in for my next tryout and as an opportunity to pass along my experiences to the younger players. However, Southwest Conference officials decided my television commentating contract with the conference and my playing in Hoop It Up competition precluded my involvement with the SMU program.

Perhaps not making the 1990 USA national team taught me a valuable lesson and gave me some important insight into my life. I couldn't try out for the Pan-American Games team in the summer of 1991 because of scheduled elbow surgery. I knew that to have a shot at my ultimate goal, the 1992 Olympic team, I'd probably have to make the 1990 Goodwill team and the 1991 Pan Am Games.

Now that the sequence isn't in place, I have to decide if my goals are the same. I realize now that I don't have to make the Olympic team to be enthusiastic about my sport. I don't have to run through walls, be hopelessly motivated, and train with a vengeance to be happy. Looking back, I think I can say I've been happy and more than satisfied with my career as an athlete.

What am I chasing? It is hard to say. I just can't get basketball out of my system. I look at the great women's basketball players, and I thank God that I have been so durable. Cheryl Miller was probably the greatest player ever. Boom, she blows her knee out and she's gone. Annie Meyers was a big hit and even got the professional tryout with the Indiana Pacers. Then poof, she was gone. Carol Blazejowski was one of the best outside shooters ever. She had some great years, but in the long haul she was gone, too.

The fact that I can still compete into my 30s is a bonus. To still command the same respect as I had rising up through the ranks as a youngster is what excites me about the game.

I'll still train with my eye towards 1992, but it won't be a be-all, end-all goal. It would be great if I could do it, but I don't need the approval of the USA Basketball Women's Games Committee or the U.S. Olympic Committee to tell me I can still play the game. When I'm ready to hang up my Converse sneakers, I will go out on my own terms, nobody else's. That's the way it's always been.

Epilogue

 On Feb. 18, 1991, I was sitting in Martina Navratilova's hotel suite at the Red Lion in Omaha, with our friend Debby Jennings. Martina was getting a post-match massage after playing Zina Garrison in an event my company, Pro Motion Events, produced. We were talking about my book, what should and should not be included. After lots of discussion, old stories, jokes and laughter, Martina solemnly told me, "Nancy, Judy and I have split and I don't think it can be fixed."

I really didn't know what to say. I had been so removed from the situation. For almost eight years, Martina and Judy Nelson had been like one.

It's so important not to interfere in other people's personal affairs. I'm friends with Judy and her parents as well as Martina, so there's no room for taking sides. But if I had to speculate, I'd guess that Judy drove Martina crazy just like I had done years before by pressing too hard on business matters. Martina just plain doesn't like to deal with that topic.

Months passed, but Martina and I kept in touch. During one conversation she said she was returning from Italy to shoot something for *Sports Illustrated*. She was having dinner in New York with friends at an upscale restaurant and invited me to join them. Conversation was light and free-spirited, not much talk of the problems with Judy. I mentioned hearing that columnist Liz Smith had implied on her TV show that she had viewed a video of Martina and Judy. She then went on to give her uneducated legal advice on Martina's plight. I said in my normal sarcastic tone, "Hey, Martina, nice video!" Having been out of the country, she hadn't heard anything about it yet, and she kind of looked at me strangely. When she realized I wasn't referring to her workout video, she came alive with questions. I believe this was the time Judy was planning her suit against Martina.

I began to watch from a distance. I understood both sides and the pain involved, and I didn't want to get dragged into one side or the other. I have too many commitments — to my husband, my work with kids, companies I deal with, broadcasting, not to mention my Christian commitment. In May I spoke to Judy. I had a conversation earlier with her mom, Frances, who was terribly hurt that Martina left Judy. Judy's family was very close and loved Martina very much. As I spoke to Judy from my mom's house in New York, I wanted to be there to listen, but I had no advice for either party. That was the last time I spoke to Judy, until I saw her in the courthouse in Fort Worth, Monday, Sept. 9, 1991.

Martina and I always chat and tell jokes — "How's your family, Nance? How's Momma Lieb, still eating?" "Martina, how's your game, your family? Can I use your villa in Antigua to vacation?" See how easy that last part flows? Actually, she's been telling me for years to take a vacation there. It wasn't until I had elbow surgery that I took her up on the offer, ten days at the St. James Club. After that I would be ready to lace up my hightops again and start training.

Before Wimbledon I received a phone call from Martina's publicist, Linda Dozoretz, an old friend. She said Mike McCurly, Martina's attorney, wanted me to sign a release waiver. Martina and I had a confidentiality clause in our agreement, drafted by her former attorney, Jerry Lofton. I guess they were afraid I'd exploit our relationship in a book. Well, I wouldn't exploit her anyway, so the clause was fine with me. Now, though, for Martina to establish her case we needed to share personal and business information at the Sept. 9 hearing. I was leery, but I called McCurly's wife, his partner, who again asked me to sign the waiver. I said I'd have to talk with my attorney, Robert Rose.

Robert, who handled my settlement with Martina in 1986, is one of the brightest and most personable defense attorney in Dallas. He's been a great friend and is the hardest-working attorney I know. Besides, in my book, any man who runs marathons is either mentally and physically tough or just crazy. Either way, he's a guy I want in my corner.

After he and I spoke, he conferred with McCurly, who also wanted Robert as a witness. We could indeed prove Jerry Lofton was Martina's lawyer and should be disqualified from representing Judy. He had too much privy information on Martina's finances and personal life. I finally went to Robert's office, signed the waiver and a power of attorney, in case I was out of town and Robert needed to act on my behalf.

The Sept. 9 hearing date was quickly approaching. Before the U.S. Open, I called Martina to see where all this stood. She said, "Nancy, Robert's testimony is more than we'll need. It's only a small part of the case." Then on Friday, Sept. 6, I had just returned from a run when my doorbell rang. "Are you Nancy Lieberman-Cline?" the man there asked. I noticed the subpoena and took it, saying "I'll give it to her when she returns." With this in hand, I called Martina at Kathleen Sullivan's apartment, where she was staying during the Open.

"Martina," I asked naively, "what about Monday?" "No problem, Nancy," she said. "My attorney said you won't be testifying, only Robert. You don't need to be there."

"OK, that's great," I said, "but what about the subpoena I just got served with?"

"Don't worry, you don't have to be there."

I wished her luck, then immediately called Robert Rose.

"Nancy, as your attorney I have to advise you that when subpoenaed, you must be present or be in contempt of court," he said. "I'll meet you Monday morning at 7:30 at my office and we'll drive to Fort Worth together."

Not knowing what to expect, Robert and I arrived at the third floor court room Monday morning . Already there was a slew of cameras, and reporters from radio, newspapers and tabloids along with the witnesses. I'm feeling so uncomfortable: I know virtually all the participants. I see Martina, we talk briefly and at 9 a.m. it's show time in Judge Harry Hopkins' courtroom — or should I say circus? The only thing missing was the tiny car with the dozen clowns climbing out.

Witnesses waiting to testify must stay outside the courtroom in the hall. Not knowing what's being said just makes the tension worse. Robert, Judy's brother Sargent Hill Jr., her sister Jan and I were talking, expressing our feelings on why this has come to pass. I like Jan and Sarge, they're nice people. I have nothing against them, and I think they feel the same about me. Finally there was a recess and some people came up to me and told me Martina had taken the stand, and that she looked calm, relaxed and ready to get on with it.

Apparently Mike McCurly's strategy was to draw parallels to my relationship with Martina, while Lofton wanted to paint a business-only picture. So the inevitable happened.

McCurly's questioning to Martina went something like this. "Martina, what did Nancy Lieberman do for you? Did she change your hair color?" "Yes!" "Did she buy your clothes?" "Yes!" "Did she handle your everyday business affairs?" "Yes!" "Did she secure endorsement contracts for you?" "Yes!" "Did she handle PR and marketing for you?" "Yes!" "Did she train you?" "Yes." "Did you have a physical relationship with her?" "Yes!" "Were you two lovers?" "Yes!"

That night, Martina told me she had felt violated answering those questions. How did she think I felt? By the afternoon, it didn't really matter any more. Innocent people were getting their lives dragged down with Martina and Judy. It's times like that when I'm grateful for my faith, and that I've never taken people for granted. I've developed long-lasting, strong relationships not only with friends, but with the media and corporate folks. It's nice to know that throughout this mess they have always believed in the quality person I am and the hard work I've provided.

For some strange reason witnesses could watch the afternoon show. I didn't know if I'd be called up or not. I knew Robert would be, but it wasn't certain when. I have to commend Judge Hopkins for maintaining his sense of humor during Jerry Lofton's cross-examination. Lofton's line of questioning was redundant; he couldn't find the right pieces to the puzzle. It was apparent during the course of the questions and objections that Jerry Lofton was outclassed by "Team McCurly."

All the while, though, I had one question in my mind: If this case was between Martina and Judy, why was I the focal point?

I settled with Martina a long time ago. My agreement was not greed, it was pure business. I didn't ask her to pay me for living with me. I helped her make over seven million dollars in three years, not to mention contributing to the success she enjoyed thereafter. I have always been self-sufficient and capable of making a good living for myself. I was doing that long before I met Martina and will continue to do so long after my jumper and her volleys at the net are gone. As for writing a book back then, I turned down high-six-figure offers, no to mention articles for the scandal rags. That's not my style; that's why I waited eight years to do my life story. Yes, it includes Martina, yes, she's a part of it, but my story goes well beyond her. I've been a world class athlete since I was 15 years old, and I'm still doing it at 33. That's what I'm proud of. I appreciate the opportunity to honestly share the good and the bad.

And believe me those two days in court were bad. It was so emotional, so difficult for me, seeing Judy's family, people I worked with, like Jim Shaffer and his assistant Bea Maulden — they were all first-class people and I believe they appreciated my contribution to Martina's career.

Robert testified Tuesday night and was absolutely a star. Any time you get three attorneys questioning each other it's comical. Robert left no shadow of a doubt: Jerry Lofton was Martina's lawyer. With that our job was done. The press talked to me for quite some time, and they were terrific to me. They could have tried to sensationalize my role, but they treated it as no big deal, old news. I was willing to be there in an uncomfortable situation because it was the right thing to do for Martina. She was telling the truth about Jerry, and my settlement with her was a key only because Jerry handled it. I can live with my decision to appear. Like every other decision I've made in my life, for better or worse, I have no regrets at all.

It sounded like Judy and Martina were close to settling later that week, but there were so many elements involved. It's hard to be fair and objective when emotions are running high. I know! I left hoping it would be settled before Thanksgiving; that was when either Judge Hopkins would rule or we'd be looking at another ugly courtroom scene. And I wondered if Martina's Villa in Antigua would be available that week.

AWARDS

Wade Trophy winner 1979 and 1980
Broderick Cup 1980
Kodak All-American 1978, 1979, 1980
Kodak All-Region 2, 1978, 1979, 1980
National Scouting Association All-American 1979
National Women's Invitation All-American 1977 and 1978
MVI NWIT 1978
MVP Detroit Coca-Cola Classic
Best Defensive Player Detroit Coca-Cola Classic 1979
Optimist Classic All-Tournament 1980
AIAW Division 1 National Championships All-Media Team 1980
Jewish Athlete of the Year 1979
Young American of 1980 Boy Scouts of America
MVP Virginia State Tournament 1978, 1979, 1980
Virginia Player of the Year 1978, 1979, 1980
1st Team All-State 1978, 1979, 1980
MVP First Annual All-American Basketball Classic 1978
U.S. National Team 1976-1980
Captain of 1977 Pan-Am Team
Pan-Am Games 1979
1976 Olympic Team (youngest member on U.S. squad)
Selected to final trials of 1980 U.S. Olympic Team
ODU Outstanding Female Athlete of the Year 1977, 1978, 1979
Norfolk Sports Club Athlete of the Year 1979-80
ODU all-time career assist leader (and single season)
ODU all-time leader in steals (and single season)
2nd ODU all-time leading scorer (behind Inge Nissen)
Street & Smith pre-season All-American 1978, 1979, 1980
Street & Smith pre-season Player of the Year 1978, 1979, 1980
Basketball Weekly All-American (second team) 1978

Nancy Lieberman
ODU Career Statistics

Yr.	G	FG-FGA	PCT.	FT-FTA	PCT.	RB	AS	BL	ST	PTS-AVG
76-77	27	240-507	.473	83-117	.709	272	212	—	—	563-20.9
77-78	34	281-651	.432	119-163	.730	325	200	—	—	681-20.2
78-79	36	243-508	.478	139-176	.790	276	254	16	144	625-17.4
79-80	37	208-390	.533	145-186	.779	294	295	24	142	561-15.2
Totals	134	972-2,056	.472	486-642	.757	1,167	961	40	286	2,430-18.1

AMERICA'S MOST COMPLETE ATHLETIC FOOTWEAR STORE.

233 BROADWAY • NEW YORK, N.Y. 10279-1099 • (212) 720-3700

NANCY LIEBERMAN-CLINE
BASKETBALL CAMPS
SCHOLARSHIP APPLICATION

Please answer the following questions as accurately as possible. Scholarships will be determined by the NLC-Camp selection committee.

PLAYER INFORMATION

Name _____ Birthdate _____

Address _____

Parent's Name _____ Phone _____

School Attending _____

Address _____

Grades: (Circle the correct answer)

          100-91   90-81   80-71

Attendance Record: Excellent   Good   Average   Poor

Describe any awards, honors, or special recognition the applicant has received from the school and/or community:

Describe any activities (clubs, athletics, music, interests, hobbies, etc.) in which the applicant is involved:

List any additional information that would be helpful to the selection committee as to why you feel this applicant is deserving of a NLC Basketball Camp scholarship.

Name of person filling out the questionnaire _____

Why do you feel you can recommend this person for the scholarship?